A. P. HILL: *Lee's Forgotten General*

A. P. HILL

Lee's Forgotten General

By

WILLIAM WOODS HASSLER

★ ★ ★

The University of North Carolina Press
Chapel Hill

Manufactured in the United States of America
ISBN 0-8078-0973-X (cloth : alk. paper)—
ISBN 0-8078-4548-5 (pbk. : alk. paper)
Library of Congress Catalog Number 57-13027

99   98   97   96   95   12   11   10   9   8

DEDICATED TO
THE FAMILY

CONTENTS

MAPS AND ILLUSTRATIONS

Distinguished in every engagement, his death in front of Petersburg, April 2, 1865, was a serious loss to the army. Upon him as perhaps none of his other young officers, except Stuart, General Lee implicitly relied, and to him the memory of the great commander seemed to revert on his deathbed, for among his last words were: "Tell A. P. Hill he must come up."

DOUGLAS SOUTHALL FREEMAN

PREFACE

As soon after the Civil War as 1879, W. E. Cameron in *Annals of the War* called attention to "the remarkable fact that no history of A. P. Hill has yet been given to the public." General Hill's continued neglect by biographers of the Confederacy is still "remarkable" in view of the conspicuous role he played in the conflict and the high esteem he enjoyed in the hearts of his countrymen. Lee ranked him next to Jackson and Longstreet; his was the fourth monument which the impoverished South erected to the memory of her heroes; and the Virginia edition of Hardesty's Historical and Biographical Encyclopedia published in 1884 devoted almost as much space to A. P. Hill as to R. E. Lee.

However, as time thinned the ranks of the Army of Northern Virginia even cracker-barrel testimonials to A. P. Hill were muted, and he soon became a nebulous, almost forgotten figure. In 1911 Mrs. B. A. C. Emerson in *Historic Southern Monuments* neglected to include the A. P. Hill statue in her otherwise complete list of Confederate monuments in Richmond. And by 1931 a University of North Carolina Extension Bulletin by F. M. Green entitled, "Studies in Confederate Leadership," omitted A. P. Hill from a list which included Stuart, Pelham, and Forrest in addition to Lee, Jackson, and J. E. Johnston.

My own interest in A. P. Hill was stimulated principally by Dr. Douglas Southall Freeman's extensive studies in Confederate leadership. Scattered allusions to the tempestuous Virginian silhouetted a seemingly complex character. As a commander he could be brilliant, but he was frequently erratic; as a superior he was considerate and intensely loyal, but as a subordinate he was generally intolerable; and despite his inordinate ambition he apparently gave little thought to the preservation of his place in history.

Inasmuch as no biography of Hill had been published, I decided to assemble and collate the available material pertaining to him in the hope that it would provide sufficient information to restore his faded portrait to a recognizable degree. Shortly after embarking on this task I discovered that my subject's modesty coupled with a self-acknowledged distaste for writing has left posterity a dearth of personal papers and correspondence. This situation is further aggravated by the fact that the bulk of what correspondence he did leave was either destroyed by fire or scattered to autograph seekers. Hence the difficulty in fixing with certitude a number of traits of what Dr. Freeman has aptly termed "the elusive personality of A. P. Hill."

Nevertheless, within these limitations (which of course preclude the writing of a definitive biography) I have endeavored to sketch an accurate study of A. P. Hill against a background of the distinguished commands with which he was intimately associated. To this end I have employed the documentary technique in order to minimize any personal astigmatism I might have toward my subject. It is my hope that this work may help bridge the last major biographical gap in the high command of the Army of Northern Virginia.

I am indebted to many kind people who generously assisted in various ways with the preparation of this biography. My wife, Mary, patiently acted as a sounding-board for every chapter, and with the cooperation of

xiii

Virginia, Martha and Tom provided the atmosphere and encouragement conducive to writing. My parents helped with the tedious chore of copying records and original manuscripts. In addition, I wish to acknowledge the contributions of the following persons whose cooperation made possible this work: Mrs. W. W. Ammen, Mr. C. M. Applegate, Mr. Louis Fabian Bachrach, Mr. J. H. Baptist, Miss Mildred Bispham, Colonel Paul L. Burke, Mr. Virginius Dabney, Mr. Peter Dulac, Mrs. F. B. Dogan, Mrs. W. Elliott Fox, Dr. Kenneth Goodner, Colonel F. M. Hinshaw, Mr. Ralph Happell, Mr. C. D. Hill, Mrs. Evelyn Hill Kight, Miss Maude S. Hill, Mr. Henry L. Hill, Miss Mildred Hill, Mrs. Emlyn H. Marsteller, Mrs. Leo Maloney, Mr. George H. Miller, Lt. Col. Robert H. Morrison, Mr. Jeffry Montague, Colonel W. J. Morton, Dr. Robert B. Nye, Mr. Quinn, Mrs. Ruth S. Rodgers, Mr. Frank B. Sarles, Mrs. William M. Sweeny, Mayor L. Frank Smith of Culpeper, Miss Mary Lee Somerville, Miss Alice B. Palmer, Mr. William H. Stauffer, Mr. Floyd B. Taylor, Miss India Thomas, Miss Burke Thompson, Dr. Thomas H. Tomlinson, Jr., Mrs. Marshall C. Tucker, Mrs. Daisie Brown Williams, and Colonel Willard Webb.

WILLIAM WOODS HASSLER

A. P. HILL: *Lee's Forgotten General*

CHAPTER I

"The Commander The Army Idolized"

BY RAIL, surrey and horseback, droves of proud Virginians converged on Richmond for a special "Decoration Day" ceremony this hot Monday, May 30, 1892. The day on which the South annually decorated the graves of her Confederate dead was set aside this year to dedicate a statue of one of the state's most illustrious heroes, General Ambrose Powell Hill.

Not since the unveiling of Lee's statue two years earlier had the capital witnessed such a reunion of soldiers in gray. Veterans of the Thirteenth Virginia Infantry Regiment and artillerists of Pegram's Battalion were conspicuous with their oversize badges and tattered battle flags which proudly identified their former association with General Hill. Also present were battle-scarred veterans of other units who shouldered gleaming muskets as they fell in at Capital Square.

At the command "Forward march," gray-haired marchers in jaunty strides wended the dusty three mile parade route to the monument on Hermitage Road. Here, to the accompaniment of martial strains and artillery salvos, tiny Virginia Meems, granddaughter of General Hill's Chief-of-Staff, in her fluttering white dress pulled the red cord which unveiled the commanding figure of A. P. Hill.[1]

Facing south, Hill's statue overlooks the scene of his valiant defense of the Confederate capital. His monument was the fourth which the South from her postwar poverty had erected to her distinguished war-time leaders. Only Lee, Jackson and A. S.

---

[1] Southern Historical Society Papers (cited hereafter as S.H.S.P.), *20*, 352 ff. A full account of the dedication of the A. P. Hill statue is also detailed in the May 31, 1892 edition of the *Times*—Richmond, Va. General Hill's monument surmounts a sarcophagus containing his remains. Two days after his death relatives buried him in a hastily dug grave in Chesterfield. From this unmarked grave his body was moved several years later to Hollywood cemetery in Richmond, and thence transferred in 1891 to the A. P. Hill monument. S.H.S.P., *19*, 183 ff.

Johnston had been similarly honored.[2] However, with the passing
of time Hill's fame has dimmed in the lengthening shadows cast
by Lee and Jackson whose deathbed calls for "A. P. Hill" constitute his principal footnote in history.[3] Yet despite history's neglect of this youthful patriot who served conspicuously from pre-
Manassas to the debacle at Petersburg, A. P. Hill possessed the
chivalrous manners, sure skill, and fiery impetuosity which truly
exemplify the Confederate commander who is cherished in tradition
and legend. As one Sourthern writer has stated: "His personal
purity, his devotion to the South, his military renown, have become
the heritage of his people."[4]

In many respects Hill was the infantry counterpart of cavalry
cavalier "Jeb" Stuart. Only thirty-five at the outbreak of war, Hill's
rise was meteoric. In ninety days he rose from Colonel of the
Thirteenth Virginia Infantry Regiment to the rank of Major General in command of the Light Division, one of the largest and
most distinguished in Lee's Army of Northern Virginia. Following
the death of his celebrated chief, "Stonewall" Jackson, he was promoted to Lieutenant General in charge of the newly formed Third
Corps. Lee constantly relied on him as a trouble-shooter and
ranked him next to Jackson and Longstreet among his commanders.

In common with Stuart, Hill's habitat was the battlefield. He
possessed what one compatriot termed "an unquenchable thirst for
battle,"[5] and nothing exhilarated him like "the fierce joy of victorious fight."[6] To miss a battle was simply unthinkable, and consequently as one of his veterans remarked at a Confederate reunion,
"He was either there or always came up."[7]

---

[2] S.H.S.P., *20*, 376.

[3] D. S. Freeman, *R. E. Lee* (cited hereafter as *R. E. Lee*), IV, 492. In his
deathbed delirium Lee cried out: "Tell Hill he must come up." See also, J. Wm.
Jones, *Personal Reminiscences of General R. E. Lee*, 451.

Dabney, R. L., *Life and Campaigns of Lieut-Gen. Thomas J. Jackson* (cited
hereafter as Dabney), 719. Jackson's dying thoughts also reverted to the battlefield, and through his final murmurings he called out sharply: "Order A. P. Hill
to prepare for action."

[4] *Confederate Military History* (cited hereafter as C.M.H.), *I*, 681.

[5] J. C. Wise, *The Long Arm of Lee* (cited hereafter as Wise), *II*, 615.

[6] S.H.S.P., *20*, 187.

[7] W. J. Robertson, " 'Up Came Hill'—Soldier Of The South," (cited hereafter
as Robertson), *Richmond Times-Dispatch*, October 14, 1934. Part I, p. 10 of
the magazine section.

Hill's battle attire included a picturesque red shirt, black felt slouch hat, and drawn sword. Arriving on the battlefield at a critical juncture as so frequently happened, he would assess the situation at a glance and then hurl his inspirited troops furiously upon the enemy. Once the battle was joined he was bold, skillful, tenacious and utterly oblivious of his personal safety. Withal, he extended every courtesy and consideration to a captured or fallen foe.

A natural leader, Hill possessed that "commanding resolution"[8] which "inspired by his voice, his example, and his personal appearance."[9] A comrade-in-arms admiringly noted that "his every posture and movement was full of grace, and in any dress, however remote from camps, his military bearing and martial step would betray the soldier by birth and training."[10]

In appearance, he stood five feet ten inches and weighed about one-hundred-and-sixty pounds. His frame was so slight that Private J. William Jones and President Jefferson Davis alike referred to him as "little A. P. Hill."[11] His handsome face was graced with long curling hair and a luxuriant red beard which, like Stuart's, disguised his youth. High cheekbones, a Roman nose, and intense hazel eyes which blazed when angry and lit up with a steely glint in battle were relieved by a "slight but very pleasant smile which seemed to light up his face all the time."[12] His slender arms merged into long, slightly tapering, virile hands.

Hill normally spoke in a soft, low Virginia drawl, but when excited his voice rose to a high metallic pitch. Possessing a teasing sense of humor, he laughed a repressed coughing sound terminating in "key, key, key." His speech was patterned after the dialect of the cavaliers ("gyel" for "girl"), interspersed with Negroisms such as "whar" for "where."[13]

A thoroughbred Virginian, Hill epitomized the southern cava-

---

[8] S.H.S.P., *2*, 302.
[9] "Souvenir—Unveiling of Hill Monument, May 30, 1892" (cited hereafter as Souvenir Booklet).
[10] S.H.S.P., *20*, 386.
[11] S.H.S.P., *27*, 452; S.H.S.P., *9*, 558.
[12] Confederate Veteran (cited hereafter as C.V.), *21*, 433.
[13] Robertson, Part III, 8, October 28, 1934.

lier possessing sensibilities of rare refinement. Contemporaries referred to his manners as "strangely fascinating and magnetic," and to his intellect as "quick and retentive."[14] One veteran who observed him under varied circumstances stated: "General Hill was firm without austerity, genial without familiarity, and brave without ostentation. The gentleman and the soldier were so completely blended in him that he never had to deviate from one to the other. He was both all the time."[15] And General "Stonewall" Walker, who succeeded to the command of Jackson's famous brigade, maintained that "of all the Confederate leaders he (Hill) was the most genial and lovable in disposition . . . the commander the army idolized."[16]

However, beneath Hill's genial exterior smoldered a nervous and sensitive nature. He was extremely volatile and quick to take offense, especially if an act violated his punctilious concept of justice or protocol. When aroused his anger flashed and he was hard to appease.[17] These traits led to serious differences with both Longstreet and Jackson under whom he served during the early years of the war. His dispute with Longstreet nearly culminated in a duel shortly after the Seven Days battles, and his feud with Jackson constituted probably the longest and most confused "family quarrel" with which Lee had to deal during the war.

Militarily, these handicaps in temperament were offset by Hill's exceptional administrative and tactical abilities which contributed substantially to the army's successes in Virginia. A soldiers' general, he thoroughly understood the character of the soldier-citizenry and treated them with due respect and consideration. A courier who carried messages between corps headquarters of the Army of Northern Virginia remembered that of all generals, only A. P. Hill never failed, even during the heat of battle, to have a kindly word and perhaps a little joke for the couriers who served him.[18] Though ambitious and zealous, he never needlessly exposed or

[14] E. A. Pollard, *Lee and His Lieutenants* (cited hereafter as Pollard), 447; "The Land We Love," April, 1866-67, 289; S.H.S.P., *20*, 383.
[15] S.H.S.P., *19*, 183.
[16] S.H.S.P., *20*, 386.
[17] *Ibid.*, 384.
[18] J. W. Thomason, Jr., *Jeb Stuart* (cited hereafter as Thomason), 166.

sacrificed his men to enhance his reputation.[19] He made frequent rounds of the camps and hospitals in a constant effort to improve conditions for his men. Intensely loyal to his men and officers, he disbursed praise liberally and insisted upon assuming full responsibility for mistakes such as the disastrous headlong attack at Bristoe Station. Therefore, it is not surprising that his leadership evoked devotion of the stripe expressed by G. W. Tucker, Sergeant of couriers in the Third Corps, who wrote: "Those attached to his person or often in contact have simply to say, 'We loved him'."[20]

Unlike Jackson and Longstreet, Hill did not have an opportunity to test his ability as a strategist, although at one time a movement was started to send him West to supplant Bragg.[21] However, his skill as a tactician was demonstrated repeatedly as his responsibilities increased from command of a regiment to a brigade to a division. Then a minor but incapacitating injury at Chancellorsville frustratingly deprived him of the opportunity to consummate Jackson's master stroke.

Appointment to corps command prior to Gettysburg provided Hill the chance to play a major though controversial role in the war's latter campaigns. With Jackson fallen, Longstreet wounded, and Ewell ailing, Lee relied increasingly upon his able, dashing commander of the Third Corps to spark what offensive drive remained in the waning Confederacy.

---

[19] S.H.S.P., *20*, 384.
[20] S.H.S.P., *11*, 565.
[21] *The Making Of A Soldier*, Letters of General R. S. Ewell arranged and edited by P. G. Hamlin (cited hereafter as Hamlin), 119. The letter pertaining to Hill's transfer to the West was written from Ewell to J. A. Early, March 8, 1863.

CHAPTER II

"Two Long Miseries And No Fighting"

W HEN BIOGRAPHY is writ-
ten collaboratively by geneticists, psychologists, and historians we
may gain a deeper insight into the influence of ancestry and early
environment on the intriguingly complex character of A. P. Hill.
Until then we shall have to content ourselves with a recital of
the known facts.

Both of Hill's parental strains were English. His mother, Fannie
Baptist Hill reputedly was descended from the Earl of Gainsboro
in Charles II's reign. On the paternal side his ancient forbears
belonged to the noble family of Hull who changed the name to
Hill during the reign of Henry VI. During the early part of the
17th century several members of the Hill family emigrated to the
eastern shore of Virginia. Here they prospered as tobacco growers
and actively participated in colonial affairs.[1]

In 1740 Russell Hill, a later descendent, moved westward with
his wife into the wilderness which subsequently became Culpeper.
Here they built a homestead and christened it "Stranger's Rest."
Their youngest son, Henry, served with Lighthorse Harry Lee
during the Revolution. He married Ann Powell, daughter of
Captain Ambrose Powell, Indian fighter, adventurer, and surveyor
who settled the boundary line between Virginia and Kentucky.[2]

Colonel Henry Hill's seventh progeny, Major Thomas Hill,
became a leading politician and merchant of Culpeper County.

---

[1] *Hardesty's Historical and Geographical Encyclopedia* (Special Virginia Edi-
tion), 389.
N. M. Nugent, *Cavaliers and Pioneers,* 6, 93, 324, 405, 457.
Records of Christ Church, Middlesex County, Virginia, 1635-1812.
Communications from Lenora H. Sweeny, genealogist, and the following
descendents of General A. P. Hill: Miss Maude S. Hill, Mrs. Evelyn Hill Kight,
Mrs. Isabelle Hill Maloney, and Miss Alice Burwell Palmer.
[2] J. G. Keys, *Virginia Heraldry,* "The Hill Family and Some of Its Distin-
guished Sons."
*Genealogical and Historical Notes on Culpeper County Virginia, Embracing a
Revised and Enlarged Edition of Dr. Philip Slaughter's History of St. Mark's
Parish,* Part I, 111; Part II, 85-86.

He was affectionately respected for his courage, hospitality, and benefactions. Shortly after his twenty-second birthday in 1811 he married Fannie Russell Baptist of Mecklenburg County, Virginia. On November 9, 1825 their third son was born. They named him Ambrose Powell Hill in honor of his distinguished great-grandfather.[3]

General James L. Kemper, a boyhood playmate of Hill's, recalled that "in his early boyhood he was self-reliant, forceful, and bright."[4] He learned his three R's at the neighborhood school under the tutelage of Reverend Andrew Broadus. From this classroom Hill advanced to nearby Bleak Hill Seminary presided over by Professor Simms, a bespectacled Pickwickian character with a penchant for Latin mottoes.[5]

With his mother, who called him Powell, young Hill formed a strong bond through their mutual fondness for books. Powell's tastes ranged from the Bible and Shakespeare, through the poets and current novelists, to the exploits of Napoleon. His later correspondence and even his military reports are tinged with poetic expressions which reflect his early reading.

From his mother, Hill inherited a spare physique and a proud, sensitive nature. Fannie Hill was a slight demure woman who spent her days brooding and knitting by a small window overlooking the distant mountains. Although her seven children were devoted to her, they evinced little sympathy in her imagined ills.[6]

Summers, Powell hunted and fished on the nearby Rappahannock and Rapidan with his tall, taciturn father. These two also enjoyed riding together, a sport in which the son soon acquired a graceful mastery of which an admiring Confederate private was

---

[3] *Ibid.* Also, communications from Mr. J. H. Baptist and Miss Mildred Bispham, descendents of A. P. Hill.

The uncertainty surrounding many aspects of Hill's career beclouds even the location of his birthplace. Culpeper, Botetourt, and Mecklenburg have been cited as possible sites. Although the birth records of Culpeper County do not go back to 1825, this writer favors Culpeper, because Hill in an autobiographical letter dated October 25, 1863 listed Culpeper County as his birthplace. In addition, Pollard's *Lee and His Lieutenants* (1867), Slaughter's *History of St. Marks Parish,* and Keys' *Virginia Heraldry* all state that Hill was born in Culpeper County.

[4] "Souvenir Booklet," Letter from J. L. Kemper to Colonel W. H. Palmer.

[5] Robertson, Part I, 10, October 14, 1934; "The Land We Love," April 1, 1866-67, 289.

[6] Robertson, Part I, 10, October 14, 1934.

later to write: "He was a perfect picture in the saddle and the most graceful rider I ever saw."[7]

At the impressionable age of fifteen, Powell Hill suddenly found his youthful activities narrowly circumscribed by a new influence. In 1840, an ardent evangelist named Ireland, proselyted hordes of Virginia churchgoers, including the Hill family, into the Baptist "New Light" movement. Thenceforth, cards, dancing and the theater were added to the forbidden list in the Hill household.

Being high-spirited and independent, Powell eagerly anticipated an early release from this oppressive blue-stocking environment. Influenced by the exploits of his military forbears together with his adolescent hero-worship of Napoleon, he decided upon a military career. Through his father's political crony, John S. Barbour, he obtained and accepted (over his mother's strenuous objections) an appointment to West Point.

*   *   *   *

Exactly five months before his seventeenth birthday, Powell Hill arrived at the United States Military Academy, and with a scratchy pen proudly inscribed "Ambrose P. Hill" on the "Descriptive List of New Cadets for the Year 1842." Divesting his pockets of fifty-five dollars, he exchanged his civilian garb for a gray cloth, gilt-buttoned coatee, white drilling "trowsers" for summer drilling, black cap with round crown, white gloves, and an unbleached fatigue jacket worn during summer encampment.[8]

"Plebe" Hill's quarters consisted of a combination medieval-type bedroom and study. A mattress on the floor served as the bed. His roommate was George Brinton McClellan, diminutive son of a Philadelphia physician. A year younger than Hill, "Little Mac" had been required to obtain special permission from the Secretary of War to hurdle the sixteen year age requirement for admission to the Academy.[9]

Among Hill's other classmates in this largest class to enter West Point up to that time, were Dabney Maury, George Pickett

---

[7] S.H.S.P., *28*, 374. During the war Hill had two favorite mounts: Champ, an iron gray, and Prince, a jet black.
[8] *Regulations Established for the Organization and Government of the Military at West Point*, 1839.
[9] *Ibid.*

and Cadmus Wilcox. On the afternoon of the last day entering cadets could report for duty, Hill and several of his new acquaintances were standing together in the south barracks when they saw a new cadet enter in the charge of a cadet Sergeant. The newcomer was dressed in gray homespun, coarse felt hat, and carried a pair of weather-stained saddlebags slung over his shoulder. As the Sergeant returned from installing the new arrival in his quarters, he was asked the stranger's name. He replied, "Cadet Jackson of Virginia."[10]

July and August the plebes spent in encampment, drilling and learning the standard army regulations as revised by General Winfield Scott.[11] Although the exercises were rigorous, cadets regarded these periods under canvas as the most enjoyable part of their four-year program.[12]

September 1 the Cadet Corps returned to barracks, whereupon the Fourth Class commenced its academic curriculum with the study of French and mathematics. Classes were small, averaging about fifteen students per section, following the prevailing practice in France and Germany. Mornings were devoted to solving problems in algebra, geometry and trigonometry. Afternoon classes were spent in wrestling with Lévizac's Grammar, Berard's Leçons Francais, and translating the *Voyage du Jeune Anarcharsis.*[13]

The first Monday in January, semi-annual examinations were held in the library from 8 to 1 and from 2 to 4. One of Hill's classmates, Bill Dutton, described this ordeal in a letter to his cousin. "The long agony is at last over," he wrote, "& it may well be called 'The Agony'; for I have never seen more anguish depicted in the countenances of any than the U. S. Corps of Cadets have manifested."[14]

Hill successfully survived "The Agony," thereby terminating his probationary period. He received his warrant as a cadet, and on February 20 signed the "Engagement for Service and Oath of

[10] S.H.S.P., *27*, 335 ff.
[11] S. Forman, *West Point,* (cited hereafter as Forman), 51.
[12] Heth MS., 5.
[13] Official Register of the Officers and Cadets of the U. S. Military Academy, West Point, New York, (cited hereafter as Official Register U.S.M.A.), 12, 1843.
[14] Forman, 100.

Allegiance" binding him to defend the United States against enemies from within and without.

Next major hurdle was the oral examination in June, when each cadet was interrogated in all branches of his studies before the Academic Board headed by Major Delafield, Superintendent and Commandant, and a Board of Visitors graced by Major General Winfield Scott. Hill passed, finishing the year 39th in a class of 83. He stood ahead of Jackson who was 51st and behind McClellan who placed 3rd. On the conduct rolls, he was charged with 53 demerits, ranking 142nd in the entire cadet corps of 223.[15]

During the following year as a Third Class cadet, Hill improved his rating in all subjects, rising to 23rd in order of general merit. As Hill's classmates laid out gaudy "furlough uniforms" for their only extended leave of absence from the Academy, Special Orders No. 72 were posted directing each student to proceed directly home without stopping en route at New York. The Commandant's directive was occasioned by "improper conduct" of the previous class in the gay metropolis.[16]

Hill headed straight for Culpeper where he enjoyed a summer of socializing and freedom from regimen. On returning to the Academy that fall, he commenced the study of Kane's Chemistry, Drawing, and Natural and Experimental Philosophy which then encompassed the field of Physics. Soon he became ill, and on resuming his studies he was permitted to recite after class to the instructor.[17] However, his condition rapidly deteriorated, and by the middle of November the Academy surgeon recommended that he be sent home on a twenty day leave of absence.[18]

The twenty day leave apparently was extended several months, for in February Hill wrote from Culpeper requesting pay that would become due on March 1.[19] This request is of interest in that

---

[15] Official Register U.S.M.A., p. 12, June, 1843.
[16] Post Orders No. 2, U. S. Corps of Cadets, Sept. 1842-Dec. 1848, Special Orders No. 72, June 25, 1844, p. 169.
[17] *Ibid.*, Special Orders No. 125, Nov. 7, 1844, p. 199.
[18] *Ibid.*, Special Orders No. 128, Nov. 19, 1844, p. 200.
[19] Adjutant's Letter Book, Feb. 19, 1845. Letter from Lt. McDowell to A. P. Hill.

although the $16 per month pay he received as a cadet did not materially affect his finances, he firmly insisted upon his due to the extent of bringing the matter to the Commandant's attention.

Unable to make up the work he missed while ill, Hill was turned back to repeat his Second Class studies. He reported to camp that summer, and struck up friendships with his new classmates that included Ambrose Burnside, Egbert Viele, Julian McAllister who was to be his roommate, and Harry Heth, a fellow Virginian. Heth and Hill became devoted beaus of two "wild though not bad" ladies (or "gyels" as Hill called them), who with their mother spent the summer of 1846 at West Point.[20]

In recognition of their social savoir-faire, Burnside, Heth and Hill represented the class of '47 as party managers. The interpretation of their prerogatives as social luminaries evoked a Post Order stating that "the managers of cadet parties who have permission to be absent from camp until taps the night of the parties, will report their return to the officer of the Guard, who will keep a record of the time they enter camp."[21]

That fall, Hill was appointed ranking Sergeant of his class in the Battalion of Cadets, a promotion based primarily upon leadership qualities. He again plunged into his Second Class courses, and passed them all finishing in the upper half of his class.

With considerable envy Hill watched his former classmates of the class of '46 receive their commissions and head for action in Mexico. Hoping that the war would last long enough for him to join in the hostilities, he began what doubtless seemed his longest year at the Academy. Fortunately, the First Class studies were heavy and challenging, comprising Engineering, Ethics, Artillery, Infantry Tactics, and Mineralogy and Geology.[22]

In February an episode occurred to break the monotonous winter routine. It had been the custom for army officers stationed at West Point to give a dinner on Washington's birthday in recognition of the approaching commissioning of First Class cadets as

---

[20] Heth MS, 17.
[21] Post Orders No. 2, U. S. Corps of Cadets, Sept. 1842-Dec. 1848, Special Orders No. 41, July 24, 1846, p. 133.
[22] Official Register U.S.M.A., 1843.

officers. For years the Cadet Captain and Adjutant had been invited to attend this banquet. For some reason the class of '47 was not accorded this recognition, whereupon the class indignantly voted that it had been "grievously insulted." Feeling that a more vigorous protest was in order, Harry Heth concocted a plan which he outlined one evening after taps to a group of ten cadets assembled in Hill's room. Hill, now a Lieutenant in the Cadet Corps, was not personally affected by the officers' snub as was his roommate who was Adjutant, but his sense of justice had been violated.

Heth's proposal, based on personal reconnaissance, was endorsed enthusiastically and set in motion. On the appointed evening, the vindicators, equipped with clothes bags, stealthily gained access to the storeroom of the officers' mess. Quickly they filled their bags with a variety of delicacies including sweetmeats, oranges, nuts, apples, wine and cigars which they lugged back to Hill's quarters. Then Heth and a small but fleet classmate named Burns returned to swoop the pièce de résistance.

As the serving man cautiously carried a luscious turkey from the kitchen across a yard to the officers' mess, Burns clipped him behind the ear sending him reeling toward Heth. Grabbing the bird, Heth stuffed it in his bag and bolted for the barracks. As he fondly reminisced years later, "Never were ten boys happier, never did a turkey have before or since, the flavor of this turkey," while the wine, drunk from a tin dipper, possessed "a bouquet flavor superior to old Madiera."[23]

More serious sessions in the barracks and at Benny Havens' tavern were devoted to discussions of the Mexican campaign and to mounting sectional rumblings. All of the provincial attitudes then current were mirrored in the conflicting views of the cadets. Through the interchange of opinions and the strong friendships formed there, the Academy served as a nationalizing influence. Thus, Powell Hill could vigorously espouse states' rights and at the same time form his closest friendships with McAllister,

---

[23] Heth MS, 12-13.

McClellan and Viele, all Northerners who believed just as firmly in a strong Federal government.

*   *   *   *

Graduating fifteenth in a class of thirty-eight, Brevet Second Lieutenant Powell Hill received his coveted orders to join the Light Battery of the First Regiment U. S. Artillery in Mexico.[24] Stopping briefly at Culpeper, he proceeded to New Orleans where he embarked for Vera Cruz. Some distance at sea the transport collided with a ship from Galveston. Hurled from his berth, Hill bounded onto deck where he saw that the wheelhouse had been shorn away. In addition, the ship was listing sharply as a result of the horses and mules below having been knocked to one side. Hill sounded the alarm, then ran back to his room where he hastily gathered his watch, purse, and a table leaf to serve as a raft in the event it became necessary to abandon ship. Fortunately the boat righted itself, and after returning to New Orleans for repairs it sailed without incident to Vera Cruz.

Arriving on Mexican soil, Hill was assigned command of a cavalry detachment and ordered to join General Lane who was marching on Mexico City. When two of the wagons broke down, orders were issued for the men to stay with them until help arrived. Some of the raw troops grew impatient and urged Hill to push on. Refused, several malcontents attempted to slip away only to find the road blocked by Lieutenant Hill, mounted and fingering a pair of cocked horse pistols. The mutineers decided to stay.

Joining General Lane at Jalopa, Hill participated in several of the closing engagements at Huamantla and Atlixco.[25] Upon T. J. Jackson's promotion to First Lieutenant in the same regiment, Hill was elevated to Second Lieutenant on August 20, 1847, and assigned to the battery of Captain John B. Magruder.[26]

When the capital fell, General Winfield Scott permitted his officers to obtain quarters in private residences. Making inquiry at an inviting house, Hill and a fellow junior officer were met by

---

[24] "Souvenir Booklet." Letter from A. P. Hill, Oct. 25, 1863, to a friend who had asked for an outline of his career. For many years this letter hung in the State Library of Virginia.

[25] G. W. Cullum, *Biographical Register of the Officers and Graduates of the U. S. Military Academy from 1802 to 1867,* (cited hereafter as Cullum), 189.

[26] *Ibid.*, "Souvenir Booklet," Hill's letter of Oct. 25, 1863.

a squat woman who energetically vented her indignation and resentment on the pair of would-be boarders. From her expostulations and gesticulations, Hill finally deduced that the matron was none other than a sister of Santa Anna. Thinking quickly, he managed to convey to her the indignities she might suffer were her relationship to the Mexican commander made so conspicuously apparent to the conquering troops. Sobered and partially convinced, she admitted them to tenancy.

In the conquered capital, Hill succumbed to the beautiful senoritas who inspired even Tom Jackson to learn Spanish and dancing. Writing to his father, Hill confessed, " 'Tis a fact that the ladies of Mexico are beautiful—and oh how beautiful—but very few of them have ever read Wayland's *Moral Science . . .* You know my failing. 'Tis an inheritance of this family, this partiality for the women."[27] One affair grew so serious that he queried his parents: "How would you relish a Mexican daughter-in-law?" However, this romance was terminated by consummation of the peace negotiations in the spring of 1848. Hill left Mexico full of romantic memories as compensation for disappointingly minor fighting.

* * * *

In the fall of 1849, Lieutenant Hill began an extended and unexciting tour of duty in the South. The First Artillery Regiment, of which Hill had been appointed Quartermaster, was ordered to subdue the marauding Seminole Indians who had escaped transfer to western reservations under the Treaty of Payne Landing in 1832.

The elusive Seminoles under Chief William Bowlegs led the mountain-climbing veterans of the Mexican campaign a lively chase through the mosquito-infested swamps and thickets of the Everglades. Failure of the campaigns of 1849-50 and 1853-55 to resolve this situation did not perturb the young Quartermaster who wrote his sister Lucy that an all-out expedition against Bowlegs " 'twould be unwise in Uncle Sam to engage in such an expensive war as 'twould prove to be, and only to drive a few poor, lazy, harmless devils from the country that no white man could, or would live in."

---

[27] Robertson, Part II, 8, Oct. 21, 1934.

In September, 1851, Hill was promoted to First Lieutenant. The following year he undertook a brief assignment at Fort Ricketts on the Texas frontier. Otherwise, he relieved the dull routine of garrison existence at Key West and Barrancas by fishing, hunting and reading.[28]

Life in this swampy climate progressively impaired Hill's health, and an attack of yellow fever[29] finally necessitated a leave of absence. After recuperating at Culpeper he wrote directly to Jefferson Davis, Secretary of War, requesting a transfer to the U. S. Coast Survey Office in Washington.[30] The request was granted in November, 1855, to this ambitious Lieutenant just turned thirty, who described himself at this period as the veteran of "two long miseries and no fighting."[31]

With characteristic enthusiasm and efficiency Hill embarked upon his new duties under Professor A. D. Bache, Superintendent of the Coast Survey. In 1856 he assisted a team studying the triangulation of the Hudson River between Albany and New Baltimore.[32] Upon completion of this project he served as general assistant in the Washington office. Here, in addition to his regular duties, Hill devoted considerable attention to improving printing operations within the department. His efforts resulted in the development of a process which markedly increased the distinctness of map printing.[33]

Within a short time he was so familiar with departmental operations that he was placed in charge of the office during absences of his superior.[34] The high regard in which he was held is indicated by his chief's report for 1857 stating: "Lieutenant A. P. Hill continues to occupy this position (viz, general assistant), and the interest as well as ability, displayed by him in performing the requirements of the office cannot fail to meet your warmest commendation . . ."[35]

---

[28] S.H.S.P., *20*, 376.
[29] "The Land We Love," April, 1866-67, 288.
[30] *Ibid.*
[31] Robertson, Part II, 8, Oct. 21, 1934.
[32] Report of the Superintendent of the Coast Survey, Report of 1856, 38-39.
[33] *Ibid.*, 1857, 190, 212-17.
[34] *Ibid.*, 1857, 119.
[35] *Ibid.*, 1857, 192.

CHAPTER III

"As Necessary To Me As My Dinner"

POWELL HILL once reminded his sister Lucy, "You know than I am so constituted that to be in love with some one is as necessary to me as my dinner . . ."[1] His warm, affectionate nature which found expression as a gay blade at West Point and in Mexico, subsequently sought permanent rapport in a strange series of romances.

His first fiancée was Emma Wilson, a Baltimore schoolmate of Lucy's at Potapsco Female Seminary in Ellicott City, Maryland. Hill courted this beauteous brunette while stationed at Fort McHenry, prior to his assignment in Florida. Although they were affianced, the engagement was broken for unknown reasons.

Upon assuming his duties in the Coast Survey Office, Hill quickly became involved in one of the Capitol's more celebrated affaires du coeur. Object of his affections was blonde, blue-eyed Ellen B. Marcy, daughter of Captain and Mrs. Randolph B. Marcy. "Miss Nelly" as she was known among the younger set, spent several winters in Washington where she became noted for her charm and beauty.

Among the dashing Virginian's more ardent competitors was his close friend, Captain George McClellan, who had gained the respect and friendship of Nelly's father during the latter's Red River expedition in 1852. "Little Mac's" suit was further strengthened with Nelly's domineering and socially ambitious parents, by his announced intention of resigning from the army to become an executive of the Illinois Central Railroad.[2]

Nelly, however, brushed aside McClellan's proposal of marriage, and before long she was seen constantly in the company of Lieutenant Hill. When rumors that Nelly Marcy was engaged to Powell Hill became the topic of Washington society, Papa Marcy

---

1 Robertson, Part IV, 8, Nov. 4, 1934.
2 *Photographic History of Civil War, X,* 164.

acted promptly from his remote post in Texas. On May 28, 1856 he wrote anxiously to his first-born from Laredo:

In regard to Mr. Hill I know but little of him, he seemed to be a gentlemanly man, and if he was not in the army but engaged in some business that would insure you a comfortable home I should not have so much objection, but I should suppose you would have more ambition. You have such ample powers of pleasing and if you chose could make a much better match. You say you are not ambitious but you are fond of attention and gaiety, and you certainly never have these in the army. There are plenty of men who have wealth and position in society who are equally agreeable as Mr. Hill, and who (would) make you fully as good a husband. You do not think these things of any moment now, but you will see that it is a stubborn truth in a few years. And if you do not consider the wishes of your parents who are your truest friends you may have cause to regret it. I understood you to tell me before I left Washington that I had no cause to fear on your account. That you would not allow any of the young officers to pay you special attentions. Have you violated the solemn pledge to me or not? You say you have not made any promises to Mr. Hill, then how does it happen that you have become so interested. You should when you saw he was attentive consulted your mother, she would have given you the proper advice. She has spent the greater part of her life in devotion to your welfare, and the dearest wish of her heart has been to see you occupy an honorable position in life. And it has always given her more pleasure to have you well spoken of than to be complimented herself. Such kind and devoted attention deserves some return and the least you could do would be to confide in her . . .

You have been gratified in every wish except this and I think it is no more than right that you should pay some little regard to the wishes of your parents. I feel too proud of you to have you throw yourself, or to marry a man who cannot place you in a prominent position in society, and I was greatly grieved when I learned that you had allowed yourself to go so directly in opposition to my wishes. You say you cannot control your feeling—that is an error. You should have gone directly to your mother when you discovered that you were beginning to favor the visits or attentions of any one and consulted her judgement. If I am not mistaken I asked you if Mr. Hill was not with you too often, and expressed my entire disapprobation to such attentions from him, and that you led me to believe that you would not encourage him or any other officer . . . Did my affection for you merit such a breach of confidence.

I inquired about Mr. Hill's family at Corpus Christi and I am inclined to believe that they are in very moderate circumstances so far as property goes.

A. P. Hill. From a photo probably taken at the outbreak of the war.

Mrs. A. P. Hill, the former Kitty Morgan McClung, whom Hill affectionately called "Dolly." From a painting courtesy Calvin M. Applegate.

I have written a letter to your mother when I first received your letter and given her instructions to go into the country and remain there. I forgive you, but I shall expect that you at once abandon all communication with Mr. Hill. If you do not comply with my wishes in this respect I cannot tell what my feelings toward you would become. I fear that my ardent affection would turn to hate. Do nothing therefore my dear child without choosing between me and him. If I cannot trust you who can I trust.[3]

This imploring letter from Nelly's possessive father was followed shortly by another reiterating the hardships of army life and urging a suspension of the affair for six or seven months.[4] In her dilemma, Nelly spiritedly reminded her father that he had voiced no objections against McClellan, although he, too, was an army officer. She also relayed her father's concern over Hill's financial status to her suitor who took pains to state it specifically in a letter to Captain Marcy.

Unmoved by Nelly and unimpressed by Hill, the Captain replied:

If it had not been for your affair with Mr. Hill I should have been exceedingly pleased at your visit to Washington and at the many good acquaintances you have made. You know how proud I am of you and how much I idolize you, and I cannot think of your marrying any man that is not occupying a prominent position in society . . .
I received a letter from Mr. Hill in which he says he is worth about $10,000. This is something but not much. I have not yet answered his letter. Although I should not have objected to your marrying Captain McClellan, yet I had no great desire for it after he went into the line of the army, as the same hard fate would have awaited you as with other officers. His talents and well known high character with the warm friendship which exists between us would have caused me to discard all other considerations and given you to him.[5]

Under such implacable pressure Nelly gradually weakened. She confided in her father who finally persuaded her to return Hill's engagement ring in which was inscribed "Je t'aime." A letter from

---

[3] G. B. McClellan MSS, Letter from Capt. R. B. Marcy to Nelly Marcy, May 28, 1865.
[4] *Ibid.*, Letter of June 3, 1856.
[5] *Ibid.*, Letter of June 12, 1856.

father to daughter written on the last day of July, 1856 reveals
his joy:

> . . . on my return found your letter in which you express a determination to be governed by our wishes in regard to Mr. Hill . . . You are the pride of my heart and a dear good girl![6]

Meantime, Powell Hill's persistent but futile efforts to hold
Nelly against the united opposition of her parents had engendered
considerable bitterness, particularly with Mrs. Marcy. This feeling
against his on-the-scene antagonist reached a climax when Hill
traced "calumnious" reports to her. With characteristic insistence
on his rights, he composed a four page indignation letter to Captain
Marcy:

My dear Sir:

I have been most deeply injured but the peculiar nature and unknown
source of the calumny prevents my seeking that redress which would be most
pleasing and most satisfactory—You know that last Spring I asked that
you would consent to my marriage with your daughter, to which you postponed giving a decided reply—This was made by me in all *honor* and good
faith, and I supposed then and *now* that your opposition touched not my
personal character—Mrs. Marcy has evidenced a decided(ly) hostility to
my suit, which though it pained me much, yet was conceded to her as her
right, and I was silent as long as I conceived the grounds of her opposition
to be such that neither *you* nor *I* should blush to hear—I now find that
I have been in grievous error.

I have heard from truthful lips and with delicacy, that Mrs. Marcy's
objections (one at least and the only one to which I reply), as stated to
me, is that from certain early imprudences, (youthful indiscretions I suppose), my health and constitution had become so impaired, so weakened,
that no mother could yield her daughter to me, unless to certain unhappiness—This is the substance. The ornaments may be imagined—Now
I do Mrs. Marcy the justice to believe that this has been told her, and that
she without weighing the matter calmly has believed it, for I have ever
thought her a woman of good feeling though somewhat warped against
me—I hope you appreciate my situation, and the deep feeling of mortification which must be mine—the charge is simply indicative, yet fatally
blighting—True or untrue the mere rumor is sufficient to make a man bow
his head in shame—hence I cannot meet and refute it, as in any other
case, and as my inclination would lead me to do in this, for this would give

---

[6] *Ibid.,* Letter of July 31, 1856.

it the publicity I desire to avoid—At present, as I hope it has reached but few, and these I wish to scotch it, if not kill it—I can trace no farther back than your wife, and to you as the proper person I address myself—If this charge were true, and knowing it to be so, I had asked your daughter's hand, my honor indeed be but a name, and my simple denial would be of no weight—With my friends and those who know me a simple denial would be unnecessary, and the enclosed notes are only to convince those of the injustice done, who, I hope, believed in the truth of the report, before making use of it against me—I have but little more to say—I ask it of you as one gentleman from another, as one officer who has been wronged, from a brother officer, who can right him, that you put this matter right in the proper quarter, and that your wife correct this false impression with whomever she may have had any agency in hearing it—I think too that in justice both to herself and myself she should make known the name of her informant to be used by me as I see fit.

Very respectfully,

A. P. Hill[7]

Marcy annotated the back of Hill's letter with a statement that he had answered the maligned young suitor and that he believed the rumors to be "a base fabrication." He promised to write his wife and let Hill know the result. True to his word, Captain Marcy wrote Nelly's mother peremptorily that if Hill's charges were true, "I should insist upon Ellen's marrying Mr. Hill at once as a just reparation."

Mrs. Marcy apparently allayed her husband's fears, and Hill —contrary to his later custom—did not press the matter. In fact, after the affair had become a memory, he wrote generously to McClellan:

I have heard a report lately which has annoyed me a good deal, that the Marcy's have given their consent to My marrying Miss Nelly, and that I had declined—Now you would of course know that this was untrue, but others might believe it—If you should ever hear it, flatly contradict it for me—The last communication I ever had with Miss Nelly about two years ago, she positively and without leaving a ray of hope, rejected me—and that's the truth—This much is certainly her due.[8]

These letters to Captain Marcy and McClellan afford an interesting insight into Hill's character. Angrily aroused and offended

---

[7] *Ibid.*, Letter from A. P. Hill to R. B. Marcy, May 29, 1857.
[8] *Ibid.*, Letter from A. P. Hill to Capt. G. B. McClellan, June 18, 1859.

by Mrs. Marcy's rumors, Hill bluntly aired his grievance and sternly demanded that proper redress which would be "most pleasing and satisfactory." On the other hand, his letter to McClellan was equally concerned with correcting a false impression at the expense of his own vanity. He was genuinely "annoyed" that a rumor unflattering to Nelly might be credited. And to set the record straight—"this much is certainly her due"— he frankly recounted a painful memory to his rival suitor whose persistent efforts finally won Miss Nelly.

Although Powell Hill soon transferred his affections to another, his proud, sensitive nature was profoundly jarred by this blighted romance. His dynamic temperament would not permit him to brood over a frustrated affair, but he could not forget it. During the war a mutual friend wrote to Nelly, "I have seen at different times many of your old army friends, Gen'l A. P. Hill, Edward Johnson, and many others and I assure you 'Miss Nelly,' as they still call you, is often spoken of."[9]

As for McClellan, the patient and successful suitor, his Army of the Potomac was to be assailed repeatedly in front and flank by A. P. Hill's Light Division. Tiring of this rough treatment, McClellan's soldiers formulated a theory that Hill was wreaking vengeance on his erstwhile rival. Early one gloomy morning Hill reportedly was fiercely at it again. As one of "Little Mac's" veterans rolled out of a comfortable blanket and shouldered arms in the surrounding confusion, he exclaimed disgustedly, "My God Nelly, why didn't you marry him (Hill)!" When this anecdote was related to McClellan at an 1885 reunion in Sharpsburg, he smiled and commented: "Fiction no doubt, but surely no one could have married a more gallant soldier than A. P. Hill."[10]

In 1857 Hill sustained another loss in the death of his father. Although he possessed the sensitive nature of his mother who had passed away in 1853, he patterned his personality after that of his modest, affable father. Father and son had been very close, and with his mentor's passing, Powell turned to Lucy as confidante.

---

[9] *Ibid.*, Letter from Mary T. Jackson to Nelly Marcy, Nov. 3, 1863.
[10] H. Kyd Douglas, *I Rode With Stonewall*, (cited hereafter as Douglas), 178.

Soon he had important news for her. From Washington he wrote:

> I can reach you and you can reach me so easily that in case either of us is married, we can surely attend the other. Look out for mine at any time! . . . There is now a little siren who has thrown her net around me, and I know not how soon I may cry 'Peccavi!' and yield up my right to flirt with whom I please. She is a sensible little beauty, and if the spasm will stay in me long enough, and she will say 'yes,' why I don't believe I could do better . . ."[11]

The "little siren" who had "thrown her net" around Hill was a wealthy young widow, Mrs. Kitty Morgan McClung of Louisville, Kentucky. With her older sister, Henrietta Morgan, she paid a visit to the capital in 1857, staying at the Willard Hotel. Hill met her at a party given by a mutual friend, Dr. Wood, of Washington.[12]

As his letter to Lucy discloses, the young assistant in the Coast Survey quickly succumbed to the charms of this vivacious, blue-eyed songbird whose luxuriant light brown hair fell gracefully over her slender shoulders. Kitty's doll-like appearance as a child prompted her Negro mammy to nickname her "Dolly," an appellation her suitor readily adopted.

Unhampered by parental opposition from Calvin and Henrietta Morgan, Hill's courtship proceeded smoothly. On June 18, 1859 he wrote elatedly to McClellan of his impending marriage:

My dear Mac

> I have been waiting for some time in the expectation that you would wend your way in this direction, and that I might have the opportunity of telling you over a cigar, that which I have been wanting to tell you for the last month—I'm afraid there is no mistake about it this time, old fellow, and please God, and Kentucky Blue-grass, my bachelor life is about to end, and I shall swell the number of blessed martyrs who have yielded up freedom to crinoline and blue eyes . . . She is young, 24 years . . . gentle and amiable, yet lovely, and sufficiently good looking for me—and what's more I know that you will like her, and when you have come to know her, say that I have done well—I believe, too, that her income is equal to mine—and if this be so I am glad for her sake, and if not I shall not be disappointed—I expect to be married in Lexington, Ken. on the 18th of

[11] Robertson, Part IV, 8, Nov. 4, 1934.
[12] *Ibid.*

July and if you could come down from Chicago, you know that there is no
one whose presence would delight me more . . .

Hill[13]

The marriage took place as scheduled at Hopemont, the
Lexington home of Dolly's mother.[14] The bride's older brother,
John Hunt Morgan, soon to achieve fame as "The Rebel Raider,"
was best man at the Episcopal ceremony officiated by Reverend
J. H. Morrison. Little did Dolly envision on the morning of her
wedding that five years later her net covered taffeta wedding dress
would be made into a colorful, glistening battle-flag for her
husband's first command, the Thirteenth Virginia Infantry Regiment.[15]

Following the ceremony the newlyweds honeymooned en route
to Washington where Hill resumed his duties in the Coast Survey.
Throughout their five and a half years of marriage, the two were
devoted to each other. Powell was proud of his wife's charm and
musical talents. Discovering that she was jealous and sensitive
about his previous affairs, he considerately requested Lucy not
to "tease Dolly about Miss Wilson and my other affair."[16]

Although the war necessitated frequent and prolonged separ-
ations, Hill spent as much time with his family as duty permitted.
Dolly, in turn, followed him wherever possible, bundling her money
and jewels in her hair which she rolled into a chignon. Her habit
of remaining with the General until a battle was imminent caused
him repeated anxiety, and her departure signaled action to the
troops.[17]

With the birth of his two daughters, Frances Russell and Lucy
Lee, Hill became a doting father. For Lucy, born in 1863, his men
built a rough-hewn cradle and General Lee, her godfather, held
the child in his arms during the christening ceremony at St. Thomas
Parish in Orange, Virginia. During the siege of Petersburg Lucy's

---

[13] G. B. McClellan MSS, Letter from A. P. Hill to G. B. McClellan, June 18,
1859.
[14] H. Swiggett, *Rebel Raider,* (cited hereafter as Swiggett), 13.
[15] This flag is preserved in the Confederate Museum in Richmond, Va.
[16] Robertson, Part IV, 8, Nov. 4, 1934.
[17] W. D. Pender MSS, Letter to his wife, June 7, 1863.

godfather visited the Hill household, on one occasion bringing "some delicious apples."[18]

Years after the war, Dr. J. William Jones, army chaplain and friend of Hill's, wrote of the General that "perhaps his noble traits of mind and heart shone most conspicuously in the intercourse of private friendship, or in the midst of his family. It was the writer's proud privilege to have enjoyed his friendship, and to have often seen him in the midst of domestic bliss; but he may not lift the veil or expose to the public gaze these sacred scenes."[19] A more intimate source revealed that in private life he was "genial, approachable, and affectionate"[20] as well as "tender and generous."[21] Removed from the turmoil of the battle-field, his restless, fiery nature found repose in the little family circle.

---

[18] *R. E. Lee, III,* 527.
[19] J. W. Jones, "Sketches of Southern Generals," (cited hereafter as "Sketches of Southern Generals"), Metropolitan Record and New York Vindicator, Part V, 1866. Furnished to the author through the courtesy of the Virginia Historical Society.
[20] *Dictionary of American Biography, IX,* 25.
[21] The *Times-Dispatch,* Richmond, June 11, 1905. Quoted from an interview with the General's wife. Clipping furnished to the author through the courtesy of the Confederate Museum, Richmond.

CHAPTER IV

"War's Labor Lost"

AS POWELL HILL witnessed the impending sectional collision from the crossroads of the nation's capital, he was clear in his own mind which course he would take. Long discussions with his politically-minded father supplemented by independent study had strengthened his belief in the doctrine of states' rights and concurrently confirmed his antipathy to the evils of slavery. He never owned a slave,[1] and when a young negro, subsequently proved innocent, was mob-lynched in Culpeper for the alleged murder of a white man, Hill fumed to his brother that "Virginia must crawl unless you vindicate good order or discipline and hang every .... connected with the outrage."[2]

However, Hill regarded states' rights as the fundamental issue with slavery simply providing the popular occasion. Therefore, despite insistent appeals of associates to remain in Washington with assurances that in the Coast Survey he would not be required to bear arms against Virginia, Lieutenant Hill left the Washington office in the spring of 1860 for an extended leave of absence from the army, following which he resigned his commission on March 30, 1861.[3]

Before tendering his resignation, Hill talked with McClellan, now a prosperous railroad executive in Cincinnati. As they exchanged views on friendly terms, Hill stated that he could not engage in a war against his native state but would "defend her to the death." As he prepared to depart the next day, McClellan said, "Hill I am truly sorry you are going to leave us; but to be frank I cannot blame you. If I were in your place, I would do as

---

[1] B. B. Munford, *Virginia's Attitude Toward Slavery and Secession*, 157.
[2] Robertson, Part II, 8, October 21, 1934.
[3] Cullum, 189.

you are about to do; but I am an Ohioan and will stand by my state, too."[4]

On April 17, Virginia passed an ordinance of secession, where-upon Hill at Culpeper immediately proffered his service to Governor Letcher. He bolstered his petition for a commission with letters of recommendation from Charles H. Smith and James L. Kemper.[5]

May 9, Hill received his commission as a Colonel of the Virginia Volunteers, assigned to command the Thirteenth Virginia Infantry Regiment. He was ordered to report to Harper's Ferry, gateway to the rich Shenandoah Valley and one of the half dozen strategic points selected by General Lee as vital to the state's defense. Here, late in May, General Joseph E. Johnston assumed command of the Army of the Shenandoah. In addition to Colonel A. P. Hill, Johnston's command included such soon-to-be-distinguished Confederate heroes as his Chief-of-Staff, Colonel E. Kirby Smith who would command the Trans-Mississippi forces, Lieutenant Colonel J. E. B. Stuart who would win laurels as chief of the cavalry, Captain W. N. Pendleton who would serve as chief of Lee's artillery, and Colonel T. J. Jackson whose fame was to rival that of Lee.

Johnston found his 7,000 raw volunteers equipped with little except the customary initial flush of enthusiasm and optimism. "They were," Johnston wrote, "undisciplined, several regiments without accoutrements, and with an entirely inadequate supply of ammunition."[6] Added to these woes was an epidemic of measles which confined nearly forty percent of the men in hospitals.[7]

In the camp of the Thirteenth Virginia, Colonel Hill rigorously drilled his regiment consisting of 550 fellow Virginians and one company from Baltimore. Infusing his command with the "forward spirit" for which his troops were to become renowned,[8] the regiment

---

[4] C.V., *16*, 178.

[5] *Calendar of State Papers of Virginia.* Letter from James L. Kemper to the Governor, April 22, 1861; Letter from Charles H. Smith to the Governor, May 7, 1861.

[6] *War of the Rebellion. Official Records of the Union and Confederate Armies. Series I* (cited hereafter as O.R.), *2*, 471.

[7] C.M.H., *III*, 71.

[8] S.H.S.P., *2*, 302.

soon caught the eye of General Johnston who commented on its "veteran-like appearance."[9]

A situation was brewing on Johnston's front which soon required Hill's "veteran-like" troops. At Chambersburg, just inside the Pennsylvania border and almost due north of Harper's Ferry, sixty-nine-year-old General Robert Patterson was organizing a force of 14,000 to invade the Shenandoah Valley; while in northwestern Virginia, another sizeable Federal army under General George B. McClellan was poised to march down the Northwest Turnpike and unite with Patterson at Winchester.

On June 10 General Patterson ordered Colonel Lewis Wallace (who achieved more enduring fame after the war as the author of *Ben-Hur*), to occupy Cumberland, Maryland with his Eleventh Indiana. There Wallace heard reports that "several hundred rebel troops were quartered at Romney . . . drilling there, impressing Union men, and in other ways oppressing the local citizens."[10] Aroused, he decided to surprise the Confederate garrison under Colonel A. C. Cummins.

Leaving Cumberland Tuesday night, June 12 with about 500 men, Wallace travelled by rail to New Creek, thence by foot over rough mountainous roads to Romney. When within a short distance of the town early the next morning, the head of Wallace's column was fired upon by a mounted picket, who turned and dashed back to warn the garrison.[11]

Colonel Cummins hurriedly formed his three companies of raw volunteers into line along the bluff on which Romney is situated. Each man pocketed a few rounds of ammunition and readied his flintlock musket sent from Harper's Ferry. Lacking artillerists, Cummins nevertheless hoped to bluff the enemy by posting two cannon from the John Brown raid behind the infantry from which position they could ostensibly sweep the town's approaches.[12]

After exchanging several shots with the charging Hoosiers, the

---

9 Robertson, Part V, 8, Nov. 11, 1934.
10 O.R., *2*, 123.
11 *Ibid.*
12 Casler, J. O., *Four Years in the Stonewall Brigade* (cited hereafter as Casler), 21-23.

defenders broke and fled as a flanking party advanced within rifle range. The Virginians headed for Winchester while the Eleventh Indiana entered the town. Following a brief search for arms, Wallace marched his troops back to New Creek.[13] In his dramatic style, he reported to Patterson, "One good result has come of it, the loyal men in that region have taken heart."[14]

Through usually reliable sources in Winchester, Johnston was notified that Romney had been occupied by 2,000 Federals, presumed to be the vanguard of McClellan's army. Fearing that McClellan was moving to effect a junction with Patterson, Johnston dispatched Colonels A. P. Hill and S. B. Gibbons with their regiments by special train to Winchester. He then burned the bridge across the Potomac and readied the rest of the army to follow as soon as transportation could be provided.[15]

Hill, who had been placed in command of the advance troops, picked up Colonel Vaughn's recently arrived Third Tennessee regiment at Winchester and moved toward Romney in accordance with Johnston's orders to "take the best position and best measures to check the advance of the enemy."[16]

At Romney, Hill learned the details of Wallace's raid together with the welcome news that a Federal force was stationed at New Creek Depot astride the Baltimore and Ohio Railroad linking Washington with the West. Without hesitation, Hill determined to avenge Cummins' rout. In an almost exact reversal of the Romney engagement, he sent Colonel Vaughn with companies from the Third Tennessee and the Thirteenth Virginia on an all-night march over the same country trails recently trod by Wallace's Eleventh Indiana.

Arriving at New Creek about dawn, Vaughn found the enemy, about 250 strong, posted on the north bank of the Potomac near the railroad bridge but with no pickets stationed. Vaughn's troops enthusiastically executed his order to charge, surprising the Federals who fled in all directions after firing a few token shots. With their

   13 *Ibid.*, O.R., *2*, 123.
   14 O.R., *2*, 124.
   15 C.M.H., *III*, 73; O.R., *2*, 471; A. H. Noll, *General Kirby-Smith*, 178.
   16 O.R., *2*, 471.

long head-start, the defenders managed to escape capture. Only one casualty, a private wounded in the arm, marred Vaughn's victory.[17]

After collecting a stand of enemy colors and two loaded pieces of abandoned artillery, Vaughn burned No. 21 railroad bridge of the Baltimore and Ohio system to its piers. Then he marched his proud fighters eighteen fatiguing miles back to Romney where Hill commended the Tennessean for the "handsome manner" in which orders had been executed "to the letter."[18] In transmitting Hill's and Vaughn's reports to Richmond, Johnston observed that the engagement "exhibits (the) difference between the spirit of our troops and those of the United States."[19]

While Hill was directing the Romney-New Creek expedition, Johnston moved his command to Bunker Hill, a hamlet midway between Martinsburg and Winchester. He considered this position more advantageous than Harper's Ferry from which to prevent a junction of Patterson and McClellan. When McClellan failed to move toward Winchester, Hill was withdrawn to the new encampment, and a cavalry regiment under Colonel McDonald was left to defend the area around Romney.[20]

Powell Hill's successful campaign was duly acclaimed in the camps of the Army of the Shenandoah, and friends confidently predicted his speedy promotion to brigadier general in command of the regiments he had just led.[21] Consequently, he was keenly disappointed when the Richmond authorities held that Virginia already had more than her share of brigadiers and that no more appointments from the "Old Dominion" state would be made at this time. Instead, the three regiments recently entrusted to his command together with the First Maryland Infantry Battalion were organized in the Fourth Brigade and placed under the command of Colonel Arnold Elzey of Maryland.[22]

With his army directly across Patterson's invasion route to the

---

[17] C.M.H., *III*, 76; O.R., *2*, 130.
[18] O.R., *2*, 130-31.
[19] O.R., *2*, 130.
[20] O.R., *2*, 472.
[21] S.H.S.P., *20*, 379.
[22] O.R., *2*, 470; S.H.S.P., *20*, 379.

Valley, Johnston daily anticipated an attack. From his headquarters he issued a stream of petitions to Richmond for more men and ammunition. With his fixation for the offensive, Hill undoubtably abhorred his chief's cautious and defensive tactics which prompted Jackson to write his wife, "I hope the General will do something soon . . ."[23]

Nor did Hill disdain the possibility of an enemy attack as flagrantly as his senior Colonel, Arnold Elzey. One evening this crusty Marylander invited the sentinel guarding his quarters to join the officers in a round of drinks. After imbibing freely, Elzey retired and the sentinel returned to his post. At daybreak the guard stuck his head in the tent and roused his slumbering chief by raucously exclaiming: "Ain't it about time for us to take another drink?" Thus awakened, Elzey's expansiveness of the previous evening evaporated, and he ordered the sentinel taken to the guard-house for insolence.[24]

Early in July, Patterson again bestirred his command briefly. Crossing the Potomac he drove in Johnston's pickets and occupied Martinsburg. There his advance foundered due to expiration of the ninety-day enlistment period which threatened to deplete his ill-clad, underfed volunteers who longed to return home.[25]

Ignorant of Patterson's plight, Johnston sent Jackson forward, while he continued to appeal for reinforcements. However, instead of strengthening him, Richmond telegraphed Johnston on Wednesday, July 17, to reinforce Beauregard at Manassas against General Irvin McDowell's "On To Richmond" drive. Receiving the telegram at 1 A.M. Thursday morning, Johnston determined to join Beauregard as soon as possible, because "the best service which the Army of the Shenandoah could render was to prevent the defeat of that of the Potomac."[26]

After arranging for the care of his 1,700 sick and wounded

---

[23] B. Davis, *They Called Him Stonewall,* 142.
[24] Casler, 25.
[25] G. F. R. Henderson, *Stonewall Jackson and the American Civil War* (cited hereafter as Henderson), 100; O.R., 2, 169-79.
[26] O.R., 2, 473. During this period of the war, Beauregard's command was known as the Army of the Potomac, a name which McClellan subsequently appropriated for his Federal army.

in Winchester and leaving some militia and Stuart's cavalry to screen his departure, Johnston started his command, now 11,000 strong, toward Manassas. Chief-of-Staff Kirby Smith was assigned command of Elzey's Fourth Brigade which brought up the rear.[27]

A creeping pace coupled with frequent delays were the despair of officers as troops forded the cold, swift Shenandoah, crossed the Blue Ridge at Ashby's Gap, and proceeded along the damp country road to the Piedmont station of the Manassas Gap Railroad where they boarded a long line of freight and cattle cars for a jolting thirty-five mile journey to Manassas Junction.[28]

By Sunday morning, July 21, three of Johnston's four brigades had arrived at Manassas. However, the non-arrival of the Fourth Brigade upset Beauregard's plan for a general offensive predicated on assurances from the president of the railroad that his line could deliver all of Johnston's troops by Saturday.

The circumstances delaying the Fourth Brigade would have been ludicrous had they been less critical. Bringing up the rear, this brigade entrained the overtaxed railway at 2 A.M. Sunday morning. For almost two days the train had been shuttling between Piedmont and Manassas on a single track road sporting only a single engine. Soldiers got no rest as they hauled derailed cars back on the track and shoveled water into the trough when the engine's water supply became exhausted. So frequent and frustrating were the interruptions that the press called for an investigation claiming that "the evil is too enormous to be longer overlooked."[29]

As the train finally approached Manassas Junction about noon Sunday, the rattle of musketry swelled so deafeningly that Kirby Smith halted the train and debouched his men. Hill was ordered to strengthen a garrison on the Confederate right while Smith hurried the other three regiments through clouds of dust to the hotly engaged left.[30]

During the Fourth Brigade's exasperating struggle to reach

---

[27] C.V., *7*, 108: A. H. Noll, *General Kirby-Smith*, 178.
[28] S.H.S.P., *19*, 87; Henderson, 101; D. S. Freeman, *Lee's Lieutenants* (cited hereafter as Lee's Lieutenants), *1*, 44.
[29] *Richmond Daily Examiner*, July 27, 1861, p. 2, col. 1.
[30] *Ibid.* Letter from an officer in the Maryland Brigade to his wife, August 17, 1861. See also C.V., *7*, 108; O.R., *2*, 476, 496.

Manassas, McDowell had assumed the offensive with a wide
flanking movement which threatened to roll up the Confederate
left. Concurrently, Federal batteries demonstrated in concert against
Johnston's right. Smith had sent Hill with the Thirteenth Virginia
to reinforce this sector against a possible thrust by large Union
forces concentrated opposite the lower fords of Bull Run. Hill
reported to Colonel Terrett at Camp Pickens, a fort constructed
earlier in the summer to protect the railroad and supply depot at
Manassas Junction. His artillerist's eyes noted with interest the
entrenchments which bristled with light field guns and fifteen 24-
pounder smoothbore guns mounted on naval carriages.[31]

Powell Hill doubtless cared little to which end of the winding
eight mile front he was assigned as long as his regiment engaged
in heavy fighting. Therefore, he must have experienced indescribable
gnawings as he waited at Camp Pickens that afternoon for the
attack which did not come, while from the hotly contested left came
envy-inspiring news. Kirby Smith had been wounded while putting
his troops into position on the Federal flank, and Elzey succeeded
to the command. Joined at the critical moment by Early, the
Confederate line swept irresistibly forward. Assailed on front and
flank, McDowell's 30,000 bluecoats turned and fled toward
Washington.[32]

Hill watched with misgivings the failure to consummate this
rout with a march on the capital. Nor were his spirits lifted by
Beauregard's and Johnston's official reports, neither of which
understandably lauded Hill and his regiment for their passive role
during the battle. Being human, the ambitious colonel of the Thirteenth Virginia may have reflected on the quirk of fate which had
catapulted Elzey rather than himself into fame as Beauregard's
"Blücher of the day."[33] He could not foresee, of course, that fourteen months hence on a critically-contested field 50 miles distant,
he would earn the similar title, "Blücher of Sharpsburg."[34]

---

[31] J. M. Hanson, *Bull Run Remembers* (cited hereafter as Hanson), 33; *Prince
William,* 145.

[32] *Battles and Leaders of the Civil War* (cited hereafter as B. and L.), *1,* 249.

[33] *Richmond Dispatch,* August 5, 1861, p. 2, col. 3.

[34] *Richmond Examiner,* May 22, 1863, p. 2, col. 2.

General and Mrs. George B. McClellan. Mrs. McClellan, the former Ellen B. "Nelly" Marcy, was engaged to Powell Hill before parental pressures shattered the match.

Lee and His Generals. A. P. Hill Stands at Lee's Right.
From the Mural by Charles Hoffbauer in Battle Abbey, Richmond.

CHAPTER V

"The Thorough Soldier"

(Williamsburg)

After the dust of First Manassas had settled and been wetted by the disillusionment of a short war, General Johnston found himself at Manassas confronting a new antagonist, Major General George B. McClellan, Powell Hill's former intimate and the officer he considered ablest in the Union Army.[1] "Little Mac" had recently emerged triumphant from a campaign in Northwestern Virginia. Hailed by the Northern press as "the young Napoleon," he had been called to Washington and placed in command of the Army of the Potomac.

While McDowell's successor undertook to organize a huge army for another invasion, Johnston wrestled with his own problems of command. Generals Beauregard and Kirby Smith had been detached for duty in the West. He was further crippled by a lack of sufficient officers of lower rank. Five brigades were without generals, and at one time half of the army's field officers were incapacitated by illness. Early in February, Johnston petitioned Richmond to promote qualified colonels to the rank of Brigadier General. Heading the list was Colonel A. P. Hill, whom Johnston had previously recommended.[2] For some obscure reason, Beauregard also pressed for Hill's promotion together with a request that he then be assigned to his new command.[3]

Hill's own feelings at this time are reflected in the following letter to a friend:

. . . What changes, my God what changes since last we met. Even though we looked forward to this rupture, yet how little idea we had of the reality of things as they now are—and how many of our old friends, upon whom we would have staked our last dime, have shown the cloven foot and are now most bitter in this war of subjugation—yet notheless (sic) by

[1] C.V., 16, 178.
[2] O.R., 5, 1058.
[3] O.R., 7, 918.

the blessing of God, and hearts that never grow faint, we will whip the damned hounds yet and then God grant that a gulf as deep and wide as hell may interpose between us . . .

Our men are in fine condition, and better still are confident of success, and mean to fight for it. I am commanding the 6th Brigade in Kirby Smith's Div, and have been ready now to move for two days. Burnside's fleet having left Annapolis and rendezvoused at Old Point. The Generals rather think he is coming up the Potomac to make an attack at Evansport. I hardly think so, but that if he moves at all against any point in Virginia, it will be up the Rappahannock, to strike at the Richmond and Fredericksburg RR— and if so, Lord won't there have to be some tall walking done by this Reserve Division! That move would I think consternate us here considerably, though of course, the Head Devils who are paid for thinking, have thought all over it . . .

My wife remained in Kentucky until November, when I smuggled her out, and she is now at Culpeper, and though within 30 miles of me, I have seen her but once since April.[4]

In addition to the problem of obtaining adequate officers, Johnston at winter's end faced the same problem which had vexed Patterson the previous summer at Martinsburg. The one-year enlist-period for Confederate volunteers was expiring, and to encourage re-enlistment the government offered a two-month furlough plus a fifty-dollar bonus. With furloughs being granted by thousands, Johnston despaired as he saw his army of less than 50,000 dwindle in the shadows of McClellan's 185,000 behemoth.[5]

In this dilemma, Johnston decided early in March to withdraw from his advanced position to a line along the Rapidan and Rappahannock rivers. From Alexandria, McClellan leisurely followed as far as Johnston's abandoned camps. Then the Federal commander enlisted his generals' support in persuading President Lincoln to accept a bold plan for the invasion of Richmond. McClellan envisioned moving the bulk of his army on four hundred transports down the Chesapeake Bay to the tip of the Peninsula which lay between the York and James rivers. From that base of operations and supplies, and flanked by strong naval forces on each of these tidal rivers, the Army of the Potomac would march up the Peninsula to Richmond.[6]

---

[4] Letter from A. P. Hill presumably to Dr. S. H. Stout, Director of Hospitals, Department and Army of Tennessee, dated Manassas, January 6, 1862. This letter was furnished to the author through the courtesy of Major L. N. Fitzhugh.
[5] O.R., 5, 732.
[6] *Ibid.*, 55-56.

First intimation in the Confederate capital of any such movement occurred the last day of March when General Huger at Norfolk telegraphed that over twenty steamers had disgorged swarms of Federals at Old Point on the tip of the Peninsula.[7] General Lee, acting during this period as unofficial Chief-of-Staff to President Davis, quickly countered with a plan to transfer most of Johnston's army to the lower Peninsula.[8]

The prospect of a major engagement coupled with his long-coveted promotion to Brigadier General,[9] raised the spirit of Powell Hill. With sentimental regrets, he bade farewell to the Thirteenth Virginia which he had molded from a motley group of raw recruits into one of the finest regiments in the army. Of his first command Hill could take considerable pride and credit in the commendations it later received. General Lee called it "a splendid body of men," and doughty General Ewell commented with unqualified admiration that, "It is the only regiment that never fails."[10]

The new brigadier was appointed to command of the First Brigade comprising the 1st, 7th, 11th and 17th Virginia regiments and Rogers' Virginia battery. Longstreet had previously commanded this brigade which now constituted one of the four (later six) brigades in his Second Division.[11] On assuming command at Camp Taylor, Hill issued the following terse order:

The undersigned hereby assumes command of the First Brigade. All orders and regulations heretofore existing will continue in force unless otherwise specifically directed.[12]

Powell Hill initiated his new command with a march through Virginia mud to Richmond. On April 17, weary bespattered youths in gray paraded through petticoat-lined streets of the capital to such sprightly airs as "Dixie" and the "Bonnie Blue Flag."[13] Turning eastward, the regiments proceeded to the aid of General "Prince John" Magruder who occupied a defensive line stretching across the Peninsula from Yorktown to the Warwick river. While awaiting

---

[7] O.R., *11*, Part 3, 394.
[8] *Ibid.*, 393-400.
[9] O.R., *51*, Part 2, 514.
[10] S.H.S.P., *20*, 378.
[11] O.R., *11*, Part 3, 531.
[12] O.R., *51*, Part 2, 575.
[13] *R. E. Lee, II*, 23-24.

reinforcements, Magruder, the master bluffer, had deceived McClellan into believing he had several times the 11,000 men defending the eastern approaches to the capital.[14]

Lee had hoped that Johnston's forces concentrating on the Lower Peninsula would contest McClellan's advance from strategic defensive positions. Delaying tactics, he felt, would provide precious time in which to complete the capital's defenses and also concentrate additional troops from scattered points. However, after inspecting Magruder's defenses, Johnston concluded that they would not withstand McClellan's superior fire power from combined land and naval batteries. Fearful lest his army be pinched off from the capital, he ordered Yorktown evacuated.[15] On Saturday night, May 3, Johnston's 56,500 effectives quietly began the retreat while Stuart's cavalry covered the rear.[16] Hill's brigade of Longstreet's self-styled "Walking Division" was among the last to file onto the almost impassable muddy road to Williamsburg.

By early afternoon on Sunday the army had passed the series of field works just east of Williamsburg which Magruder had constructed as a second line of defense across the Peninsula. Then suddenly the creeping but orderly retreat was interrupted by an attack on Stuart. Johnston immediately decided to launch a rearguard action from Magruder's fortifications, pregnable though they were, in order to let the rest of the army slip away. Accordingly, he counter-marched two of Magruder's brigades to Fort Magruder, pivot of the flimsy defenses. Heavy fire from these two brigades checked the enemy advance, and that evening they were relieved by two of Longstreet's brigades under Brigadier General R. H. Anderson.[17]

Shortly after dawn on Monday, Hooker's Federal sharpshooters drove in Anderson's pickets from the felled woods in front of the four redoubts to the left of Fort Magruder. After an unsuccessful attempt to recover this ground, brisk skirmishing continued for more than an hour. Meanwhile, Hooker in his concealed position

---

[14] *Ibid.*
[15] O.R., *11*, Part 3, 489.
[16] *Ibid.*, 479-84.
[17] O.R., *11*, Part 1, 580.

was rapidly reinforcing with infantry and artillery. Realizing that the enemy was not to be shaken easily, Longstreet recalled Wilcox's brigade to reinforce Anderson, and Powell Hill was ordered to take a position within supporting distance.[18]

Late in the morning Longstreet decided it was pointless to subject his men further to the enemy's long-range guns and superior batteries. Thereupon he ordered all brigades to attack at the first opportunity. Soon Hill was directed to take a position in the woods to the right of Wilcox and assail the enemy who was then deploying in force.[19]

Forming his lines quickly, Hill unleashed three cheering regiments on the bluecoats, who gave ground. The Seventh Virginia under Colonel Kemper paused behind a fence to exchange leaden volleys at forty-five yards, when Hill came up on foot to appraise the situation.[20] After consulting a moment with his boyhood chum, Hill decided, "Then was the time, and Kemper's regiment was ordered to charge them, and led by their gallant colonel, they bounded over the fence, Colonels Garland and Corse at the same moment, with that military quickness and intuition that proves the thorough soldier, advanced their own lines, and the enemy were forced back step by step . . ."[21]

When the Federals reached an expanse of felled timber, they were reinforced and staged a rally. However, Hill's men were not to be denied. For two hours his regiments maintained a heavy fire from their advanced position. When ammunition ran low, Hill ordered the entire brigade to charge with the bayonet. Jubilantly they reeled back the enemy and captured eight guns together with a color standard bearing the inscription "To Hell or Richmond."[22]

It was now late in the afternoon. Hill halted his First Brigade which had been actively engaged for seven hours. Cartridge boxes were refilled from those of the enemy dead, arms were collected, and the wounded removed. Then Hill permitted the men to lie

---

[18] *Ibid.*, 564.
[19] *Ibid.*, 565, 570.
[20] "Souvenir Booklet," Letter from J. L. Kemper to W. H. Palmer.
[21] O.R., *11*, Part 1, 576.
[22] *Ibid.*, 577.

down in line until sunset when the brigade was withdrawn.[23]

While Powell Hill's brigade spearheaded Longstreet's attack on the right of Fort Magruder, Daniel Harvey Hill, his unrelated namesake, checked Hancock's vigorous demonstration on the Confederate left in a confused and costly struggle. Night ended action along the entire front, and Longstreet's scrappy brigades resumed their march early the following morning.

The exploits of Powell Hill and his brigade quickly became a cheering topic of conversation throughout the retiring army. Statistically, his brigade captured 160 prisoners, 7 stand of colors, and, with the aid of the Ninth Alabama, eight pieces of artillery— all at a cost of 326 casualties, highest of any brigade engaged on the right.[24]

More impressive to those who witnessed the action, was Hill's bold and skillful handling of men under fire. Even the normally stolid Longstreet singled out Hill's command for commendation. Hill, he wrote, "ably led" his brigade whose "organization was perfect throughout the battle, and it was marched off the field in as good order as it entered it."[25]

Hill's own report is both interesting and revealing.[26] In an expansive vein he distributed praise liberally among men in all ranks from Colonel Corse who was "calm and equable as a May morn," to Private Hunt, a courier, for "activity and cool courage." He neglected, of course, to mention that twice with his own hands he had saved a private struggling in personal combat.[27] Lamenting his losses, he added, "But all the regiments fought with a heroism that, if persisted in, must ever drive the foe from our soil."[28]

Portentous were Hill's specifications, as stated in his report, for the "thorough soldier." "Military quickness and intuition" he listed as the qualities which enabled a commander to recognize the critical moment and thereupon seize the initiative. Faithful adherence to this standard was to guide, with momentous results, this impetuous young brigadier.

---

[23] *Ibid.*, 577.
[24] *Ibid.*, 569, 577-78.
[25] *Ibid.*, 567.
[26] *Ibid.*, 575 ff.
[27] Pollard, 447.
[28] O.R., *11*, Part 1, 578.

CHAPTER VI

"Courageous And Impetuous, But Exceedingly Imprudent"
(Mechanicsville)

IN THE overall theater of Confederate operations on the Peninsula the rearguard action at Williamsburg merely enabled Johnston's army to hold its own in the race against McClellan's flanking force steaming up the York River.[1] But to Powell Hill this battle also provided a long-awaited opportunity to demonstrate his capabilities as one of the most promising young officers in the army.

However, even the ambitious commander of the First Brigade who superbly handled over 2,500 men at Williamsburg scarcely could have anticipated that this would be his sole engagement as a Brigadier. Troops from Fredericksburg and Gordonsville under Generals J. R. Anderson and L. O'B. Branch were being withdrawn to the defense of Richmond, and President Davis wrote to Johnston on May 26 that their addition "seemed to require another major-general, and upon the recommendations before me, Brigadier-General Hill was selected."[2] Hill, now in his thirty-sixth year, had served the Confederacy just slightly over a year.

The same day (May 27) that Hill received his commission as Major General,[3] Johnston received word that McDowell was moving overland to effect a junction with McClellan.[4] Thereupon the Confederate commander decided to overwhelm McClellan before McDowell arrived.[5] Hill, in compliance with Johnston's instructions to concentrate his division for this offensive, rushed his troops to Mechanicsville on May 28 and reported to Major General G. W. Smith who commanded the three divisions constituting the left wing of Johnston's army. This unofficial grouping of divisions

---

[1] Longstreet, in his official report of this action, estimated that 9,000 Confederates engaged 12,000 Federals. O.R., *11*, Part 3, 481.

[2] O.R., *11*, Part 3, 547.

[3] *Ibid.*, 555.

[4] G. W. Smith, *Confederate War Papers*, 147, 156.

[5] *Ibid.*, 147.

under a single commander circumvented a Confederate law which established the division as the largest military unit within an army.

Hill's orders were to carry the Federal outpost at Mechanicsville and then push on to the right of the enemy's main line along Beaver Dam Creek.[6] This movement would clear the way for Smith's other two divisions under Whiting and D. R. Jones to cross the Chickahominy and join Hill in a combined assault on McClellan's right. The Chief Engineer of the Army together with Johnston's Chief-of-Staff examined the enemy's position and reported it to be naturally formidable, especially against an attack from the direction of Mechanicsville. Although the high command anticipated "bloody work," Smith reported that "every confidence was felt that A. P. Hill would take the works at Mechanicsville with certainty and without delay."[7]

Just as Hill was getting his troops into position for this eagerly anticipated operation, Johnston—learning that McDowell had returned to Fredericksburg—countermanded the order for an offensive. In a directive to Whiting, Johnston wrote: "I think it will be best for A. P. Hill's troops to watch the bridges."[8] Accordingly, Hill withdrew his division and took position on the extreme left of the army.[9]

Johnston now decided to shift offensive operations to the south side of the Chickahominy. Scouts had reported that McClellan, advancing cautiously as usual, had pushed Keyes' IV Corps across the Chickahominy to Seven Pines, a small settlement about five miles east of Richmond.[10] With heavy rains swelling the Chickahominy and thereby hindering McClellan from reinforcing this isolated force, Johnston determined to destroy it in an effort to prevent a Federal siege of the capital.[11]

Johnston issued orders for D. H. Hill, Huger, and Longstreet to converge upon the enemy on Saturday, May 31, while at Meadow

[6] *Ibid.*, 159.
[7] *Ibid.*, 148.
[8] *Ibid.*, 152.
[9] *Ibid.*, 150.
[10] This Federal force actually comprised Keyes' IV Corps supported by Heintzelman's V Corps.
[11] O.R., *11*, Part 1, 933.

Bridges, Powell Hill, in temporary command of the left wing, guarded against any enemy demonstrations north of the Chickahominy.[12]

In the ensuing battle, Powell Hill and his troops remained inactive in a manner reminiscent of First Manassas. After dark he reported to Smith that "all had been quiet during the day near Meadow Bridges."[13] However, this time there were few laurels won by his hotly engaged colleagues. A combination of faulty staff work, conflicting orders, and unexpected enemy reinforcements resulted in a confused and costly battle ending in a fruitless draw.

Unquestionably the most important result of this battle of Seven Pines was the transfer of command from the wounded Johnston to Robert E. Lee of what henceforth was to be known as the Army of Northern Virginia. News of this change of commanders was withheld awhile, and McClellan's first intimation of it was disclosed in a letter of June 9 to his wife stating: "I had another letter from our friend A. P. H. (A. P. Hill) yesterday in reply to Joe Johnston, so I am now confident Joe is badly wounded. In my reply sent this morning I ignore Hill entirely and address mine to the 'Commanding General,' etc., so G. W. Smith will have to come out this time."[14]

The day after Lee assumed Johnston's mantle, he held a conference with his general officers. No record is preserved of Powell Hill's participation, nor of his reaction to the new commanding General. Although Hill had risen rapidly as a protégé of the cautious Johnston, the youngest Major General in the army must have been impressed by Lee's bold, aggressive approach.

Shortly after this council, Lee notified Hill that his division was being enlarged by the addition of three brigades. As these troops were suffering from illness, Lee suggested that they be placed in reserve.[15] Hill's enlarged division now included the following six brigades and artillery:[16]

---

[12] G. W. Smith, *Confederate War Papers*, 162.
[13] *Ibid.*, 184.
[14] G. B. McClellan MSS, Letter from Major General McClellan to his wife, June 9, 1862. Hill's letter dealt with the exchange of prisoners.
[15] O.R., *11*, Part 3, 589. Letter from R. E. Lee to A. P. Hill, June 11, 1862.
[16] O.R., *11*, Part 2, 487.

First Brigade commanded by Brigadier General Charles W. Field; 40th, 47th, 55th, and 60th Virginia regiments.

Second Brigade commanded by Brigadier General Maxcy Gregg; 1st, 12th, 13th, 14th South Carolina regiments and 1st South Carolina Rifles.

Third Brigade commanded by Brigadier General Joseph R. Anderson; 14th, 35th, 45th, 49th Georgia regiments and 3rd Louisiana Battalion.

Fourth Brigade commanded by Brigadier General Lawrence O'Brien Branch; 7th, 18th, 28th, 33rd, and 37th North Carolina regiments.

Fifth Brigade commanded by Brigadier General James J. Archer; 1st, 7th, 14th Tennessee regiments, 19th Georgia regiment, and 5th Alabama Battalion.

Sixth Brigade commanded by Brigadier General W. Dorsey Pender; 16th, 22nd, 34th, 38th North Carolina regiments, 2nd Arkansas regiment, and 22nd Virginia Battalion.

Artillery commanded by Major R. Lindsay Walker[17] comprising the batteries of Andrews, Bachman, Braxton, Crenshaw, Davidson, Johnson, Masters, McIntosh and Pegram.

Hill proudly christened his command the "Light Division." Unfortunately, he did not elaborate on the significance of this sobriquet. Lacking an explanation from the coiner, several possibilities have been advanced. An obvious one is that Hill simply paraphrased the name of the "Light Artillery" with which he served in Mexico. Or it may have symbolized the marching speed he demanded,[18] and which was to compare favorably with General Crawford's "Light Division" in Wellington's army that marched 62 miles in 26 hours to Talavera.[19]

W. F. Dunaway, a veteran of the Light Division, offered the following interesting commentary on its name: "Why it was called the Light Division I did not learn; but I know that the name was applicable, for we often marched without coats, blankets, knapsacks, or any other burdens except our arms and haversacks, which were never heavy and sometimes empty."[20]

Lieutenant Cathey of the 16th North Carolina regiment of Hill's division, linked his recollections of the Light Division with admiration for its youthful commander. He wrote: "Next to her

---

[17] During Walker's illness at the Seven Days' Battles, Hill's artillery was commanded by Lewis M. Coleman.

[18] *Dictionary of American Biography, IX,* 25.

[19] S.H.S.P., *13, 9.*

[20] W. F. Dunaway, *Reminiscences of a Rebel* (cited hereafter as Dunaway), 25-26.

own native commanders the Sixteenth learned to respect the person of A. P. Hill. He was one of the great leaders that the Civil War developed. I remember how he looked perfectly. He was one of the handsomest men I have ever seen . . . a fearless man and a brilliant commander, and his Light Division will go down side by side with the illustrious soldiers of history."[21]

Having invested his division with a "suggestive designation,"[22] Hill spent most of June whipping his six brigades into "perfection in organization." Half of his troops had yet to experience their first ordeal under fire, and all of Hill's organizational ability was required to train and integrate the disparate units of his division. However, the troops were soon "well-drilled, thoroughly disciplined, and in the highest spirits."[23] He had fulfilled Lee's Special Orders No. 22 directing divisional commanders to "have their commands in readiness at all times for immediate action."[24]

One day early in June, Lee sent Colonel Long, his military secretary, to inspect Hill's lines near Mechanicsville, about two miles northeast of Richmond. In his notebook Colonel Long reported: "Hill's defences are as well advanced as those of any part of the line. His troops are in fine condition. He designates his division 'the Light Division'. Hill is every inch a soldier and is destined to make his mark."[25]

While McClellan's army was mired in the mud around Richmond, Federal aerialists in silken observation balloons scouted Lee's defenses. However, when the roads dried, Lee realized that unless he assumed the offensive, Richmond soon would be under the scrutiny of seige guns instead of air-borne observation glasses. Accordingly, Stuart was ordered to take his 1,200 cavalrymen and learn the enemy's positions and movements. On this memorable ride which eventually encircled McClellan's army, Stuart ascertained

---

[21] *North Carolina Regiments* (cited hereafter as *N. C. Regts.*), *I*, 765.
[22] C.M.H., *I*, 680.
[23] J. F. Caldwell, *The History of a Brigade of South Carolinians Known First as "Gregg's" and Subsequently as McGowan's Brigade* (cited hereafter as Caldwell), 12. This remarkable book, written from memory in 1866, provides an intimate insight into Hill's command.
[24] *R. E. Lee, I*, 78.
[25] A. L. Long, *Memoirs of Robert E. Lee,* 167 (cited hereafter as Long). Notebook entry for June 7, 1862.

that General Fitz Porter's V Provisional Corps, which formed the right wing of McClellan's army north of the Chickahominy, was exposed to attack. Furthermore, Stuart reported that the Army of the Potomac was being supplied from a base in the vicinity of White House on the Pamunkey river.[26]

On the basis of Stuart's information Lee outlined a plan which he proposed at a council of war held in his headquarters on Monday, June 23. Present at this conference were Longstreet, D. H. Hill, A. P. Hill, and T. J. Jackson, the latter arriving after an exhausting journey from the Valley. In substance, Lee planned to prevent a foredoomed defense of Richmond by rolling back Porter's corps, followed by a thrust at McClellan's supply line along the York River Railroad. This maneuver would force McClellan to abandon his entrenchments in front of the capital and either retreat or fight at a disadvantage.[27]

Execution of the plan called for Jackson and D. H. Hill to assail Porter's right flank, while A. P. Hill supported by Longstreet attacked frontally. During this attack on Porter, Huger and Magruder were to pin down the larger part of McClellan's army south of the Chickahominy by vigorous demonstrations in front of Richmond.

Following the adoption of this plan, Lee recapitulated its details in Confidential Orders No. 75,[28] a copy of which was sent to each divisional commander. Screened by Stuart, Jackson was to leave Ashland, cross the Central Railroad, and march toward Beaver Dam. He was to communicate his approach to General Branch, whose brigade Powell Hill would post at Half Sink, seven miles north of the rest of the Light Division which was to be stationed at Meadow Bridges. When contact was established with Jackson, Branch would march southward, clearing Meadow Bridges for the crossing of Powell Hill's division. The Light Division in turn would advance to Mechanicsville, thereby clearing the Mechanicsville bridge for the crossing of D. H. Hill's and Longstreet's waiting

[26] O.R., *11*, Part 1, 1031.
[27] *R. E. Lee, II*, 110 ff.
[28] O.R., *11*, Part 2, 498-99.

divisions. The combined force of over 50,000 men would then press forward to establish contact with Huger and Magruder.

Lee's well-conceived plan for relieving Richmond from the prongs of a numerically overwhelming foe hinged on the smooth transmission of movement from Jackson to Branch to Powell Hill to D. H. Hill and Longstreet. Of these commanders, only Longstreet and D. H. Hill previously had worked in harness during a major engagement. Jackson, secretive and accustomed to independent command, was weary and in unfamiliar country. As for Powell Hill, this was to be his first active engagement as a Major General, and being entrusted with the pivotal role, he was eager, perhaps overly so, to justify Lee's confidence in him.

Confidential Orders No. 75 were delivered to Powell Hill on Wednesday night, June 25. Pursuant to these orders he directed Branch to move his brigade to the bridge at Half Sink. While the North Carolinians marched northward, Hill concentrated his remaining five brigades and batteries in a concealed position behind trees at Meadow Bridges. Everything was in readiness to move shortly after dawn on the 26th.[29]

Daybreak ushered in a fair June day. Hill's troops waited in the shade of trees for Branch's skirmishers to sweep the enemy from the opposite bank. As the hour hand of his watch reached 8 o'clock, Hill dispatched a reassuring note to Branch stating: "Wait for Jackson's notification before you move unless I send you other orders."[30]

Shortly after 10 A.M. Branch finally received from Jackson the message he had been awaiting since 4 A.M. In Jackson's terse style, the note stated simply: "The head of my column is crossing the Central Railroad."[31] Within ten minutes, Branch set in motion his troops which had been resting on their arms for six hours. However, his march to Meadow Bridges was beset by ambuscades which delayed the brigade's arrival until late afternoon.[32]

Meanwhile the green troops of the Light Division at Meadow

---

[29] *Ibid.*, 834.
[30] *Ibid.*, 881.
[31] O.R., *11*, Part 3, 620.
[32] O.R., *11*, Part 2, 835, 882.

Bridges grew fidgety as Richmond bells tolled the noon hour and still there was no word from Jackson or sign from Branch. As the afternoon sun penetrated a cloudless sky, Powell Hill's patience melted—then it geysered. In his own words: "Three o'clock having arrived, and no intelligence from Jackson or Branch, I determined to cross at once rather than hazard the failure of the whole plan by longer deferring it."[33]

Thereupon, without consulting Lee who was less than two miles distant,[34] or ascertaining the proximity of Jackson, Hill assumed the responsibility of disregarding Lee's orders by engaging McClellan's entire right wing with the Light Division. It was a bold maneuver strikingly similar to the one Johnston and G. W. Smith had planned for him a month earlier. Plainly attired in his gray flannel fatigue jacket and felt slouch hat, he advanced Field's brigade to seize the bridge. Encouraged by Hill's constant exposure to enemy fire,[35] the cheering Virginia regiments flushed a picket line of Pennsylvania riflemen from the woods on the opposite bank and sent them scurring toward Mechanicsville. The Light Division then crossed, formed in line of battle behind the skirmishers, and swept across the rolling plain in pursuit. The artillery[36] and wagons were directed northeast to Atlee's Station whence they advanced southward to Mechanicsville along the same route Branch was expected.

---

[33] *Ibid.*, 835.

[34] E. P. Alexander, *Military Memoirs of a Confederate* (cited hereafter as Alexander), 118.

[35] Ayres and Wade, *The War and Its Heroes*, 55.

[36] Wise severely criticized Hill's handling of artillery during the Seven Days. "The errors of A. P. Hill," he wrote, "with respect to his artillery are attributable to A. P. Hill. When preparing for operations on the north side of the Chickahominy, he issued orders that but one battery would accompany each of his 6 brigades, and that the rest of his batteries including those of his reserve battalion would remain in the position previously prepared for them on the south side. He did not take the precaution of carrying with him 6 teams of spare horses for each of his batteries, but drew them, nevertheless, from his remaining batteries, thus crippling the latter for effective use." Wise, *I*, 213.

Of Hill's employment of artillery at Mechanicsville, Wise stated that the "attack was too headlong to have permitted an artillery preparation had the guns been on hand. The general who hurls his infantry columns upon the enemy's positions at sight simply chooses the precipitate assault in preference to the more deliberate attack with the artillery support which he might have elected." Wise, *I*, 208.

Lee had planned (Special Orders No. 75) to aid Hill's advance by having "the heavy batteries on the Chickahominy . . . open at the proper time upon the batteries at Mechanicsville." Hill's hasty attack, of course, nullified this plan.

Hill's line supported by artillery quickly advanced a mile and a half to the edge of the little hamlet of Mechanicsville where enemy batteries beyond the town opened a heavy concentric fire on the head of Field's column. Throwing the advance regiments into line as they neared the village, Hill, his shirt torn in several places,[37] ordered them to drive the foe from the town. Pegram's six-gun battery was placed in support of the cheering infantry, and it soon drew a converging fire from thirty Federal guns.[38] Soon the cannonading became so continuous as to drown the sound of musketry.[39]

Shortly after Field's troops captured Mechanicsville, Lee arrived. He learned for the first time that Hill had begun his assault without first establishing contact with Jackson. However, this was no time for lamentations or indictments. The battle had been joined and was now raging furiously. Retreating Federals had retired to a previously prepared position along Beaver Dam Creek, about one mile east of the town. This natural line of defense fronted on high perpendicular banks from which artillery and entrenched infantry commanded the open fields over which Hill's advancing troops must cross.

A "spiteful" fire from Porter's eighty guns dampened even Powell Hill's enthusiasm for a frontal attack, and he "forebore to order the storming of their lines" in the hope that Jackson's guns soon would open on the enemy's flank and rear. Meanwhile, he formed his leading brigade into line of battle along the mile and a quarter front facing Beaver Dam Creek. He ordered Anderson to take in flank a particularly annoying battery on the left while McIntosh's battery was sent forward to attract its attention and keep it occupied. In pursuance of this order Colonel Thomas' 35th Georgia

---

[37] W. P. Snow, *Southern Generals* (cited hereafter as Snow), 397.

[38] *Lee's Lieutenants, I,* 649. Four of Pegram's guns were disabled, but during the night he somehow thoroughly equipped the remaining two, and in the morning he requested and received Hill's permission to remain in action. S.H.S.P., *14,* 12.

[39] G. Spencer Welch, *A Confederate Surgeon's Letters to his Wife* (cited hereafter as Welch), 15. Although Welch was not an admirer of A. P. Hill, his letters vividly describe army life in the Light Division and the Third Corps.

regiment of Anderson's brigade succeeded in crossing the creek and holding its own until the battle closed.[40]

As action mounted on the left, Lee sent Hill an order to halt and hold the position he then occupied. This directive was occasioned by information Lee received from Lieutenant Sydnor, a local inhabitant, that quicksand lining the bottom of Beaver Dam Creek on Hill's left would render an attack there suicidal. As this treacherous condition did not exist on his right, Hill felt free to attempt a passage there. After Pender's exposed brigade in line of battle passed Mechanicsville and veered defiantly to the right in the face of heavy fire, Hill directed the North Carolinians to force a crossing and attack a strong, well-serviced battery and force near Ellerson's Mill.

Then meeting General Ripley, whose leading brigade of D. H. Hill's division had just crossed the Mechanicsville bridge over the Chickahominy, Hill requested him to cooperate with Pender in turning the enemy's left further down the creek.[41] Both brigades attacked fiercely but in vain. Pender's assault was thrown into confusion, and Ripley's flankers were slaughtered as they misguidedly charged down a hill directly into enemy guns.[42]

About 9 o'clock the battle ceased save for an artillery engagement which persisted for some time in the darkness. Leaving word with his Assistant Adjutant to notify him of any important enemy movements,[43] Hill left the front to attend a conference at the Lumpkin house in Mechanicsville. On his way he found the streets blocked with ambulances, litter bearers, and wagons.[44] At this meeting of divisional commanders, Lee assessed the day's events and surveyed possibilities for the morrow. Neither at this council nor in his official report did he censure Hill for his impetuous attack contrary to orders. However, Lee's disapproval of Hill's blunted assault on Beaver Dam Creek was manifest in his

---

[40] O.R., *11*, Part 2, 835.
[41] *Ibid.*, 647-48.
[42] *Ibid.*, 835-36; *R. E. Lee, II*, 134.
[43] O.R., *11*, Part 3, 620.
[44] *N. C. Regts., IV*, 156.

calling Lieutenant Sydnor to testify in Hill's presence concerning the latter's receipt of orders to refrain from attacking.[45]

Hill himself suffered no compunctions regarding his initiation and conduct of the battle. He had attacked in the belief that further delay would hazard the whole plan, and when it ended he was satisfied in "the object of this attack, viz, clearing the way for Longstreet, having been fully accomplished."[46]

A plausible though inexcusable explanation for Powell Hill's precipitate attack is that by mid-afternoon, having received no word that Jackson was unavoidably delayed, he felt confident that the ever-prompt hero of the Valley must be nearby. In this event he would feel justified in taking the calculated risk of ordering a frontal attack in the expectation that before long Jackson would assail Porter's flank and rear. However, Hill failed to take even the simple precaution of sending a courier to ascertain the proximity of Jackson or Branch. In tragic consequence, Jackson arrived at his designated meeting place with D. H. Hill to find it unoccupied. Puzzled, Jackson bivouacked for the night, while to the south casualties mounted in the Light Division.

Thus, Powell Hill impetuously and injudiciously precipitated a battle which Lee had planned to avoid by a skillful flanking maneuver rather than by a costly tour de force. Impartial students of the battle of Mechanicsville must agree with Hotchkiss that Hill's attack "was courageous and impetuous, but exceedingly imprudent."[47]

---

[45] *Lee's Lieutenants, I,* 514-15, Letter from T. W. Sydnor to Jed Hotchkiss, Dec. 27, 1897.
[46] O.R., *11,* Part 2, 836.
[47] C.M.H., III, 286.

CHAPTER VII

"With Undiminished Ardor"

(Gaines' Mill)

Before DAWN on Friday, Federal artillery and long-range musketry opened a rapid fire on Mechanicsville. When the two-hour barrage, which reminded one participant of myriads of hailstones falling on a house top,[1] was not followed by blue infantry Lee ordered Powell Hill's division to press the attack in anticipation of Jackson's arrival on Porter's flank.[2]

Hill assigned Maxcy Gregg's brigade, which he had held in reserve the previous day, to lead the advance. Two companies handsomely dashed across Beaver Dam Creek and cleared the redoubts and rifle pits of the lively token force covering Porter's withdrawal. The entire Light Division then crossed and took the country road running eastward toward Powhite Creek, the next natural defensive position available to Porter.[3]

As Hill's pursuing brigades passed the enemy's deserted camps they saw huge heaps of blazing commissary and quartermaster stores, piles of knapsacks, arms, and accoutrements which their fresh ardor prevented them from pillaging as freely as they later learned to do.[4] About 10 A.M. the head of Gregg's column arrived at an intersection near Walnut Grove Church where Hill stopped to exchange greetings with Jackson, whose division had finally arrived. Soon Lee rode up to greet and confer with Jackson, whereupon Hill excused himself to hurry his command.[5]

Lee had ordered Hill to attack with his full division as soon as he could bring the retreating foe to bay, which presumably would occur near Powhite Creek. A frontal attack by the Light Division supported by Longstreet would drive the Federals into

---

[1] Welch, 15.
[2] O.R., *11,* Part 2, 836, 882; *R. E. Lee, II,* 491.
[3] O.R., *11,* Part 2, 836.
[4] Caldwell, 15.
[5] Douglas, 100.

the guns of Jackson and D. H. Hill who were marching to cut off the Federal line of retreat toward the York River Railroad.

Early in the afternoon Gregg's advance guard glimpsed a group of Federals behind a pine thicket on the opposite bank of Powhite Creek. While the South Carolina regiments formed their battle lines, Gregg directed his skirmishers to effect a lodgement as Andrews' battery shelled the woods. Without delay the skirmishers rushed down the creek to Gaines' Mill and cleared the crossing. After engineers repaired the bridges, Gregg quickly filed his men across. Up the hill they clambered unopposed to find the bluecoats retiring in haste over an open table-land.

As each regiment reached the crest, Gregg formed it into line. When the entire brigade was ready, it swept forward to the southeast in what Powell Hill admiringly described as "the handsomest charge in line I have seen during the war."[6] A number of the enemy fell as they retreated, but one of them, after lying a moment, attempted to follow his fleeing comrades who were disappearing into the woods at the edge of the field. This lone target, like the proverbial hare pursued by hounds, drew the undivided fire of Gregg's charging line. Excitement mounted as a shower of bullets kicked up the dust around him, to the accompaniment of shouts to "Shoot him!" and "Down with the fellow." Miraculously, he staggered on and succeeded in reaching a clump of trees where his pursuers found him exhausted by fatigue and loss of blood.[7]

After advancing several hundred yards over flat fields, the South Carolinians brushed aside a skirmish line and descended a wooded slope leading to a ravine. On the opposite eminence rode a Federal officer encouraging and instructing his gunners. On sighting Gregg's troops, the Union battery opened. Gregg notified Hill, further on the right, that he had brought the enemy to bay, and requested permission to charge. However, as the other brigades were not yet in position, Hill ordered him to halt and await orders. Thereupon, the weary, sweating foot soldiers of the Second

---

[6] O.R., *11*, Part 2, 836.
[7] Caldwell, 16.

Brigade crossed the ravine where, concealed by young pines, many dropped into a sound sleep.[8]

While Gregg's brigade rested, Lee and Hill pondered the changing situation. Both were unaware that news of Jackson's approach coupled with Hill's attack at Mechanicsville had prompted McClellan to establish a new base on the James, and that Porter's retreating V Corps had offered only token resistance at Powhite Creek in order to occupy the far more formidable defensive position along Boatswain's Swamp—a location not indicated on Lee's incomplete and inaccurate map.[9]

Hill formed his brigades and batteries into line facing woods dense with tangled undergrowth and traversed by a sluggish stream of variable width which converted the soil into a deep morass. On the far side of the swamp, Federals felled trees to obstruct a crossing, while swarms of Yankee sharpshooters sighted their targets. On the side of the hill a second line of infantry was posted behind breastworks, and on the crest above this bristling girdle loomed a third tier strengthened with rifle trenches and crowned with artillery.[10] This range of hills curving southwesterly from the vicinity of McGhee's house to beyond the Watt farm, was manned by Porter's reinforced V Corps.

Convinced that McClellan would maneuver to defend his supply line along the York River Railroad, Lee intended to attack Porter frontally with the Light Division while Jackson threatened his right flank. When the enemy extended to meet Jackson, Longstreet was to assail his left.

Hill prudently restrained his impatient lines, sweltering in the glaring sun, until 2:30 when he received word that Longstreet was readying his division. Then with what Lee termed "the impetuous courage for which that officer and his troops are distinguished,"[11] Powell Hill unleashed his brigades in succession: Gregg, Branch, Anderson, Pender, Field, and Archer. With wild cheers and waving banners the graycoats charged into the swamp.[12]

---

[8] *Ibid.,* 17.
[9] *R. E. Lee, II,* 144-45.
[10] O.R., *11,* Part 2, 492.
[11] *Ibid.*
[12] Caldwell, 19.

The entrenched foe responded with a continuous roar of musketry and artillery.[13]

For two hours the battle raged on Hill's front with varying success. On the left Gregg made several desperate but unavailing hand-to-hand attempts to rout Hiram Duryea's red-breeched zouaves.[14] Three of Gregg's regiments, the Fourteenth South Carolina and the Sixteenth and Twenty-Second North Carolina, daringly charged and pierced the enemy line but were later compelled to retire before overwhelming numbers.[15]

On Gregg's right, Branch's confused line was hard pressed, whereupon Hill supported him with Pender who stubbornly maintained his position despite heavy casualties. In the center, Anderson charged three times, and his Thirty-Fifth Georgia regiment under Colonel Thomas drove a wedge in the enemy's line only to be thrown back. Amid the storm Anderson himself seized a regimental color which he planted on the crest of the line in an attempt to rally his men.[16] On the right, Archer and Field moving to turn the Federal left braved a withering fire to press within twenty yards of the enemy entrenchments at the base of a long, wooded hill. There they recoiled before a hail of lead. Re-forming, they charged again with no better success.[17]

Butting Porter's 30,000 entrenched bluecoats supported by long-range guns south of the Chickahominy had proved a futile task for the Light Division alone. Convinced that "these brave men had done all that any soldiers could do," Hill directed his brigadiers to break off the engagement where possible and rest until help arrived.[18]

Shortly, General Ewell's veterans of the Valley relieved Hill's decimated left, while Longstreet finally demonstrated in force on the right. To the aid of Hill's right also came General Whiting's division of Jackson's command. Massive John B. Hood commanding the Fourth Texas Brigade of Whiting's Division rode forward with Powell Hill to survey the wide swamp in front of Hill's right.

---

[13] O.R., *11*, Part 2, 837.
[14] *Ibid.*, 381.
[15] *Ibid.*, 837.
[16] S.H.S.P., *19*, 417.
[17] O.R., *11*, Part 2, 837.
[18] *Ibid.*

The commander of the Light Division inquired whether the Fourth Texas could sweep the enemy from the opposite slope. Candidly but eagerly Hood replied, "I don't know whether I can or not, but I will try!"[19]

Moving his tall Texans through Hill's gaping lines, Hood (followed by Law) led his determined brigade through the swamp. Closing ranks to fill the gaps left by the fallen, they rushed the first and second lines which fled in confused panic. Quickly the rapid firing Texans bounded to the crest and captured 14 hot artillery pieces which had sprayed destruction on Hill's right most of the afternoon.[20]

As Hood breached the Federal left, Powell Hill executed Lee's order for a general advance. Relaying the commanding General's directive to other divisional commanders, he pushed forward the Light Division wearied though it was by five hours of relentless fighting.

It was now 7 o'clock, and the sun had slipped below the horizon as Lee's army swept forward and planted flags along the length of the Federal line. Porter's attempts to rally and reinforce his shattered divisions proved futile as gray waves forced his troops back to the Chickahominy where indistinguishable shadows ended the battle.[21]

Although Powell Hill had yet to win a decisive battle as a divisional commander, he demonstrated at this battle of Gaines' Mill his ability to execute orders promptly and diligently. Even a severe critic conceded that "A. P. Hill before leaving one field of battle was ordered to follow up the enemy and attack. Without hesitation and with undiminished ardor, he complied."[22]

Against the entire Federal army north of the Chickahominy, Hill had vigorously and persistently hurled his unsupported division. During this formative period of Lee's command when plans were frustrated by hesitant, tardy and confused commanders, the commanding General would long remember the incisive leadership displayed this day by Powell Hill.

---

[19] *Lee's Lieutenants, I,* 532.
[20] O.R., *11,* Part 2, 493.
[21] *Ibid.*
[22] Wise, *I,* 213.

CHAPTER VIII

"Always Ready For A Fight"

(Frayser's Farm)

E ARLY Saturday morning Lee's
skirmishers, scouring the woods, found the front vacated by all
save enemy dead and wounded together with a Federal general
who overslept.[1] Columns of dust rising south of the Chickahominy
signalled McClellan's withdrawal.[2] Lee prudently restrained a pursuit until he could ascertain whether the foe was retreating down
the Peninsula or across it to the James.

Reports trickling into headquarters during the day disclosed
that the enemy's sole activity down the Chickahominy had been
to burn a railroad trestle in his supply line.[3] This satisfied Lee
that McClellan probably had cut loose from his old base and
was heading for a new one on the James. After posting Ewell
and Stuart on the northern bank of the Chickahominy, just in
case the Federals turned down the Peninsula, Lee ordered the
rest of the army to cross the river and head off the retreating
bluecoats.

Richmond was relieved. Kaleidoscopic developments had played
havoc with Lee's original plan to maneuver McClellan from his
entrenchments and force him to retreat or give battle, but regardless
of the manner the objective had been achieved. McClellan's entire
army had abandoned its entrenchments in front of Richmond,
and now constituted a moving target encumbered by an enormous
wagon train.

Determined to seize this fleeting opportunity, Lee planned by
rapid marches and smooth coordination to fling 70,000 men on
McClellan's rear and flank. An aggressive attack delivered in concert conceivably could annihilate the Army of the Potomac.

---

[1] O.R., *11*, Part 2, 571, 593.
[2] *Ibid.*, 494.
[3] *R. E. Lee, I*, 163.

Lee accordingly issued orders for a general assault on Monday. Jackson was to attack McClellan's rear while the rest of the army assailed his flank. The divisions of Powell Hill and Longstreet were assigned the same route and placed under the command of Longstreet, who ranked Hill.

On Sunday the Light Division followed Longstreet's sweating troops across the Chickahominy at New Bridge and trod the dusty Darbytown road to within six miles of the enemy's column. Bivouacking that night in the rain at Atlee's farm, the troops resumed the march early the next morning. Proceeding through the woodland for several miles, the column turned left onto the Long Bridge Road leading to the Quaker Road along which the Federals were retreating.[4]

About a mile from this intersection Powell Hill halted his division behind Longstreet's, closed his brigades, and established field hospitals. Soon a staff officer rode up and delivered an order for Hill to take command of the field during Longstreet's absence. Thereupon the commander of the Light Division inspected the ground with Brigadier General R. H. Anderson, now in temporary command of Longstreet's division.[5] They found the front facing the enemy densely tangled with woods and underbrush which would render it virtually impossible to charge any distance and keep order.[6] Nearby was the 214 acre Frayser Farm from which the brewing battle was to acquire its name.

Swiftly, Hill disposed the troops in an arc astride the Long Bridge Road—Longstreet's division and Branch's brigade in front supported by the Light Division. Before the battle was joined Longstreet returned and resumed command of the combined divisions.

By prearrangement, General Huger on Longstreet's left was to fire a gun signalling the coordinated attack on McClellan's flank and rear. About 2:30 the sound of gunfire on Huger's front was naturally taken as the spark for the giant offensive. But before the Confederates could advance, Federal guns opposite Longstreet

---

[4] O.R., *11*, Part 2, 838.
[5] *Ibid.*, 838.
[6] Caldwell, 22.

and Hill swept the Long Bridge Road with a round which crashed precariously close to Lee and Davis who had ridden into a small clearing to observe the impending fray. Years later Davis fondly recalled how "gallant little A. P. Hill" dashed up and exclaimed in the high pitched tone his voice assumed when excited: "This is no place for either of you, and as commander of this part of the field, I order you both to the rear."[7] In token obedience, Davis and Lee moved to a nearby observation post. This did not satisfy Hill who followed and solicitously demanded: "Did I not tell you to go away from here, and did you not promise to obey my orders! Why, one shot from that battery over yonder may presently deprive the Confederacy of its President and the Army of Northern Virginia of its Commander!" Such an ardent appeal impelled compliance.[8]

As the afternoon passed with no signs of activity by Huger or Jackson, Lee was forced to the same conclusion Powell Hill had reached while waiting impatiently the previous Thursday at Meadow Bridges, namely, that further delay would hazard the entire plan. To retard McClellan's escape to the James, Lee therefore decided to attack with Hill's and Longstreet's divisions which together constituted less than a third of the striking force he had originally contemplated.

About 5 o'clock Longstreet's brigades surged through the woods forcing the enemy back and capturing a number of his batteries. Before dark the Federals rallied, checked the advance, and threatened to envelop Longstreet's flanks. With his entire division committed, "Old Pete" calmly called on Hill for support. Holding Anderson's Georgia brigade in reserve, Powell Hill thrust forward the rest of his division. Gregg's brigade was dispatched to the left to thwart a flanking movement; Archer, in shirtsleeves, led the Fifth Brigade to the aid of Longstreet's two brigades on the right which had fallen back; and Field and Pender rushed forward to relieve an Alabama brigade heavily engaged in the woods along the Long Bridge Road. Field's Virginians pressed forward so impulsively that a regiment of Federals interposed between them and Pender's men. A volley by the latter scattered the enemy,

---

[7] S.H.S.P., *14*, 452.
[8] *B. and L., II*, 400; O.R., *11*, Part 2, 838.

and the advance was resumed. Colonel Mayo's 47th Virginia regiment of Field's brigade took possession of a Federal battery and
turned its guns on the bluecoats thereby relieving pressure on
Gregg who was hotly engaged on the left.[9]

Twilight now descended and in the dimness a lone Federal
officer on horseback approached Colonel Mayo's troops which
he mistook for his own. Hearing numerous cries to halt, backed
by leveled muskets, the braided figure dismounted and led his
horse to the captors where he identified himself as Brigadier
General George McCall, commander of the Third Division of
Porter's V Corps. Having commanded the Pennsylvania Reserves
which had inflicted such heavy casualties on the Light Division
at Beaver Dam Creek, McCall was fearful of the treatment he
might receive. Upon being conducted to Colonel Mayo, he pleaded,
"For God's sake Colonel, don't let your men do me any harm."
Indignant at the implied accusation, Mayo demanded in strong
language whether McCall thought his captors were a set of bar-
barians. With that, the relieved but disgruntled general was started
on his way to Richmond.[10]

Meanwhile, the enemy pressed hard along the entire line as
the struggle approached a climax in the gathering darkness. Powell
Hill now ordered forward Anderson's reserve brigade and directed
it to advance cautiously so as not fire on comrades. After forming
in line of battle, two regiments on each side of the road, Anderson
advanced his brigade in the face of enemy fire before engaging
at close range. A terrific volume of fire rolled along the line, and
Federal reinforcements held the issue in doubt until Hill espied
his staff rallying part of Wilcox's brigade of Longstreet's division.
Hill rapidly formed them into line, and with moist eyes appealed
to the jaded troops to save the day. In earnest tones he ordered
them to shriek the curdling "rebel yell" as they advanced so as
to give the impression that heavy reinforcements were attacking.
Within five minutes the inspirited troops had broken the enemy
lines and decided the contest.[11]

---

[9] O.R., *11*, Part 2, 838.
[10] Dunaway, 31-32.
[11] O.R., *11*, Part 2, 838; Pollard, 441.

As firing ceased the Light Division rested on the costly-won field until relieved near dawn by Magruder's division which Lee had placed in general reserve. A fraction of Lee's army had delayed but not halted the retreat of McClellan's forces. Again Powell Hill's division had borne a conspicuous share of the fighting which netted fourteen pieces of artillery and two stands of colors. But in a larger sense these tangible trophies were overshadowed by what D. H. Hill described as Powell Hill's habit of "being always ready for a fight."[12] Lee himself regretfully concluded that "could the other commanders have co-operated in the action the result would have been most disastrous to the enemy."[13]

*   *   *   *

Tuesday's dawn revealed that McClellan again had withdrawn under cover of darkness. Lee doggedly pursued in the fading hope of destroying the enemy before he reached the James. Huger, Jackson, and Magruder were directed to lead the attacking column, while the battle-weary divisions of Longstreet and Hill trailed as a reserve.

Moving toward the James by the same road along which McClellan was retreating, the head of Lee's column encountered Federal infantry and artillery formidably massed on an elevation known as Malvern Hill. Longstreet located a position on the Confederate right from which he felt Lee's batteries could cut a swath in the Federal lines, through which Huger and Magruder could then pour their troops. As few guns were immediately available, Powell Hill ordered Pegram's and Davidson's batteries of the Light Division to cooperate. These tireless gunners, joined by others, engaged massed Federal batteries for two hours in a gallant but unequal duel.[14]

As the batteries on Lee's right were shattered in a futile attempt to dent the enemy's left, Lee called on the exhausted but reliable combination of Longstreet and Powell Hill to assail McClellan's right flank. These two divisions were already moving late in the afternoon to execute this order when suddenly they

[12] *B. and L., I*, 388.
[13] O.R., *11*, Part 2, 495.
[14] *Ibid.*, 839.

were halted. Lee, on receiving news that the enemy was retiring and that the Federal right had been hurled back, ordered a general offensive. Magruder with 15,000 men stormed the Federal left, followed shortly by D. H. Hill's attack on the center. Without adequate artillery support the attackers were mowed down in droves as they charged up the hill into a torrent of artillery and musketry fire. In response to Magruder's call for assistance, Powell Hill dispatched Branch's and Anderson's brigades.[15] Other reinforcements also arrived, but darkness halted further costly efforts on this confused field.

Wednesday and Thursday the Light Division trudged through the mud with Jackson's and Longstreet's divisions in a final effort to destroy McClellan, now ensconced at Harrison's Landing on the James. However, Lee found the Federals, ringed in front by artillery and bulwarked behind by gunboats on the James, too strong to assail. The Army of Northern Virginia would have to content itself with having relieved Richmond.

---

[15] *Ibid.*

CHAPTER IX

"Hill Versus Longstreet"

Following THE Seven Days Battles, Powell Hill encamped the Light Division on the flatlands several miles east of Richmond.[1] En route from Harrison's Landing his penchant for comfortable, unadorned garb led to an amusing incident. Major J. G. Field, Chief Quartermaster of the division, had placed a faithful sergeant at the head of the wagon train with explicit orders to hold it at a certain point until ordered forward by him. When a "courier" approached the sergeant and directed him to move the wagons which were obstructing the progress of an artillery train, the guardian recited Field's orders. Undaunted, the "courier" replied, "General Hill orders the wagons forward."

Obligingly the sergeant put the wagons in motion. Further on the train passed a shady grove where a group of officers were resting their steeds and enjoying a fresh breeze on this hot, dusty July day. In passing, the sergeant observed one of the officers salute the "courier" and address him as "General." Upon inquiry, the custodian of the wagon train learned that this same "courier" who had ordered him to move the wagons was none other than General A. P. Hill.[2]

Powell Hill spent July rehabilitating his tattered division which had sustained over 4,000 casualties in the recent campaign. Two of his brigadiers, Anderson and Pender, had been wounded, and although both recovered, Anderson resigned shortly to manage a munitions plant in Richmond. Subsequently, he was succeeded by Colonel Edward L. Thomas of the Thirty-Fifth Georgia.

Hardy survivors of the Light Division subsequently boasted with pardonable pride that they had endured one of the longest continuous ordeals of the entire war. As one participant wrote:

"Had not Hill's division been made of steel rather than flesh and blood,

---

[1] Caldwell, 24.
[2] S.H.S.P., *19*, 179.

they could not have withstood the many hardships of these trying days; for after fighting desperately at Mechanicsville on Thursday, they marched to Gaines' Mill and fought five hours on Friday; rested part of Saturday; traveled a circuitous route, and a terrible road of many miles on Sunday and Monday, achieving another brilliant victory against great odds. Hill, however, is a military genius, and had it not been for the scientific handling of his men, few would have rested uninjured on the torn and bloody field of Monday night. All were prostrated with fatigue, and lay on the ground without fires, covering, or food, too weary to think of anything but rest."[3]

Such exposure took its inevitable toll. An epidemic of typhoid and dysentery soon occupied Hill's attention as his camp hospitals and sick quarters overflowed with patients.[4] Hordes of lice also made their appearance, adding to the general discomfiture in the hot, damp camps. The annoyance of these parasites was further aggravated by the necessity of wearing the same clothing day after day. Not only were clothes scarce, but during the first year of the war the Confederate government compensated each enlisted man twenty-five dollars annually for apparel. With clothing prices trebled their pre-war cost, one veteran plaintively noted that this allotment "was hardly enough to cover one's nakedness."[5]

On the brighter side, Hill's commissary succeeded in supplying plentiful rations. Bacon, beef, flour, and salt constituted regular fare, with occasional issues of molasses and beans for variety. Hill also reduced military exercises during this hot, recuperative period, to guard mountings and a few dress parades.[6]

One of the pleasant interludes which the men anticipated each day was reading the Richmond dailies whose headlines and columns glowingly detailed the army's achievements. Favorite paper of the Light Division was the three-cent *Richmond Examiner,* whose editor, John M. Daniel, had served as a volunteer aide on Hill's staff until wounded at Gaines' Mill. With a facile pen Daniel made the name of A. P. Hill a household word[7] as he extolled the exploits of the Light Division and its commander in such a fashion as to dwarf the feats of others. These articles naturally

---

[3] Snow, 398-99.
[4] Caldwell, 25.
[5] *Ibid.* At this time the Confederate government paid privates eleven dollars per month. J. C. Schwab, *The Confederate States of America,* 182.
[6] *Ibid.*
[7] *Annals of the War,* 698.

A. P. Hill's Troops Take Randol's Battery at Frayser's Farm. From *Battles and Leaders of the Civil War.*

From *Story of The Confederate States* by Joseph Derry

A. P. Hill Orders Lee and Davis Out of Battle Range at Frayser's Farm

aroused resentment among the various commands which finally erupted with the appearance of the July 2 edition of the *Examiner* that carried an account of the battle of Frayser's Farm. The lead article on page one stated:

"About four o'clock Monday afternoon, General Longstreet having been called away, the command of his division was assumed by General A. P. Hill, who with both divisions—that of Longstreet and his own—engaged the enemy at a later hour in the evening.

"The battle was thus fought under the immediate and sole command of General A. P. Hill, in charge of both divisions . . .

"Never was a more glorious victory plucked from desperate and threatening circumstances . . .

"One fact is very certain, and that is that the battle of Monday night was fought exclusively by General A. P. Hill and the forces under his command . . .

"Hill's division has constantly been used on the enemy's front at every stage of the contest from Beaver Dam and Cold Harbor to the late field in the vicinity of Darbytown, to which no name has yet been given. It is a melancholy evidence of the achievements of this division, that out of a force of 14,000 men, with which it went into action on Friday evening last, it now cannot probably bring more than 6,000 efficient men into action."[8]

Aside from exalting the role of the Light Division at the expense of Longstreet's fine performance, the *Examiner's* reiteration of an erroneous statement that Hill had commanded his own and Longstreet's divisions in the latter's absence throughout the battle cast untrue aspersions on Longstreet's adherence to duty. Longstreet's natural resentment was aggravated by knowledge that the *Examiner's* version was Daniel inspired, and he felt that Hill should have curbed such fanciful distortions. Had this article appeared while Daniel was still attached to Hill's command, Longstreet's plaint would have been justified, but as Daniel had severed his connection with the army before this engagement, he was beyond Hill's jurisdiction. Hill, of course, was fully aware that his role had been exaggerated, for in his report, written subsequent to his separation from Longstreet, he stated: "Before the battle opened General Longstreet returned and resumed command."[9]

Longstreet preferred to set the record straight in a more public

[8] *Richmond Examiner,* Wednesday, July 2, 1862, p. 1, col. 1.
[9] O.R., *11,* Part 2, 838.

manner. After composing a rough draft of his projected reply to the *Examiner* article, he showed it to Major Moxley Sorrel, his Assistant Adjutant General, and asked whether he would object to send such a communication under his own name to the Richmond *Whig* which at the time was engaged in a journalistic feud with the *Examiner.* Sorrel eagerly consented, and the July 11 edition of the *Whig* carried the following insertion at the top of page 1:

A CARD

In Bivouac, July 9, 1862

To the Editor of the Whig:

Since the commencement of the Chickahominy campaign some articles have appeared in the *Richmond Examiner* which are calculated to do injustice to some of the officers and to alarm our people. No one in the army has any objection to Major General A. P. Hill's being supplied with all the notoriety that the *Examiner* can furnish, provided no great injustice is done to others. His staff officer, through the columns of the *Examiner,* claims that he had command of the field on Monday for a short time, intimating an improper absence of some other officers. General Lee and Major General Longstreet rode upon the field together, and some hours before Major General A. P. Hill. Both of these officers remained upon the field and slept there, neither having left it for an instant. Major General Longstreet was absent from his usual position for an hour perhaps, for the purpose of putting one of Gen. Hill's Brigades (Gregg's) into action.

The "eight thousand" claimed to have been lost by Gen. A. P. Hill's Division alone will cover the loss of the entire army during the week's campaign. Trifling wounds will swell the list above this figure, but the actual loss will fall short of it. Exaggerated statements of casualties, like those made by the *Examiner,* are calculated to be a great injury to the army, both at home and abroad.

I am sir, very respectfully,

Your obedient servant,

G. M. Sorrel, Assistant Adjutant General[10]

Hill's reaction was immediate and direct. On July 12 he wrote succinctly to Lee: "I have the honor to request that I may be relieved from the command of Major-General Longstreet."[11] Longstreet forwarded the letter with the following endorsement: "If it is convenient to exchange the troops, or to exchange the

---

[10] *Richmond Whig,* Friday, July 11, 1862, p. 1, col. 3.
[11] O.R., *11,* Part 3, 639.

commanders, I see no particular reason why Maj. Gen. A. P. Hill should not be gratified."[12]

Lee tabled this correspondence in the hope that time would cool simmering tempers. Instead, they soon boiled turbulently. As was Hill's wont when he felt aggrieved, he marshalled witnesses and facts in legal fashion. He investigated Sorrel's counter-implication that Longstreet had absented himself at Frayser's Farm to perform Hill's duties. He queried Maxcy Gregg regarding Longstreet's alleged posting of the South Carolina brigade, and learned that Longstreet had discussed the disposition of Gregg's troops and sent an officer to guide them to the vicinity of the battlefield. Gregg added that to his knowledge Longstreet had done nothing else to put the brigade in position, and that Gregg himself had led his troops into action.[13] Although "Old Pete" had rendered some assistance to Gregg, Hill doubtless considered it incidental rather than the object of an hour long mission.

To Hill the quarrel had now become an affaire d'honneur in which his every contact with Longstreet was dominated by wrathful resentment. Upon receipt of a routine report from Longstreet's Assistant Adjutant General, he promptly returned it with the endorsement that "General Hill declines to hold further communication with Major Sorrel."[14] This maneuver, doubtless designed to smoke out Longstreet, succeeded admirably. When Sorrel showed Hill's note to his superior, "Old Pete" bounded to his feet and thundered: "Write him again, and say that note was written by my command, and must be answered satisfactorily."[15] Hill still refused, whereupon Longstreet initiated a sharp but indecisive correspondence directly with his sulking lieutenant. Becoming exasperated, Longstreet decided to take drastic action. Summoning Sorrel, he directed him to don sword and sash and place Hill under arrest with orders to confine himself to his camp and its vicinity. Fully panoplied and followed by an orderly, Major Sorrel arrived at Major General Hill's tent. As Longstreet's emissary

---

12 *Ibid.,* 640.
13 O.R., *51,* Part 2, 590-91, Letter from M. Gregg to A. P. Hill, July 13, 1862.
14 G. Moxley Sorrel, *Recollections of a Confederate Staff Officer* (cited hereafter as Sorrel), 86.
15 *Ibid.,* 87.

entered, Hill, informally attired, rose from his low chair and saluted. After Sorrel communicated Longstreet's order, Hill saluted stiffly and resumed his chair in silence.[16] Not since his third year at the Academy, when he was arrested for some unrecorded infraction, had Hill received such an order.[17] During his arrest, the Light Division was placed under the command of J. R. Anderson, who resigned on July 17 and was succeeded by L. O'B. Branch.[18]

Hill was not one to sulk resignedly. He resumed an angry correspondence with Longstreet which culminated in arrangements for a "hostile meeting" between the two. Learning of the impending duel, Lee quickly exerted his tact and influence to effect a settlement which, if not amicable, at least preserved the services of his two lieutenants who had served with greatest distinction during the Seven Days' Battles.[19] Hill was restored to command of his division, which Lee then transferred to Jackson's sphere in the Valley. As tensions ebbed, Powell Hill and "Old Pete" gradually became "fairly good friends," although Longstreet in his memoirs found little to praise in the fiery commander of the Light Division.[20]

As for Major Sorrel, Longstreet's mouthpiece, that young officer of French descent felt certain he had incurred Hill's undying enmity. Under this misapprehension he regarded Hill's attitude toward him as stiff and menacing. Therefore, he was both surprised and puzzled during the winter of 1864 upon receiving his long-sought promotion to Brigadier General with orders to report to A. P. Hill. Stopping at the War Department in Richmond preparatory to joining his new command, Sorrel met Captain John Reilly, a former subordinate who was now Assistant Adjutant General. Reilly asked Sorrel if he had seen the paper that had secured his promotion. When Sorrel indicated he had not, Reilly drew from his files a letter from A. P. Hill to Lee commenting on the poor condition and handling of a Georgia brigade in his corps. Hill concluded with a request that Lieutenant Colonel G.

---

[16] *Ibid.*
[17] Post Orders No. 2 (U. S. Military Academy), Special Orders No. 122, Nov. 2, 1844, p. 199.
[18] O.R., *51*, Part 2, 590.
[19] Sorrel, 87.
[20] *Ibid.*, 88.

M. Sorrel of Longstreet's Corps be promoted and placed in charge of this brigade.[21]

Reporting to Hill, Sorrel found that "nothing could exceed his kindness in receiving me; it continued all through my service in his corps, and I had every evidence of the good feeling of this distinguished officer."[22]

---

[21] *Ibid.* Also Letter of A. P. Hill to R. E. Lee, Oct. 13, 1864: "I will make another effort to improve Wright's almost worthless brigade—neither of the senior officers are suited for command—recommend Lt.-Col. G. M. Sorrel." This communication was furnished to the author through the courtesy of the Confederate Museum.

[22] Sorrel, 276.

CHAPTER X

"Damn The Fortunes Of War . . ."

(Slaughter's Mountain)

W HILE McCLELLAN licked his wounds and pondered the evacuation of his Army of the Potomac from Harrison's Landing, Lee turned his attention to a new threat from the north. Disappointed over the Peninsular fiasco, Lincoln had placed Major General John B. Pope, bombastic conqueror of Island Number 10 on the Mississippi, in command of the newly-formed Army of Virginia. This force, comprising the divisions of Banks, McDowell, and Franz Sigel, was assigned the task of diverting Lee's attention from McClellan.

Pope initiated his mission in the middle of July by menacing the Virginia Central Railroad, Lee's only direct rail connection between Richmond and the Shenandoah Valley. To counter this threat Lee dispatched Jackson to Gordonsville, a salient on the line. Upon Powell Hill's release from arrest at the end of July, Lee reinforced Jackson with the Light Division augmented by Colonel Stafford's Second Brigade of Louisiana Volunteers. Thus strengthened, Jackson was to "suppress" Pope as soon as possible and then return to Richmond in the event McClellan recuperated sufficiently to essay another thrust against the capital.[1]

Cognizant of Jackson's extreme reluctance to discuss plans with subordinates, and of Hill's sensitive, volatile temperament, Lee exhorted Jackson to take the commander of the Light Division into his confidence. In a letter written to Jackson the same day he ordered Hill north, Lee counseled:

A. P. Hill you will, I think, find a good officer, with whom you can consult, and by advising with your division commanders as to your movements much trouble will be saved you in arranging details, as they can act more intelligently. I wish to save you trouble from my increasing your command. Cache your troops as much as possible till you strike your blow,

---

[1] O. R., *12*, Part 2, 214; *Ibid.*, Part 3, 918-19.

and be prepared to return to me when done, if necessary. I will endeavor to keep General McClellan quiet till it is over, if rapidly executed.[2]

With characteristic attention to his division's welfare but in violation of Lee's orders to cut his transportation to a minimum,[3] Powell Hill embarked for Gordonsville with an excess of transportation which Lee notified Jackson to have him turn over to the quartermaster upon arrival.[4] Hill's movement to join his new chief was undetected by the enemy, and on July 29 the Light Division detrained at its destination.

No record exists of Powell Hill's impressions as he hitched his fortunes for the ensuing nine months to the Star of the Valley. Although the two officers had known each other since West Point days, the acquaintanceship had been formal and intermittent. Until now Hill had never served under Jackson whose eccentricities were the talk of the army. Whatever doubts he may have entertained regarding relations with his fellow Virginian were bridled by the realization that having requested to be relieved from Longstreet, he had no choice but to content himself in his new assignment.

Certainly the sharply contrasting natures of these two dedicated commanders did not portend an harmonious relationship. Jackson held himself aloof from all contacts save official ones involved in the administration of his command, and even in these he dispensed with the customary amenities. Furthermore, the mystical Hero of the Valley was as relentless in dealing with shortcomings of subordinates as he was in pursuing the enemy. Once during the Valley campaign "Old Jack" had demanded to know why a certain brigade had changed the order of march contrary to his orders. When the Colonel in command replied that it made no difference, Jackson fumed, "I want you to understand, Colonel, that you must obey my orders first and reason them afterwards. Consider yourself under arrest, sir, and march to the rear of your brigade."[5]

Hill also demanded strict adherence to duty, but he possessed a cordial, considerate manner "so courteous as almost to lack

---

[2] O.R., *12*, Part 3, 918, Letter from Lee to Jackson, July 27, 1862.
[3] *Ibid.*, 919, Letter from Lee's Assistant Adjutant General to A. P. Hill, July 28, 1862.
[4] *Ibid.*, 923, Letter from Lee to Jackson, August 4, 1862.
[5] S.H.S.P., *19*, 155.

decision."[6] A fellow officer, Colonel James A. Walker, described him as "affable and readily approached by the humblest private; but the officer next in rank never forgot when on duty that he was in the presence of his superior. No commander was ever more considerate of the rights and feelings of others under him, or sustained the authority of his subordinate officers with more firmness and tact."[7] And whereas "Stonewall" spent most of his leisure moments in prayer and meditation, Powell Hill would pull out his wooden pipe,[8] hand-carved by an admiring veteran, and enjoy a sociable smoke with his associates.

Significantly, Hill joined Jackson at a time when the latter was running out of general officers to conduct the numerous courts martial in session. These proceedings were interrupted shortly by reports that the vanguard of Pope's army under Banks had arrived at Culpeper. Jackson informed Lee that he planned to overwhelm the advancing Federals, and on Thursday, August 7, he started his three divisions over plantation paths and by-roads to Orange Court House which the Light Division reached about midnight.[9]

That night Jackson sent Hill orders to fall in behind Ewell's division at dawn on Friday. Jackson's old division under the command of Winder would then follow the Light Division. At the designated time Hill had his column waiting near the street down which Ewell's division was expected to lead the line of march. One or two brigades passed before Hill suddenly recognized that they belonged not to Ewell but to Winder. Inquiry revealed that Jackson, without notifying Hill, had ordered Ewell to march by roads to the left of the main line of march. Not desiring to interpose his large division between Winder's brigades, Hill decided to wait until the entire division had passed.[10]

During the interval between the passage of two of Winder's brigades Jackson rode up to Hill and demanded to know why his troops were not moving. Thinking Jackson was aware that part of Winder's command already had passed, Hill replied that

[6] *Annals of the War*, 703.
[7] S.H.S.P., *20*, 384.
[8] This pipe is preserved in the Confederate Museum.
[9] O.R., *12*, Part 2, 221.
[10] *Ibid.*, 214-15.

he was waiting for Winder's division to pass. Impatient, Jackson looked down the street only to see one of his old brigades standing at ease. Presuming it to be Winder's vanguard, he ordered it forward.[11]

After Winder's column finally passed, the Light Division fell in behind, but its progress was so slow that Hill rode ahead to ascertain the cause. At Barnett's Ford he found that Ewell's route converged with the road over which Winder's and Hill's men were proceeding. Hill sent word to Jackson that the passage of Ewell's troops and trains was delaying the forward movement, and inquired whether the wagon trains were to follow each division.[12]

Late in the afternoon, having progressed only about a mile and while Ewell's troops were still crossing the river, Hill received orders from Jackson to return to Orange Court House and encamp for the night.[13] Jackson subsequently denied ordering Hill back to Orange Court House, contending instead that he had sent Hill verbal and written orders to move forward.[14]

Such were the events which raised the curtain on the prolonged dispute between Jackson and his spirited new lieutenant who had joined the command only a week previously. It was a quarrel whose flames would be fed continuously until Chancellorsville. Henceforth these antagonists seldon met except in the line of duty.[15] And although Jackson did not keep a "black list" as Hill later charged, he did mentally record his observations and interpretations of his lieutenant's conduct during the ensuing month. These he subsequently compiled into a list of eight specifications to support his charge of neglect of duty against Hill. The first specification concerned Hill's alleged tardiness on the confused march toward Culpeper Court House (see Appendix).

During the night following this hectic day of August 8, Hill sent a note to Jackson requesting permission to expedite the march by taking his division over a short cut and rejoining the main

---

[11] *Ibid.*, 216.

[12] *Ibid.*, 215.

[13] Letter from Hill to Major A. S. Pendleton, March 13, 1863. The original is in the possession of the Virginia Historical Society. Hill stated as his recollection that the order had been transmitted verbally by Major Paxton.

[14] O.R., *12*, Part 2, 216.

[15] Douglas, 196.

column at any point Jackson might designate. "Old Jack" replied curtly that Hill should move immediately along the appointed route as he intended to be in Culpeper on Saturday night. Piqued but obedient, Hill started his troops before dawn and soon pressed the "foot cavalry" of Jackson's old division.[16] As the day wore on a suffocating cloud of dust enveloped the column, and the intense heat felled some of the marchers with sunstroke. Sensing that a battle was imminent, soldiers scattered their colorful playing cards along the road, thereby divesting themselves of this "device of the devil" in the event they should be killed.[17]

When Federal cavalry began demonstrating against the left of the advancing column, Hill ordered Gregg's brigade to join Lawton's troops of Winder's division and take a position which would protect the crossing of twelve hundred baggage wagons and also guard the march. Unhappy at being assigned to duty in the rear, Gregg twice appealed to Hill to be relieved and sent to the front. Although Hill sympathized with his brigadier's wishes, he had to refuse on the basis that the South Carolina brigade was in the very place it was most needed.[18]

Within six miles of Culpeper Court House, Hill heard firing ahead. He soon learned that Ewell's advance guard had encountered Federal cavalry supported by artillery. Jackson quickly disposed the two leading divisions along a front concave to the enemy. Winder occupied the unreconnoitered left of the arc which rested on Culpeper Road; Early's brigade of Ewell's division held the center; and on the right Ewell's remaining two brigades manned the apron skirting the base of a ridge known as Slaughter's Mountain (also known as Cedar Mountain). Characteristically, Jackson decided to take the initiative by rocking the enemy with artillery fire, after which the entire command would stage a general assault and overwhelm the bluecoats. But of these plans he said nothing to Hill whose rear division constituted the reserve.

On hearing the artillery fire, Hill ordered Colonel R. Lindsay

---

[16] O.R., *12*, Part 2, 215.
[17] Dunaway, 34.
[18] Caldwell, 26; O.R., *12*, Part 2, 215.

Walker, his chief of artillery, to hurry forward all of the division's long-range guns from a park in the rear. However, only Fleet's and Pegram's batteries succeeded in wending their way past the labyrinth of wagon trains and ambulances to Early's front where they unlimbered in an exposed position within close range of the enemy. As Federal skirmishers crawled forward toward these un-supported guns, Early's troops dashed up with a yell and threw a protective cordon of infantry around the guns.[19] Less fortunate was General Winder, who was mortally wounded while observing the effect of his artillery.[20]

Meanwhile the opposing artillerists staged a spirited two-hour artillery duel. As the din subsided late in the afternoon, but before the Confederate attack got underway, two Federal brigades—their bayonets glittering and banners flying—charged across the open field in front of Early while another enemy force emerged from the woods on the left and broke Winder's front line. With Jackson's center and left assailed and in confusion, the timely arrival of the Light Division was dramatic and decisive. Hill hurried Thomas' leading brigade to support and extend Early's battered line which was rallying around Hill's old Thirteenth Virginia now commanded by Colonel James A. Walker.[21] Thomas formed his line along a fence bordering a corn-field over which the enemy were advancing. Firing furiously, the Georgians held their ground and hurled back the attackers.[22]

Into the disorganized troops on the left now galloped Jackson and Powell Hill—the latter in shirt sleeves brandishing his sword.[23] Scanning the situation, Hill espied a young lieutenant scurrying to the rear. Wrathfully he seized the skulker, stripped off his insignia, and ordered him back to the front.[24] Meantime, Jackson had drawn his sword and was preparing to lead a rally in person when General Taliaferro, upon whom Winder's command had devolved, insisted his chief retire to the rear.

---

[19] O.R., *12*, Part 2, 215, 226.
[20] Henderson, 409.
[21] O.R., *12*, Part 2, 219-20.
[22] *Ibid.*, 215.
[23] "Souvenir Booklet."
[24] Robertson, Part IV, 8, November 4, 1934; S.H.S.P., *20*, 384.

Soon Jackson encountered Lawrence Branch who had just formed his brigade into line on the left of Culpeper Road. The handsome young commander had been confined to an ambulance during the march because he was too feeble to walk, but the exhilaration of battle resuscitated him sufficiently to command his brigade.[25] Jackson informed Branch that his left was beaten and broken, and ordered the North Carolinian to advance through woods and thick undergrowth to support the redoubtable Stonewall Brigade which had thrown back the earlier assault on the left only to be assailed in turn on front and flank. Branch's men had proceeded only a hundred yards when they met Stonewall's veterans retreating in disorder before the pursuing bluecoats. Opening ranks to permit the refugees to pass, Branch's brigade, unshaken by the surrounding panic, pressed forward in unbroken line and received the enemy's fire. The North Carolinians then promptly poured repeated volleys into the enemy who broke and fled through the woods where they were reinforced by a fresh brigade.[26]

Archer and Pender having now arrived on Branch's left, a general charge was made which drove the Federals across a wheat field and into the opposite wood.[27] Archer's 1,200 man brigade was subjected to heavy fire while crossing the open field and suffered 135 casualties.[28]

Among the Federal prisoners captured was General Henry Prince, who was taken to Powell Hill then engrossed in observing the battle near the front where the minie balls were whining. Prince greeted Hill by saying, "General, the fortunes of war have thrown me in your hands." Hill brusquely replied, "Damn the fortunes of war, General, get to the rear; you are in danger here." As one witness of this episode commented: "Hill's duties required him to undergo the exposure, but he could not bear the idea of having even an enemy unnecessarily exposed."[29]

With the enemy routed, Jackson's forces rallied from end to end and were advancing en masse when Banks made a last desperate

---

[25] O.R., *12*, Part 2, 223.
[26] *Ibid.*, 222; Henderson, 411.
[27] O.R., *12*, Part 2, 215, 218, 222, 225.
[28] *Ibid.*, 218.
[29] S.H.S.P., *19*, 182.

effort to seize the initiative. Uncovering two cavalry squadrons which had been concealed in the woods opposite Jackson's left, the Federal commander hurled them toward the Confederate center. But as the two lines of Federal cavalry charged diagonally they exposed their flank to Branch and Taliaferro whose combined fire emptied many saddles and dispersed the survivors.[30]

Evening shadows now shrouded 3,000 antagonists who had fallen during the afternoon. But darkness brought no respite to Jackson's command. With the aid of a full moon "Old Jack" intended to press on to Culpeper before Pope's converging forces concentrated at this strategic hub. On receipt of Jackson's orders to pursue the enemy, Hill advanced Field's and Stafford's fresh brigades together with "Willie" Pegram's four gun battery. After the guns had shelled the woods in front, Stafford's men cautiously pushed ahead, skirmishing and taking prisoners.[31]

The head of Hill's column had proceeded less than a mile and a half when Farrow, Jackson's most reliable scout, reported that the enemy was drawn up in a woodland just several hundred yards ahead. Jackson ordered Pegram to take position on a knoll and open fire, while Hill directed Field's brigade to support the battery. Pegram serviced his guns for an hour in the face of a concentric fire from three Federal batteries before severe losses in men and horses silenced the roar of his guns and halted the infantry advance.[32] Thereupon the front brigades bivouacked within listening distance of the enemy's pickets.[33] The next day both sides collected and buried their dead. Hill's casualties included his Chief Quartermaster, Major J. G. Field, and an aide-de-camp, Captain F. T. Hill. Just prior to the campaign Hill also had lost the staff services of his brother, Major E. B. Hill, Chief Commissary, who was furloughed to Richmond on sick leave.[34]

In the face of heavy enemy reinforcements, Jackson retired across the Rapidan to his camps around Gordonsville. Here Powell Hill had time to reflect on his initiation into Jackson's command.

[30] O.R., *12*, Part 2, 216, 222.
[31] *Ibid.*, 216, 224.
[32] *Ibid.*, 184, 216, 218.
[33] Dunaway, 34.
[34] O.R., *12*, Part 2, 216; S.H.S.P., *19*, 179-80.

He found Jackson to be the same uncommunicative officer he had known as a cadet. Now, however, this trait manifested itself in ways that were frustrating to the methodical and forthright commander of the Light Division. Completely ignoring Lee's suggestion to counsel with Hill, Jackson failed to acquaint his new lieutenant with his overall plan, drew his marching orders loosely, and changed them without notifying Hill. This was a bitter indoctrination for the proud and sensitive Virginian who had so distinctly outshone Jackson recently during the Seven Days' Battles.

Hill doubtless derived some consolation from the fact that confusion in the order of march had resulted in the Light Division rescuing Jackson's old division rather than vice versa, which conceivably could have occurred had the original order been followed. For the rout on Jackson's left was due to a lack of reconnaissance which subsequent events revealed to be one of Powell Hill's shortcomings. On the brighter side Hill shared Jackson's thirst for battle, and with a major engagement in the offing, he was quite certain his division would be in the thick of it.

Brigadier Generals of the Light Division

JAMES J. ARCHER
Photo National Archives

LAWRENCE O'BRIEN BRANCH
Photo courtesy Library of Congress

MAXCY GREGG

JAMES H. LANE
Photo courtesy Library of Congress

EDWARD L. THOMAS
Photo National Archives

Lt. General Thomas J. "Stonewall" Jackson. Hill quarreled
bitterly between battles with Jackson but rushed to succor
him at Chancellorsville.

CHAPTER XI

"Let Us Die Here"

(Second Manassas)

J ACKSON'S offensive victory at Slaughter's Mountain provided the South a refreshing change in outlook following the grim battles in front of Richmond. Strategically, however, it was a hollow triumph. The Virginia Central Railroad still lay exposed to Pope's army which was being reinforced by Burnside and McClellan. In the face of this enemy concentration, Lee dispatched Longstreet's ten brigades northward and hastened forward himself to assume command of his reunited forces.

When Lee joined the army at Gordonsville on Friday, August 15, he learned that Pope's horde was wedged between the Rapidan and Rappahannock rivers. In the hope of trapping Pope between these fluid jaws and crushing him before reinforcements arrived, Lee issued orders for the army to cross the Rapidan on Monday and assail the enemy the next day. But the prospect of a major victory quickly evaporated as preparations went awry, and Pope withdrew upon receiving captured orders from Lee to Stuart divulging the Confederate strategy.

Revamping his plans, Lee ordered the army to cross the Rapidan on Wednesday and form front opposite Pope's forces which now were disposed along a north-south line on the east bank of the Rappahannock. Jackson was to cross at Somerville Ford and move up the west bank of the Rappahannock, keeping to the left of Longstreet and maneuvering so as to cross the upper reaches of the river and overwhelm Pope's right flank.[1]

This operation was marred at the outset by a recurrence of friction between Jackson and Hill. Although Lee's orders specified that the movements were to start "at dawn,"[2] Jackson directed

---

[1] O.R., *12*, Part 2, 729.
[2] *Ibid.*

Hill to move "as soon as the moon should rise."[3] On Wednesday night Jackson discovered that the Light Division had not stirred, nor had Hill issued marching orders to his brigadiers. These were to constitute two additional specifications in support of Jackson's charge of Hill's neglect of duty.[4] Though Hill may have been uncertain as to the interpretation of "moonrise" he should have checked it, and his failure to instruct the brigade commanders was inexcusably negligent.

After a two hour delay occasioned by Hill's puzzling behavior, Jackson's command proceeded without incident through Culpeper County to the hills opposite Warrenton Springs where the Light Division encamped near the home of Dr. Scott.[5] On Friday, Jackson sent Early's brigade of Ewell's division across the river intending to follow with the whole command. Early's troops filed across a dilapidated dam which washed away during the rainy night, thereby isolating the brigade which faced annihilation or capture at the hands of a rapidly mounting enemy force. Fortunately, Jackson was able to construct a temporary bridge over which Early recrossed to safety before dawn on Sunday.[6]

Early on the Sabbath at least seven heavy Federal batteries took position on the hills opposite the Light Division which Hill had drawn up behind five of Colonel Walker's batteries. About 10 A.M. the enemy opened a heavy fire to which Walker's guns replied for several minutes before Hill ordered Walker to hold his fire until Federal infantry appeared. About noon long columns of bluecoats advanced down the road apparently intent on seizing the bridge. In concert, all of Hill's guns belched forth a storm of shot which scattered the enemy. Twice this reception was repeated before the enemy retired for the last time.[7] During this minor engagement the Light Division was under heavy continuous artillery fire for eight hours with a loss of only eighteen—a tribute to Hill's deployment of six brigades totaling over 10,000 men.[8]

---

[3] Appendix, specification 2 of Jackson's charge.
[4] *Ibid.*, specifications 2 and 3.
[5] O.R., *12*, Part 2, 670, 673, 678.
[6] *Ibid.*, 707.
[7] *Ibid.*, 670, 673.
[8] S.H.S.P., *13*, 31.

While Hill engaged the enemy at Warrenton Springs, Jackson conferred with Lee at nearby Jeffersonton. Frustrated in his attempt to edge around Pope's right and concerned by Federal dispatches Stuart had snatched from Pope's headquarters revealing the imminent approach of reinforcements, Lee outlined a plan whereby Jackson and Stuart were to make a wide sweep around Pope and strike at his supply lines far to the rear.

Accordingly, Hill's division, which had been relieved Sunday evening by Hood,[9] turned out promptly at dawn on Monday and fell in behind Ewell's division. Unencumbered by knapsacks the column wheeled left and moved briskly up the river to Henson's Mill where a crossing was made.[10] Skirting the base of the Blue Ridge, Hill's barefooted veterans left a blood-stained trail as they trudged over rugged roads and rocky hillsides to Salem where the command rested for the night.[11] Next morning the column turned right and hurried unopposed through Thoroughfare Gap to Manassas Junction whose outskirts the Light Division reached late on Tuesday. Hill estimated his men had marched fifty-four miles in two days.[12] The troops were ragged, weary, and famished having subsisted for two days on green corn and apples plucked along the line of march.[13]

Meanwhile, Ewell's division and Stuart's cavalry turned southeast at Gainesville and struck the Orange and Alexandria Railroad at Bristoe Station in Pope's rear. After this force derailed two empty trains and tore up some track, a detachment hastened north and captured Pope's enormous stores at Manassas Junction which were defended by only two batteries.[14] Pope's yawning cornucopia now lay invitingly open to Jackson's half of Lee's army.

There were no stragglers Wednesday morning as the ravenous soldiers of the Light Division sighted the stores at Manassas Junction. Hill's veterans brushed aside Ewell's well-disciplined guards and helped themselves to delicacies and sartorial luxuries

---

[9] O.R., *12*, Part 2, 670.
[10] *Ibid.*, 678.
[11] S.H.S.P., *13*, 9.
[12] O.R., *12*, Part 2, 670.
[13] S.H.S.P., *13*, 11.
[14] O.R., *12*, Part 2, 650.

unknown to their own commissariat. Hill made no effort to restrain his men from garnering what he doubtless considered their due.[15]

While the troops gorged their stomachs with lobster salad and stuffed soap and toothbrushes into their pockets,[16] "Old Jack" astride his cream-colored mount[17] observed an enemy brigade approaching Manassas from the north. Instantly he ordered Hill's revelers to interrupt their jubilee and form line of battle to the right of the road along which the bluecoats were marching. After two of his batteries swept the advancing line, Jackson rode forward and demanded the foe to surrender. When this summons was rejected, the Light Division supported by artillery attacked the hopelessly outnumbered enemy and drove them like "scattered partridges"[18] across Bull Run toward Centreville.[19] One of Branch's North Carolinians pausing on all fours during the pursuit to lap up some water, discovered a bluecoat hiding in a culvert. Crawling from his hideout the good-natured Yankee slapped the Tar Heel on the shoulder and conceded, "You got us badly this time, come let's take a drink."[20] As the prisoners marched past the captors, a man in Gregg's brigade without apparent provocation sprang among the captives and mauled one severely before fellow South Carolinians broke it up in the interest of fair play.[21]

By noon Hill's men returned to resume their revelry, this time with freer conscience as permission was granted to take anything in the storehouses "from a dose of calomel to a McClellan saddle."[22] They were joined later by Ewell's troops who had retired northward from Bristoe Station in the face of Pope's advancing army.

---

[15] Caldwell, 31; O. R., *12*, Part 2, 678. General Isaac Trimble who had posted the guards noted in his report: "It was with extreme mortification that in reporting to General A. P. Hill for orders about 10 o'clock, I witnessed an indiscriminate plunder of the public stores, cars, and sutler's houses by the army which had just arrived, in which General Hill's division was conspicuous, setting at defiance the guard I had placed." O.R., *12*, Part 2, 721.

[16] S.H.S.P., *13*, 12.

[17] Caldwell, 28.

[18] C. G. Chamberlayne., ed., *Ham Chamberlayne—Virginian* (cited hereafter as Chamberlayne), Letter from Ham Chamberlayne to his Mother, Sept. 6, 1862.

[19] O.R., *12*, Part 2, 678.

[20] *N. C. Regts.*, *2*, 973.

[21] Caldwell, 30-31.

[22] *Ibid.*, 31.

That night Hill's satiated veterans withdrew from Manassas Junction to Centreville, leaving Gregg's and Thomas' brigades as a rearguard to oversee the burning of sutlers' and commissary stores together with about a hundred loaded freight cars.[23]

Having destroyed vast Federal stores and severed Pope's supply line, Jackson decided to take an advanced defensive position near Groveton where he could threaten Pope while awaiting Longstreet. On Thursday morning the Light Division was marching down the Warrenton Turnpike toward Groveton when Hill received orders from Jackson to move his troops south to the lower fords of Bull Run and assail the enemy force heading northward. Two hours had elapsed since Jackson sent this order, and having just seen two intercepted dispatches from Pope to McDowell ordering a concentration of the Federal army on the Manassas plains, Hill "determined it best to push on and join General Jackson."[24] He fully realized the danger of violating Jackson's stern dictum to "obey my orders first and reason about them afterward,"[25] but he courageously disregarded his chief's directive in the belief that more recent information indicated that Pope intended to crush Jackson's isolated command.

Therefore, Hill crossed Bull Run near the Stone Bridge, turned right and took position behind an embankment of the unfinished Independent Railroad.[26] About sunset he heard brisk firing to the right where Ewell's and Taliaferro's divisions—concealed by a ridge commanding the Warrenton Turnpike near Groveton—surprised King's Federal division as it was marching sprightly behind a regimental band toward Manassas. Hill dispatched Gregg's brigade to support Ewell, but the South Carolinians did not reach the field until after dark when they learned the sad news that Ewell's leg had been shattered by a minie ball. Soon the stubborn, indecisive engagement ceased, and during the night the bluecoats slipped away to Manassas to notify Pope of Jackson's position.[27]

While this engagement at Groveton was in progress Hill turned

---

[23] O.R., *12*, Part 2, 679.
[24] *Ibid.*, 670.
[25] S.H.S.P., *19*, 155.
[26] O.R., *12*, Part 2, 679.
[27] *Ibid.*

his batteries on the advance guard of the forces Pope was massing to overwhelm Jackson. When darkness quieted the guns, veterans of the Light Division stretched out to rest on the rocky slopes of the railroad with orders from Hill to maintain complete silence.[28] But in the ensuing stillness a shout suddenly arose in the enemy camps as one unit after another took up the cry until the entire countryside resounded with spine-chilling Yankee yells.[29]

On this cold, dewy, moonlit Thursday night of August 28, some of Hill's soldiers reflected on a prophecy which had been confidently predicted two months earlier by an infantryman in Gregg's brigade. While discussing the future course of the war this prognosticator had stated unhesitatingly that the next great battle would occur on the 29th of August. His forecast was based on a blue-numeraled vision of this date in a newspaper he had read. The seer proved to be one of the casualties on the day his prediction was fulfilled.[30]

Responsibilities rather than prophecies occupied Powell Hill's attention on the eve of the impending struggle against Pope's gathering horde. With Ewell and Taliaferro wounded, he was the only experienced divisional commander on the field. Consequently, Jackson assigned him the task of defending the critical left of the one and three-quarter mile front along the railroad cut. The embankment, almost five feet high,[31] constituted an excellent fortification marred only by an isthmus of thick timber which bisected the front rendering it impossible to employ artillery effectively.[32]

Hill took advantage of the compact front to dispose Gregg, Thomas, and Field from left to right in a double line, supported in the same order by Archer, Pender and Branch. The batteries were posted in an open field behind the infantry.[33] On the extreme left Gregg's brigade was crowded onto a rocky, wooded knoll slightly in advance of the general line and flanked on the left by

[28] S.H.S.P., *13*, 14.
[29] Caldwell, 32.
[30] *Ibid.*, 33.
[31] S.H.S.P., *13*, 15, 27.
[32] O.R., *12*, Part 2, 670.
[33] *Ibid.*

a cleared field extending to Bull Run. Gregg's cramped position barely accommodated his brigade, but fortunately the South Carolinians were able to utilize the undulating terrain and copses for maximum concealment.

In a wooded thicket on Gregg's right, Hill placed Thomas' Georgia brigade, but between these two brigades he carelessly left an undefended gap about 150 yards wide. This negligence was compounded by the presence of a ten foot high embankment in front of the interval which afforded excellent cover for an enemy attacking force.[34] In his report Hill offered no explanation for this faulty disposition, nor was it the last time he was to commit this error.

Just as Hill completed his final dispositions at daybreak on Friday, German troops of Fritz Sigel's corps advanced behind skirmishers in what Powell Hill immediately discerned as a move to turn the Light Division's left and roll up Jackson's entire line.[35] Gregg's brigade promptly engaged 4,000 of the enemy in dense woods near the railroad cut, split two brigades and drove them back in confusion.[36] Rallying, the German troops repeatedly charged Gregg's front and flanks in vain.[37]

By noon Gregg's front had been cleared of bluecoats, and the defenders were further heartened by news of Longstreet's arrival. However, Pope, unaware that he now confronted Lee's reunited army, resumed hammering Hill's division. He unleashed Hooker's and Reno's divisions which crashed through the woods to assail Thomas and Field. The latter's riflemen picked out their targets at point-blank range as the Federals stormed the embankment. Hill then ordered Pender to bring forward his reserve brigade and counterattack. Thereupon the North Carolinians swept the enemy from the embankment through the woods to a clearing. Here Pender's men encountered heavy artillery fire and infantry which threatened to envelop their flanks.[38] Although Pender was knocked down by a shell he refused to leave his troops, but instead led

---

[34] *Ibid.,* 680.
[35] *Ibid.,* 670.
[36] S.H.S.P., *13,* 19; Henderson, 457.
[37] O.R., *12,* Part 2, 680.
[38] *Ibid.,* 697-98.

them back to cover behind the embankment.[39] More serious was the severe wounding of Charles Field, whose men Hill asserted "were ever ready to follow where he led." His command devolved upon Colonel J. M. Brockenbrough of the Fortieth Virginia.[40]

Frontal assaults having failed, Pope now sent Hooker's division toward the gap Hill had left between Gregg and Thomas. A fresh Massachusetts brigade crawled unobserved to the high embankment opposite the interval, and with a rush sliced between the two brigades and isolated Gregg's command.[41] Thereupon Gregg promptly wheeled McGowan's reserve infantry into the gap, and assisted by the Forty-Ninth Georgia Regiment of Thomas' brigade and Archer's cheering brigade, they steadily pressed the enemy spearhead back to the railroad track where it broke and fled under a barrage of grape and canister.[42] At one juncture McGowan's volunteers delivered and received volleys at ten paces.[43] Here, as one Confederate officer observed, "was the consummation of the grand debate between Massachusetts and South Carolina. Webster and Calhoun had exhausted the argument in the Senate, and now the soldiers of the two states were fighting it out eye to eye, hand to hand, man to man . . . Each state showed it had 'the courage of its convictions'."[44]

The afternoon was waning, but to the exhausted defenders time had "leaden wings," and the red sun seemed determined "not to go down."[45] Five times Pope had hurled his division piecemeal against the Light Division, and each attack had been received by Hill's troops with what Lee termed "their accustomed steadiness . . . (and) repeatedly repulsed."[46] Over 4,000 enemy dead and wounded lay heaped in the woods on Hill's front. Colonel McCrady of Gregg's brigade soberly reflected, "It was war, but it was not

[39] *Ibid.*, 671.
[40] *Ibid.*
[41] S.H.S.P., *13*, 27.
[42] *Ibid.*, 30; O.R. *12*, Part 2, 680-81.
[43] O.R., *12*, Part 2, 681.
[44] S.H.S.P., *13*, 30.
[45] Douglas, 137.
[46] O.R., *12*, Part 2, 554.

grand."[47] Even during the intervals between attacks, sharpshooters maintained a deadly fire on all moving targets.[48]

And now Pope ordered still another assault against the Light Division. Anticipating the attack, Hill checked his supply of ammunition which he discovered was down to about one round per man.[49] He immediately ordered details to collect cartridges from the dead and wounded. In Gregg's sector the situation was so critical that the wounded were stripped of weapons and ammunition before the Infirmary Corps was allowed to administer aid.[50]

Solicitous of his ability to withstand another onslaught, Hill notified Jackson he would do his best but was dubious of the outcome. Jackson was visibly disturbed by this message from his combative lieutenant, and he directed an aide to ride and "tell him if they attack he must beat them." On further reflection he decided to follow and discuss the situation in person. When Hill reiterated his apprehension, Jackson replied in his low husky voice, "General, your men have done nobly; if you are attacked again you will beat the enemy back." At that moment the sound of musketry rattled on the left. Hill said, "Here it comes," and galloped off as Jackson called after him, "I'll expect you to beat them."[51]

Meanwhile, Gregg rallied his South Carolinian brigade, "weakened in all things save its unconquerable spirit,"[52] to meet five enemy brigades advancing in double lines. He informed Hill that his ammunition was exhausted, but he thought he could hold his position with the bayonet.[53] To this Hill admiringly exclaimed, "He is the man for me."[54]

As Hill watched the serried blue lines advance, he anxiously realized that this assault "made the chances of victory to tremble in the balance."[55] Bolstered by reinforcements, the Federals

---

[47] S.H.S.P., *13*, 32.
[48] *Ibid.*, 26.
[49] O.R., *12*, Part 2, 671.
[50] S.H.S.P., *13*, 34.
[51] Douglas, 138.
[52] O.R., *12*, Part 2, 671.
[53] *Ibid.*, 681; S.H.S.P., *13*, 34.
[54] "Souvenir Booklet."
[55] O.R., *12*, Part 2, 671.

swarmed over the railroad and poured a deadly volley into Hill's line which slowly but steadily retired. At the extreme left, Gregg was forced back 300 yards to a ridge overlooking the field. Here he drew up the remnants of his five regiments into two lines to receive the cheering enemy's final thrust. With his Revolutionary saber drawn, Gregg strode up and down in front of his line entreating, "Let us die here, my men, let us die here."[56]

With only fixed bayonets to dispute the dreaded charge they expected at any moment, Gregg's men were suddenly paralyzed and then relieved by a shout in their rear. Coming to their assistance at Hill's order were comparatively fresh reinforcements under the command of Early. Raising the rebel yell, the welcome newcomers fell upon the enemy who halted, turned, and fled in disorder. While the bluecoats scurried down the slope, they abandoned a mule which in the midst of the confusion quietly cropped a green blade here and there among the blood-stained grass.[57]

When the sun finally descended, Hill dispatched a note to Jackson stating: "General Hill presents his compliments and says the attack of the enemy was repulsed." With a rare smile and a rarer compliment, Jackson told the courier, "Tell him I knew he would do it."[58]

Although Pegram and Braxton engaged the enemy artillery until dark, the bluecoats essayed no further demonstrations.[59] The ordeal over, Hill relieved several of his front brigades and directed the men to refill their cartridge boxes.[60] Then the leaden-boned and muscle-weary survivors slept where they dropped.

Powell Hill's handling of the Light Division this day was notable in several respects. It was his first experience in directing a defensive engagement. By nature and preference an aggressive tactician, he nevertheless displayed conspicuous ability in executing his assignment to hold the Federal objective on the left. Engaged continuously from early morning to sunset, his brigades had sustained and repelled six separate assaults by forces aggregating almost

---

[56] S.H.S.P., *13*, 34.
[57] *Ibid.*, 33, 35.
[58] Douglas, 138.
[59] O.R., *12*, Part 2, 674.
[60] *Ibid.*, 671.

twice those of the Light Division. He had maintained a steady eye on the battle's progress and closely coordinated the movements of his brigades. Reinforcements were directed to the right point at the right time. Only his puzzling failure to close the gap between Gregg and Thomas marred his performance which otherwise evoked even an eight word compliment from Jackson.

By Saturday morning Pope not only was still unaware that Longstreet had arrived and taken position on Jackson's right, but he was also under the delusion that Jackson had abandoned the field. Acting on this premise, he ordered McDowell, Porter, and Reynolds to seize the ridge Jackson had occupied. With this eminence in Federal hands, Pope envisioned his legions falling upon Jackson's forces as they retreated through Thoroughfare Gap.

In mid-afternoon one, two, and then three lines of bluecoats, their bayonets flashing in the sun, sprang from the woods and crossed the meadows to assail Jackson's right.[61] Within half an hour the initial fierce assault was beaten off at close range with bullets, rocks, and bayonets.[62] Thereupon the enemy shifted the attack to Hill's front, where, preceded by heavy shelling, they attacked furiously in force and drove in the front-line brigades of Archer, Gregg, and Thomas. Hill threw in Brockenbrough and Pender to check the infantry while his batteries opened and quickly forced the enemy guns to withdraw.[63]

Soon the relentless Federals resumed the attack with such violent intensity along Jackson's entire front that "Old Jack" urgently requested Lee to dispatch a division to his assistance. But Longstreet, who had calmly followed the battle from an elevation near the point where his line obtusely intersected Jackson's, had a simpler and quicker solution. Noting that the Federals exposed their left flank to Longstreet's batteries as they advanced against Jackson, "Old Pete" ordered his guns to open. As though mowed by a leaden scythe, the blue supporting lines withered behind the assault line which broke and fled.[64]

---

[61] Dabney, 532.
[62] O.R., *12*, Part 2, 666-67.
[63] *Ibid.*, 652, 671.
[64] *R. E. Lee, II*, 321-22; *Lee's Lieutenants, II*, 126.

As Hill had noted at Williamsburg, "then was the time," and as the tide of battle suddenly shifted into reverse Lee ordered a full-scale counterattack. Almost in unison the entire army—disposed in double lines along a five mile crescent—surged forward. Pausing only to crush islands of resistance, Lee's gray divisions, 50,000 strong, swept irresistibly forward.[65]

Hill with his customary impatience had ordered an advance in anticipation of the general order. Jackson had approved the move and directed Hill to advance en echelon. Holding back Gregg to meet a reported threat on his flank, Hill unleashed his other brigades. As though welded together, Archer, Pender, and Thomas drove everything before them. Archer captured three pieces of an enemy battery scampering to the rear, and Pender's cooperating troops overtook the remaining three pieces in the woods.[66] On the extreme right of Hill's line Brockenbrough became separated from the division and advanced with Taliaferro's veterans; while Branch, on the extreme left, encountered resistance shortly after entering the woods on his front and had to be relieved by Lawton who now commanded Ewell's division.[67]

After driving the enemy a mile and a half to Henry House, Hill's men encountered stiffened resistance. In the growing darkness troops became confused and the pursuit stalled. Some units had penetrated so far into the Federal lines that Pender's Assistant Adjutant General was captured while trying to find his way back to the brigade from Hill's headquarters.[68] Shortly after dark Archer's Tennesseans challenged silhouetted troops on their front. When they received the reply: "For the Union," each side fired a single volley into the opposing lines thereby concluding a grim day's work.[69]

Jubilation over this smashing victory at Manassas was tempered by depressing casualty lists. Losses in the Light Division totaled 1,507 of whom over 600 were in Gregg's brigade.[70]

---

[65] Hanson, 125; Henderson, 476-77.
[66] O.R., *12*, Part 2, 671, 698.
[67] *Ibid.*, 652, 671.
[68] *Ibid.*, 672.
[69] *Ibid.*, 701.
[70] *Ibid.*, 672.

Still with his "headquarters in the saddle" but with *his* back to the enemy, Pope withdrew during the rainy night after the battle to a well-fortified position at Centreville. As Stuart continued to harry him there, the Federal commander decided to retire even further to the intrenchments at Alexandria.

Desirous of striking the enemy still another blow, Lee ordered Jackson to make another sweep to the left of the retreating columns and assail Pope's flank. All day Sunday Hill's weary men sloshed through the mud, and many fell behind late in the day as the column turned east along the Little River Turnpike. Jed Hotchkiss, Jackson's topographical engineer, reported this straggling in the Light Division to Jackson who ordered Hill to slacken his pace. Jackson subsequently claimed that later the same evening Hill "permitted the head of his columns again to march too rapidly and allowed a large number of his men to straggle from the ranks."[71] This was to constitute another specification in Jackson's charge of Hill's neglect of duty. With friction developing so soon after the battle, it began to appear that these two implacable foes could effect a truce only when fighting the enemy.

Late the next afternoon Jackson's column made contact with the retreating Federals near the once fine colonial mansion of Chantilly which the bluecoats had sacked. Jackson immediately ordered Hill to ascertain the strength of the enemy troops bristling in the thick woods ahead.[72] Hill advanced Branch and Brockenbrough whose brigades pressed forward in the face of a blinding thunderstorm which burst upon the opposing lines almost simultaneously with the clash of arms.[73]

Hill's two brigades charged across an open field, met the enemy and drove him through the woods to another field beyond. Here the Federals rallied and counter-attacked Brockenbrough as Branch advanced alone on the right in the face of a murderous frontal fire. The North Carolinians replied as fast and furiously as their damp cartridges permitted. About the same time his ammunition ran out, Branch observed an enemy flanking force

---

[71] Appendix, specification 4 of Jackson's charge.
[72] O.R., *12*, Part 2, 672, 677.
[73] *Ibid.*, 672, 677, 682; Long, 199.

advancing through a field of corn on the right. He immediately notified Hill who ordered him to hold his position with the bayonet. Then Hill threw in successively the brigades of Gregg, Thomas, and Pender who in turn were fought to a standstill.[74]

In the misty dusk a one-armed Federal officer, guiding his horse with his knee, approached within recognition distance of Hill's lines. In response to skirmishers' cries to surrender, the officer wheeled and started to escape across open ground when a shot felled him. Upon recovering his body, the Confederates identified him as Brigadier General Philip Kearney, one of the ablest and most promising commanders in the Union army.[75]

With the loss of Kearney, Federal resistance wavered, and under cover of darkness the retreat was resumed. While Pope's columns fell back to the shadows of Washington, Hill paid his respects to Phil Kearney, who like himself reveled in the tumult of battle and had acquired renown as a rash but hard fighter.[76] Viewing his antagonist's spare body recumbent on the porch of a cabin behind the lines, Hill said with obvious feeling, "Poor Kearney, he deserved a better death than that."[77]

---

[74] O.R., *12*, Part 2, 672, 677, 698, 703.
[75] S.H.S.P., *19*, 173-74; C. F. Walcott, "The Battle of Chantilly," in T. F. Dwight, ed., *The Virginia Campaign of 1862 Under General Pope*, 160.
[76] S.H.S.P., *19*, 174.
[77] *B. and L., II*, 538.

CHAPTER XII

"Not A Moment Too Soon"

(Maryland Campaign)

AS POPE retired to the capital, Lee decided to invade the North. Such a move, he felt, would lure the Federal army away from the shelter of Washington without drawing it back onto Virginia soil. Accordingly, on Wednesday, September 3—just three days after the engagement at Chantilly— Jackson's troops led the advance of 53,000 ragged but confident Confederates.[1]

As though on cue, Jackson and Hill lost no time in resuming their feud. At the close of the first day's march Jackson issued explicit orders to each of his divisional commanders to march at a fixed hour early the next morning. At the appointed time Jackson was understandably annoyed to find that the Light Division was neither in motion nor ready to move. Taking matters into his own hands, he ordered Hill's troops forward, but Hill's inexplicable laxity had delayed the advance two hours and added two more specifications of neglect of duty to Jackson's list.[2]

On joining his column as it advanced toward Leesburg, Hill rode at the head of his leading brigade. Jackson noticed that his lieutenant neither observed the hourly rest period of ten minutes nor rode back and forth along the column to keep it closed. By noon Jackson's thin patience was exhausted. Riding up to Colonel Thomas commanding the leading brigade, he ordered him to halt and observe the customary half hour mid-day respite. As the Georgians subsequently fell in to resume the march, Powell Hill galloped up to Thomas and demanded to know who had ordered the troops to halt. Thomas answered, "By General Jackson."

His wrath fully aroused by Jackson's repeated issuance of orders directly to brigadiers of the Light Division, Hill accosted

---

[1] O.R., *19*, Part 2, 639.
[2] Douglas, 146; Appendix, specifications 5 and 6 of Jackson's charge.

Jackson who was sitting nearby on his horse. In his excited, high-pitched voice, Hill said tersely: "General Jackson, you have assumed command of my division, here is my sword; I have no use for it." Jackson replied calmly: "Keep your sword General Hill, but consider yourself under arrest for neglect of duty."[3] Thereupon Jackson turned to Kyd Douglas, his young aide, and ordered him to notify Lawrence O'B. Branch, Hill's senior brigadier, to assume command of the division.[4]

Stripped of his command, Hill marched on foot with the rear guard as the army headed for White's Ford to breast the Potomac. Attired in a frayed flannel shirt and a battered white hat slouched down over his blazing eyes, he strode along looking "as mad as a bull."[5] Arriving at the river, the rear ranks stretched out along the road to rest while waiting their turn to cross "this rapid Jordan" into "a Canaan."[6] Espying General Lee approaching on his gray mount, Hill asked the men to "move out of the road," but the commanding General told them to lie still while he considerately rode around them.[7]

As the Army of Northern Virginia crossed into Maryland, Lincoln relieved Pope, and over the strenuous objections from his cabinet reappointed McClellan to command the reunited Army of the Potomac. Cognizant of Lee's northward maneuver but ignorant of his objective, McClellan advanced with characteristic caution.

Meantime, Lee encamped his army for several days in the vicinity of Frederick to afford sympathizers from the border state an opportunity to enlist. However, the response was disappointingly apathetic, and one of Hill's men surmised that the number of new recruits could be expressed in two figures.[8] This undemonstrative reception coupled with dwindling supplies prompted Lee to start his army toward Hagerstown where he could establish lines of communication with the Shenandoah Valley.

---

[3] S.H.S.P., *20,* 384.
[4] Douglas, 146; S.H.S.P., *10,* 243.
[5] *N. C. Regts., IV,* 164-65.
[6] Caldwell, 40.
[7] *C.V., 30,* 45.
[8] Caldwell, 41.

First, however, it was necessary to reduce the Federal garrisons at Harpers Ferry and Martinsburg athwart the route over which Lee's supply trains would travel. While Lee accompanied the main column toward Hagerstown, Jackson was to recross the Potomac and capture both of these strongholds. Concurrently, Lee dispatched Generals McLaws and Walker to seize Maryland Heights and Loudon Heights, eminences which commanded Harpers Ferry from Maryland and Virginia respectively. Swept by artillery from these heights and enveloped from the rear by Jackson, the Federal garrison on this promontory between the confluence of the Potomac and Shenandoah rivers would have no sensible alternative but to surrender.[9]

At daylight on Wednesday, September 10, Jackson broke camp and started his divisions on a forced march. In ill-humor Hill resumed his position at the rear. He had slept the previous night in an ambulance, and arising before dawn he ordered the vehicle forward. The driver found the road blocked by a wagon driven by a stubborn Irishman who refused to budge. Furious at the delay, Hill bounced out of the ambulance and rapped the son of Erin across the shoulders with the flat of his sword. Surprised to see his arrested commander, he bellowed, "Big yer pardon, Gineral; big yer pardon, Gineral! Didn't know you were in the ambulance."[10]

Pushing westward over the green fields of Maryland, Jackson's column reached the Potomac at Williamsport where the soldiers crossed to the accompaniment of bands playing "Carry Me Back To Ole Virginny."[11] Thence Jackson hurried his men along two roads toward Martinsburg. Pushing aside enemy pickets, the advancing troops entered the town from the west. Famished soldiers who had subsisted for three days on green corn[12] now feasted on the bountiful commissary stores abandoned by General White in his haste to fall back with 2,500 men to Harpers Ferry.[13]

With an engagement obviously imminent, Powell Hill decided that he could swallow his pride easier than sit out a battle. His

---

[9] O.R., *19*, Part 2, 603-04.
[10] S.H.S.P., *19*, 180.
[11] Douglas, 155.
[12] Dunaway, 49.
[13] O.R., *19*, Part 1, 980; *B. and L.*, *II*, 612.

problem was how to approach Jackson. Since his arrest he had communicated with his chief only to the extent of requesting a copy of the charges preferred against him. Jackson had replied curtly that a copy would be furnished should the case be brought to trial; meanwhile Hill was to remain with his division.[14] Desirous of avoiding a similar rebuff in seeking reinstatement, Hill sent for Kyd Douglas and asked him to intercede on his behalf. Earnestly, he requested Douglas to inform Jackson that he did not wish anyone else to command his division in the coming battle, and that upon conclusion of the campaign he would report himself under arrest.[15]

As Kyd Douglas considered Hill a divisional commander who "had few equals," he eagerly relayed Hill's message to Jackson, appending his own opinion that "no one could command Hill's division as well as he could."[16] Although Jackson recently had refused to reinstate another subordinate who had been released from arrest, his esteem of Hill caused him to relent, and he instructed Douglas to direct Hill to assume command of the Light Division.[17]

Upon receipt of the welcome news, Hill donned his coat and sword, "and looking like a young eagle in search of his prey, he took command of his division to the delight of all his men."[18] Without delay he ordered his brigades to advance on Harpers Ferry. By Friday morning, September 13, Gregg's brigade at the head of the column came in sight of white rows of Federal tents on Bolivar Heights, an open plateau surmounting the rear of Harpers Ferry.[19] Hill posted pickets to guard the roads from the town, and then bivouacked his command at Halltown, a village about two miles from the enemy position.[20] Meanwhile, Walker and McLaws occupied the heights north and east of Harpers Ferry.

---

14 Jackson's MS Letter Book, 42.
15 Douglas, 158.
16 *Ibid.*, 147, 158.
17 *Ibid.*, 158; *B. and L., II,* 625.
18 *N. C. Regts.,* IV, 165.
19 Caldwell, 42.
20 Snow, 400.

On Sunday, Jackson's command was stretched across the promontory along a line extending from the Potomac to the Shenandoah. Having bottled up the bluecoats, plainly visible in their works,[21] Jackson ordered Hill to "move along the left bank of the Shenandoah, and thus turn the enemy's left flank and enter Harpers Ferry."[22] Hill shelled the woods on his front, and then moved his column along the river. Before he had proceeded far he espied a knoll crowning the extreme left of the enemy's line. Bare of earthworks and artillery, it was occupied by infantry protected by an abatis of felled timbers.[23]

Hill ordered Pender to take his brigade together with Archer's and Thomas' and seize this position. Proceeding along a by-road, the three brigades executed this order with but slight resistance. After dark Hill directed Colonel Walker to place seven batteries on this newly won eminence.[24] Meanwhile, Branch and Gregg continued along the river, and taking advantage of ravines and precipitous cliffs, gained the plains to the left and rear of Bolivar Heights.[25]

As the shades of night rose on Monday, they unveiled clouds of mist enshrouding Bolivar Heights. Having selected their targets the previous evening, Hill's artillerists pierced the fog with a rapid enfilading fire which was soon swelled by ten of Ewell's guns together with batteries on Loudon Heights and Maryland Heights.[26] Cessation of the artillery engagement constituted the signal for Pender to advance, but he had scarely moved forward when the Federal guns again opened. Hill noted that their fire was desultory, and he sent Pegram's and Crenshaw's batteries forward to deliver a devastating fire at close range.[27] Within five minutes after Hill's guns opened, the attacking force discerned through the rising mist a "white flag flying, and a large one it was."[28]

Hill dispatched Lieutenant Ham Chamberlayne, his adjutant

21 *N. C. Regts., 2,* 553.
22 O.R., *19,* Part 1, 659, 954, 980.
23 *Ibid.,* 980.
24 *Ibid.,* 147-48, 980, 1000, 1004.
25 *Ibid.,* 980; Caldwell, 42-43.
23 O.R., *19,* Part 1, 147-48.
27 *Ibid.,* 980, 984.
28 Dunaway, 50.

of artillery, to ascertain whether the enemy intended to surrender. When this proved to be the case, Hill received General Julius White and his staff who had just been conferring with Kyd Douglas. The Federal commander was inquiring for Jackson, to whom he wished to surrender the garrison.[29] At Hill's request Douglas conducted the party to the Confederate lines. As the cortege threaded its way through curious troops, Hill and White afforded a sharp contrast. The commander of the Light Division was dressed in his usual plain garb, while White, riding at his side, was handsomely uniformed down to polished boots and immaculate gloves. As his gleaming saber jangled at his side, White apologized to Hill for his finery, explaining that he had donned his best uniform expecting to meet top Confederate officials. Ruefully he added that his presence at Harpers Ferry was an accident—"an unfortunate accident too."[30]

The small cavalcade drew rein near a small church where Jackson was sitting reflectively on his horse. With minimum ceremony Jackson received White's unconditional surrender and turned the details of capitulation over to Hill. He then dashed off a note to Lee informing him of the surrender, adding that "as Hill's troops have borne the heaviest part of the engagement, he will be left in command until the prisoners and public property shall be disposed of, unless you direct otherwise."[31] Late in the afternoon "Old Jack" started the rest of his command toward the town of Sharpsburg, Maryland.

Hill was occupied until after midnight supervising the parole of prisoners and the collection and removal of captured supplies which included an immense stock of hard bread.[32] The fruits of victory were considerable—"11,000 prisoners, about 12,000 stand of arms, 70 pieces of artillery, harness and horses, a large number of wagons, commissary, quartermaster's and ordnance stores"— all won at a cost of only 69 casualties in the Light Division.[33]

While busily engaged in supervising these matters, a man

---

[29] Chamberlayne, 109; Douglas, 162; O.R., *19*, Part 1, 980.
[30] *B. and L., II*, 611.
[31] O.R., *19*, Part 1, 951.
[32] S.H.S.P., *19*, 180.
[33] O.R., *19*, Part 1, 981.

wearing a dusty Federal cavalry uniform stalked into Hill's provisional office and asked for a pass to Loudon, just across the Shenandoah River. Hill's suspicions were aroused when the caller claimed he was a non-combatant resident of that county who had been caught in Jackson's net. Angrily, Hill demanded: "What are you doing with those clothes on?"

"I bought them," replied the bluecoat.

Furious at this transparent alibi Hill cried, "You are lying. Get out of here you damned scoundrel." Then impatiently he grabbed the "non-combatant" by the shoulders and bodily ejected him from the room.[34]

Hill's men spent Monday and Tuesday guarding prisoners, faring sumptuously, appropriating apparel, and corraling roaming horses on which to carry their new possessions. The historian of Gregg's brigade recounted that, "The ragged, forlorn appearance of our men excited the combined merriment and admiration of our prisoners. It really looked like Pharaoh's lean kine devouring the fat."[35]

But the vagaries by which Mars suddenly changes the fortunes of war were classically illustrated only two days after the fall of Harpers Ferry. McClellan, who had been following Lee cautiously, arrived at Frederick on September 13. There Private Mitchell of the 27th Indiana stumbled upon a packet of three cigars wrapped in a copy of Lee's Special Orders No. 191 which he promptly relayed to McClellan. These orders, issued on September 9, indicated the routes and objectives of Lee's divided forces.[36] Galvanized by this windfall, McClellan immediately pressed westward planning to overwhelm Lee and Jackson in detail.

Bewildered by McClellan's unprecedented initiative, Lee plugged D. H. Hill's division into the gaps at South Mountain toward which McClellan's advance guard was streaming. Then upon learning that Harpers Ferry had capitulated, Lee ordered his scattered divisions to concentrate at Sharpsburg. This town of 1,300 nestled in a pocket which was bordered on the west by

---

[34] S.H.S.P., *19*, 180.
[35] Caldwell, 43.
[36] O.R., *19*, Part 2, 603-04.

the meandering Potomac and on the east by drowsy, tree-lined Antietam Creek. Here Lee disposed his troops, which by late Tuesday evening numbered less than 25,000, along a north-south line opposite Antietam Creek beyond which 87,000 fresh, confident bluecoats were massing.[37]

Against such odds Lee needed every available reserve. Before retiring on Tuesday he dispatched a note to Powell Hill urging him to join the main army as soon as possible. Hill received the note at 6:30 Wednesday morning, and, leaving Thomas' brigade to complete the removal of captured supplies, he had his other five brigades moving in an hour.[38]

At a rapid gait the Light Division began its seventeen-mile dusty trek along the west bank of the Potomac. Overhead early morning clouds dissolved in the hot rays of a late summer sun.[39] Spurred on by the mounting volume of cannonading ahead, Hill rested his panting troops only two or three times during the seven hour march.[40] Sporting a flaming red shirt he rode back and forth along the column, prodding stragglers with the point of his dress sword.[41] Notwithstanding the urgency, many fell by the way exhausted from the long hard march. Archer, himself ill, could muster only 350 in his four regiments when they reached the field at Sharpsburg.[42]

When Hill's column arrived at Boteler's Ford near Shepherdstown about 2 P.M., the jaded pacers gingerly waded the swift flowing Potomac which was lined here with jagged stones.[43] Meantime, Powell Hill, "always ready and impatient to begin a fight,"[44]

---

[37] *R. E. Lee, II,* 383.
[38] O.R., *19,* Part 1, 981. An interesting Federal commentary relating to Hill's march is contained in Major General Jacob Cox's description of the battle of Sharpsburg. Lamenting the inaction of Couch's division which had been left near Maryland Heights to observe Jackson's movements, Cox stated: "Why could it not have come up on our left as well as A. P. Hill's division which was the last to leave the Ferry, there being nothing to observe after it was gone? Couch's division coming with equal pace with Hill's on the other side of the river would have answered our needs as well as one from Porter's Corps. Hill came up but Couch did not." *B. and L., II,* 657-58.
[39] *Annals of the War,* 701.
[40] Caldwell, 44.
[41] Alexander, 266.
[42] O.R., *19,* Part 1, 1000.
[43] Caldwell, 44.
[44] *C.M.H., III,* 355.

galloped ahead with several of his staff to assess the situation on the smoke-veiled Confederate right. There he found Lee who had been scanning the rear for his arrival as anxiously as Napoleon awaited Grouchy at Waterloo. And a Waterloo it undoubtedly would have been save for Hill's timely arrival. In a series of assaults beginning at dawn and shifting progressively to the Confederate right, McClellan had decimated Lee's divisions without forcing a decision. Early in the afternoon Burnside's IX Corps crossed the stone bridge over the lower Antietam against only light opposition by Toombs' exhausted Georgia brigade. After gaining a foothold on the precipitous west bank, Burnside prepared to crush Lee's right, now thinly manned by 2,000 infantry, and then sweep up the slopes into Sharpsburg. If successful, this maneuver would put the Ninth Corps in Lee's rear from which it could cut the lines of retreat to the Potomac.

After reporting to Lee, Hill conferred with Brigadier General D. R. Jones, commanding the sole division in that sector, to acquaint himself with the terrain and to determine where his approaching brigades should take position.[45] At this juncture McIntosh's battery jounced onto the field, whereupon Hill sent it to strengthen Jones' right. "While his eagle eyes took in everything about him,"[46] Hill espied a second lieutenant crouching behind a tree. Wrathful at this display of cowardice, he seized the officer's sword and broke it over his back.[47]

At 3 o'clock the storm broke. In three lines Burnside's troops seemed to shake the freshly ploughed earth as they rushed Jones' attenuated line, captured McIntosh's guns, and surged to within half a mile of Lee's line of retreat.[48] But just as victory seemed within McClellan's grasp the Light Division arrived at 3:40, "which," as Colonel McGowan noted, "was not a moment too soon for the fortunes of the day."[49] Promptly, Hill disposed his brigades under the admiring eye of Kyd Douglas who noted that

---

[45] O.R., *19*, Part 1, 981.
[46] *C.V.*, *21*, 433.
[47] S.H.S.P., *19*, 181.
[48] *B. and L.*, *II*, 629.
[49] O.R., *19*, Part 1, 988.

"at the critical moment A. P. Hill was always at his strongest."[50]

Hill detached Brockenbrough and Pender to guard against an attack from the lower Antietam, and then quickly advanced the battle flags of Archer, Branch, and Gregg toward the blue line which had pierced Jones' defenses. Archer's cheering brigade formed on the right of Toombs and with a yell of defiance[51] charged the bluecoats who were about to resume their advance after a brief respite. Immediately the air was rent by hissing bullets and hurtling grape, and "the whole landscape for an instant turned slightly red."[52]

Archer's Tennessee Volunteers advanced in the face of scattered musketry fire through a tall cornfield to the edge of a freshly ploughed cornfield. Halting, Archer turned to discover that only one of his regiments had followed him, the others having mistaken a call from one of the men to "fall back" as an order from their brigadier. Re-forming his lines, Archer led his men on the double quick thereby diverting the enemy's attention from his pitifully small numbers. Steadily the brave little band surged across the fields, retrieved McIntosh's guns, and seized a strong enemy position behind a stone fence.[53]

Meantime, Branch and Gregg to the right and rear of Archer checked the advancing left of the Ninth Corps, and then joined in the general counter-attack. Moving forward into a dense forty acre cornfield, Gregg's brigade opened at close range with telling effect.[54] Some of the advance infantry fired so rapidly that the charges clogged and had to be hammered down with stones.[55] In the thick of the fray as usual, Maxcy Gregg was jolted by a freak

---

[50] *B. and L., II*, 629.
[51] *N. C. Regts.*, 2, 553.
[52] *B. and L., II*, 662. The reader may wonder how weary footsore troops could fight effectively after such a gruelling march. One of Hill's veterans in the 40th Virginia (W. F. Dunaway) described the soldier's feelings on such occasions as follows: "It may be supposed by the uninitiated that after such fatigue the soldier is not in good condition for fighting, but the sense of weariness is lost when the excitement of battle begins." Dunaway, 38.
[53] O.R., *19*, Part 1, 1001. As previously noted, Archer's brigade numbered less than 400 as it came onto the field, and nearly one-third of these were lost in taking the stone fence. O.R., *19*, Part 1, 1001.
[54] Caldwell, 46.
[55] O.R., *19*, Part 1, 992.

shot which nearly unhorsed him as it careened against his hip without breaking the flesh.

Less fortunate was Lawrence O'Brien Branch. After sweeping the enemy on his front he was joined by Gregg and Archer who directed his attention to a V-shaped Federal column advancing against his left. As Branch stepped forward and raised his glasses to obtain a better view, a sharpshooter's bullet struck him in the right cheek and emerged behind his left ear. The gallant North Carolinian fell dying into the arms of a staff officer. Respected and beloved by his men, "his death was regarded as a public calamity."[56] He was succeeded by Colonel James H. Lane.[57]

Hill's 2,000 effectives, joined by Jones' and Toombs' heartened troops and supported by a heavy enfilading fire from Walker's batteries, quickly drove Burnside's demoralized legions to the cover of high ground bordering the Antietam.[58] The tide of battle had been dramatically reversed, and as the action on Hill's front drew to a close at sunset, tension drained from many an anxious gray-clad body. Brigadier General John J. Walker, who commanded a division on the left during the afternoon, thus described the relief of many who had followed by ear their deliverance on the right:

> "For thirty minutes the sound of firing came steadily from the same direction; then it seemed to recede eastward, and finally to die away almost entirely. We knew then that Hill *was* up; that the Federals had been driven back, and that the Confederate army had narrowly escaped defeat."[59]

*   *   *   *

As McClellan gave no indication of renewing the carnage, Lee made preparations to recross the Potomac. Thursday the army turned southward, and during the evening Powell Hill quietly withdrew his Light Division to cover the army's retreat. Before noon

---

[56] *N. C. Regts.*, 2, 553-54.

[57] In his report Hill paid tribute to Branch as follows: "The Confederacy has to mourn the loss of a gallant soldier and accomplished gentleman who fell in this battle at the head of his brigade. He was my senior brigadier, and one to whom I could have intrusted the command of the division with all confidence." O.R., *19*, Part 1, 981. Lane said of his predecessor: "He was a very gallant General, stood high in the estimation of his officers, and I often heard would have been promoted but for his untimely death." S.H.S.P., *10*, 241-42.

[58] O.R., *19*, Part 1, 981, 984.

[59] *B. and L.*, *II*, 681.

the next day his brigades were back on Virginia soil and on their way toward Shepherdstown.[60]

However, shortly after dawn on Saturday morning Hill received urgent orders from Jackson to hurry his division back to the Potomac and repel several enemy brigades which had crossed, driven in General Pendleton's two depleted brigades, and captured four guns. Proud that his redoubtable division had been selected to prevent an enemy concentration against the rear of Lee's scattered and discouraged forces, Powell Hill hustled his sweltering troops along the Shepherdstown road.[61] Half a mile from Boteler's Ford, he halted his men in a cornfield opposite the enemy who were drawn up along the steep banks bordering the Virginia shore. On the Maryland hills across the river Fitz-John Porter, Hill's old antagonist of Mechanicsville vintage, had massed seventy heavy guns and lined the Chesapeake and Ohio Canal with sharpshooters to support his divisions of the V Corps.[62]

After appraising the enemy's dispositions Hill formed his division in double line of battle with Pender, Gregg, and Thomas in front, supported by Archer, Lane, and Brockenbrough. To insure close coordination Hill assigned Archer command of the first line and Gregg the second.[63] As the long butternut lines charged across the open plains they encountered what their admiring divisional commander described as "the most tremendous fire of artillery I ever saw, and too much praise cannot be awarded my regiments for their steady, unwavering step. It was as if each man felt that the fate of the army was centered in himself."[64]

Without stopping to close ranks, Gregg and Thomas hurled back the enemy in front of Hill's right and center. However, on the left the enemy massed against Pender's brigade and extended their line in an attempt to outflank the North Carolinians. Pender countered by wheeling one regiment to meet this threat and at the same time notified Archer of his danger. Archer quickly moved by the left flank to prolong Pender's front, and together the two

---

[60] O.R., *19*, Part 1, 981.
[61] *N. C. Regts.*, *2*, 555.
[62] O.R., *19*, Part 1, 982, 986.
[63] *Ibid.*, 982.
[64] *Ibid.*, 981.

brigades then advanced on the double. When they gained the crest, Hill's confident veterans raised a yell and poured a heavy fire into the backs of the bluecoats who fled headlong down the slopes into the river.[65] "Then," according to Powell Hill, "commenced the most terrible slaughter that this war has yet witnessed. The broad surface of the Potomac was blue with the floating bodies of our foe."[66]

The macabre spectacle magnified Porter's plight, as the Federal casualties were only slightly higher than those in the Light Division which totaled 261. But Powell Hill was happy in the thought that, "this was a wholesome lesson to the enemy, and taught them to know it may be dangerous sometimes to press a retreating army."[67]

---

[65] *Ibid.*, 982, 986, 1001-02.
[66] *Ibid.*, 982.
[67] *Ibid.*

CHAPTER XIII

"Closing The Gap At Fredericksburg"

FOLLOWING the strenuous Maryland campaign, Lee rested his ragged army in the vicinity of Winchester. Hill established his temporary divisional headquarters nearby at Camp Branch, named in honor of the recently fallen commander of the Fourth Brigade.[1] With characteristic appreciation of his command's performance, Hill lost no time in issuing the following congratulatory address on September 24:

Soldiers of the Light Division:
You have done well and I am pleased with you. You have fought in every battle from Mechanicsville to Shepherdstown, and no man can yet say that the Light Division was ever broken. You held the left at Manassas against overwhelming numbers and saved the army. You saved the day at Sharpsburg and at Shepherdstown. You were selected to face a storm of round shot, shell, and grape such as I have never before seen. I am proud to say that your services are appreciated by our general, and that you have a reputation in the army which it should be the object of every officer and private to sustain.[2]

For his own brilliant performance in every act of the Maryland drama, Powell Hill received significantly different commendations from Lee and Jackson. Lee, in a letter to Davis written on October 2, recommended that Jackson and Longstreet be appointed to command the two recently authorized army corps, and then added, "Next to these two officers, I consider A. P. Hill the best commander with me. He fights his troops well and takes good care of them."[3] This tribute from the commanding General was distinction indeed in an army which at the time included Early, Harvey Hill, Hood, and Stuart.

Jackson, about to be promoted to Lieutenant General in command of the Second Corps, tacitly recognized Hill's recent exploits by refraining from rearresting him. In fact, the usually unrelenting

---

[1] Welch, 34; O.R., *51*, Part 2, 626; *N. C. Regts., IV*, 167.
[2] O.R., *51*, Part 2, 626.
[3] O.R., *19*, Part 2, 643.

Presbyterian went so far in a letter to Army Headquarters as to indicate his willingness to halt the vendetta with Hill. On October 3 he wrote: "As the object in arresting General Hill, which was to secure his stricter compliance with orders has been effected, I do not consider further action on my part necessary . . ."[4]

However, Hill would not be mollified. Jackson had arrested him and refused to furnish a list of the charges. During the march into Maryland he had suffered the extreme humiliation of walking behind his division. An issue which cut so deeply into Hill's pride and violated his sense of justice was not to be dismissed or compromised. It had to be resolved in Jackson's favor or his.

Hence, two days after driving Porter's advance guard into the Potomac at Shepherdstown, Hill—in a bold, tumbling scrawl which contrasted harshly with his normal, carefully-delineated script—unburdened himself to Colonel R. H. Chilton, Lee's Assistant Adjutant General.

Col.—
I have the honor to represent that on the 4th of this month I was arrested by Maj. Gen. T. J. Jackson, whilst at the head of my Division, for neglect of duty. In reply to a respectful request to know in what I had been guilty of neglect of duty, it was replied that should the interest of the service require that my case should be brought before a court, a copy of the charges would be sent me—on the eighth day I was released and ordered to the command of my Division. I respectfully represent that I deem myself to have been treated with injustice and [here followed significantly the words 'feel it deeply' which were crossed out] censured and punished at the head of my command, and request that a court of Inquiry be granted me.
Very Respectfully
A. P. Hill, Major General[5]

In forwarding Hill's letter Jackson appended a summary of the charges against his aggrieved lieutenant. Lee tactfully endeavored to straddle this delicate situation with the following endorsement of Hill's communication:

Respectfully returned to Gen. A. P. Hill who will see from the remarks of General Jackson the cause of his arrest. His attention being now called to what appeared to be neglect of duty by his commander, but which from an officer of his character could not be intentional and I feel assured will

---

[4] *Ibid.,* 731.
[5] Letter Book, Light Division, Sept. 22, 1862.

never be repeated, I see no advantage to the service in further investigating this matter nor could it without detriment be done at this time.[6]

But Hill would have none of Lee's "let bygones be bygones." On September 30 he wrote uncompromisingly to Colonel R. H. Chilton, Lee's Chief-of-Staff:

> I have the honor to acknowledge the receipt of my letter requesting a court of inquiry, with the remarks of Maj. Gen. T. J. Jackson, and the indorsement of the general commanding, crediting the truth of the charges and refusing the court.
>
> I respectfully say to the general that I deny the truth of every allegation made by Major General Jackson, and am prepared to prove my denial by any number of honorable men including members of General Jackson's own staff. If General Jackson had accorded me the courtesy of asking an explanation of each instance of neglect of duty as it occurred, I think that even he would have been satisfied, and avoided the necessity of keeping a black-list against me. It is hardly necessary to remark that the charges made by General Jackson are of a serious character, involving my reputation and standing as an officer commanding a division of this army, and if true, I should be deprived of the command; if untrue, then censure should be passed upon the officer who abuses his authority to punish, and then sustains his punishment by making loose charges against an officer who has done and is doing his utmost to make his troops efficient.
>
> I again respectfully reiterate my request for a court of inquiry, to involve the matter of these additional allegations, and ask that a speedy answer be given me.

Then as a smoldering after-thought, he added this postscript:

> To show the spirit dictating the indorsement of General Jackson, I instance: "Instead of General H. being with his troops, I found him at his headquarters apparently just up." My headquarters had been at the place General J. saw me that morning, which was on the road, and not 100 yards from my leading brigade, but unfortunately for the truth of his conclusions, they were moved the day before. I had breakfasted that morning at 2 o'clock, and when General J. saw me, had ridden with my escort from my headquarters to where he saw me, some three-fourths of a mile.

In endorsing this outspoken petition, Jackson stated:

> . . . I spoke to him about the first neglect, and he did not give a satisfactory explanation. He had ample opportunity of knowing his neglect of duty. When an officer disobeys or disregards a known order, it is his duty to report it at once, with his explanation, without waiting to be called upon in each individual instance.
>
> No black-list has been kept against General Hill. The specifications only

---

[6] Jackson MSS.

extend over a period of about four weeks, and are of such a character as would not readily escape the memory . . ."[7]

Although Jackson was loath to press the issue, Hill, had maneuvered him into presenting formal charges. This "Old Jack" did in a carefully worded list containing eight specific instances of alleged neglect of duty, which he forwarded to Lee "in order that the commanding general can order a general courts-martial . . . should the interest of the service so require."[8]

Confronted with this impasse between two of his ablest lieutenants, Lee attempted to insulate the searing charges and counterclaims in his file of unsettled matters for future consideration. He could not afford to lose the services of either commander, and if Hill were separated from Jackson to whom could he be assigned?

Douglas recounted "a feeling of military oppression" the day Lee visited Jackson's headquarters at Bunker Hill to essay a reconciliation between the two antagonists. The three generals were closeted in Jackson's tent for some time, after which Lee mounted Traveller and rode away. Hill grimly spurred his horse in another direction and Jackson strode back to his quarters. No word of the proceedings was ever revealed by the participants, but whatever the nature of Lee's appeal, it failed to mend the rift.[9]

Hill, unable to force a showdown with his chief, devoted his energies to rehabilitating the Light Division which Pender loyally contended "stands first in point of efficiency of any Division of this whole army."[10] Numerically however, it was only a shadow of its former might, having dwindled from 12,000 on July 20 to little more than a third of that number (4,777) two months later.[11] Fortunately, this diminution was relieved somewhat by returning stragglers and new conscripts.

As a former artillerist, Hill was particularly concerned over the depleted condition of his batteries. "My gallant Captain of the artillery,"[12] as he called young "Willie" Pegram, had so few sur-

---

[7] O.R., *19*, Part 2, 729-30.
[8] *Ibid.*, 731.
[9] Douglas, 195.
[10] Pender MSS, Letter to Mrs. Pender, Sept. 22, 1862.
[11] O.R., *11*, Part 3, 645. O.R., *14*, Part 2, 621.
[12] O.R., *19*, Part 1, 981.

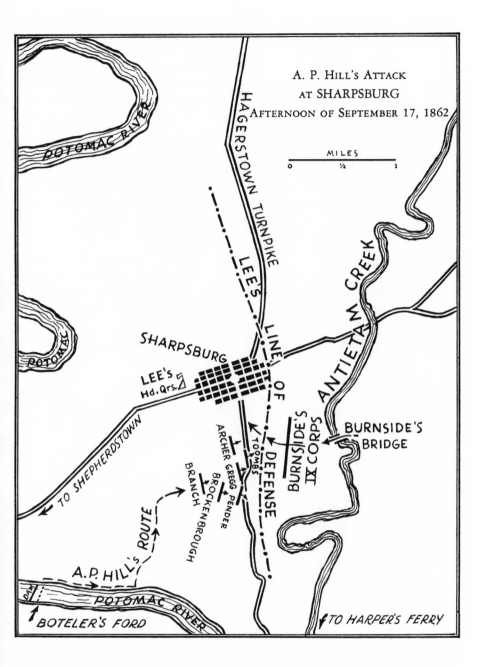

A. P. HILL'S ATTACK
AT SHARPSBURG
AFTERNOON OF SEPTEMBER 17, 1862

MILES

0   ½   1

POTOMAC RIVER

HAGERSTOWN TURNPIKE

LEE'S LINE

POTOMAC

SHARPSBURG

ANTIETAM CREEK

LEE'S
Hd. Qrs.

OF DEFENSE

ARCHER

TOOMBS

GREGG

PENDER

BROCKENBROUGH

BRANCH

BURNSIDE'S
IX CORPS

BURNSIDE'S
BRIDGE

TO SHEPHERDSTOWN

A. P. HILL'S ROUTE

DAM

POTOMAC RIVER

BOTELER'S FORD

TO HARPER'S FERRY

Burnside's Bridge Across Antietam Creek

vivors and guns that the unit was disbanded and distributed among the division's other batteries. Only by a direct appeal to Lee was Hill able to reconstitute this Virginia battery which had won laurels as one of the most celebrated in the army.[13] Hill also interceded to prevent the disbandment of Fleet's battery, but without success.[14]

Hill's most pressing problem was the restoration of his troops' health, now deteriorated as a result of exposure, irregular rations, and deplorable sanitation. One veteran thus described the pitiful plight of the Light Division's soldiers at this time: "They now stood, an emaciated, limping, ragged, filthy mass, whom no stranger to their valiant exploits could have believed capable of anything the least worthy."[15] Lice, always the scourge of fighting men, soon assumed epidemic proportions in the camps. Whereas even hard-bitten veterans hitherto had considered this affliction too disgusting a topic for polite conversation, they now spoke of "fighting under the black flag" and of "flanking them out of position." Hill insisted upon thorough ablutions for the men, who were marched by squads and companies into the Opequan river. More stubborn cases were hospitalized.[16]

Boredom of convalescence was relieved the middle of October by reports that a large enemy force had crossed the Potomac at Shepherdstown and was moving toward the Confederate camps. The Light Division was sent to support Stuart in contesting the Federal advance. However, it soon developed that McClellan was simply feeling out Lee's position and "Little Mac" retired without a fight when Hill and Stuart appeared. Later in the month Hill's men enjoyed the sporting diversion of tearing up twenty miles of Baltimore and Ohio track west of Harpers Ferry. With boyish enthusiasm they ripped up the cross-ties and heaped them on a pile to which they set fire. On this conflagration they then piled the rails which softened and bent under their own weight.[17]

McClellan now began moving his army south of the Potomac

---

13 *Ibid.,* 623, 649.
14 O.R., *19,* Part 2, 651.
15 Caldwell, 53.
16 *Ibid.*
17 *Ibid.,* 55; O. R., *19* Part 2, 623.

with the intention of staying. To cover "Little Mac's" possible thrusts, Lee posted Jackson at the gateway to the Shenandoah Valley and withdrew Longstreet across the Blue Ridge to Culpeper where his divisions could block any move toward Gordonsville and the Virginia Central Railroad. During these operations Powell Hill moved his brigades to Castleman's Ferry near Snicker's Gap. On the march his lack of insignia resulted in another of his frequent brushes with teamsters. While watering his horse, Hill watched with growing anger as a crusty driver belabored his mules in an attempt to hustle them across the stream. Exasperated, Hill employed his "lace-curtain" language in demanding the mule driver stop beating the animals, only to be told to mind his own business. In his accustomed manner, Hill then obtained compliance by applying his rapier across the back of his unwittingly disrespectful subordinate.[18]

Early in November an enemy force moving toward the Valley attempted to cross the Shenandoah river but was repulsed by Archer's and Thomas' brigades supported by Latham's and Pegram's batteries.[19] Following this brief skirmish the division enjoyed a long uninterrupted rest during which the men thrived on rations which one of Hill's commissaries bragged he had "never seen equalled in variety."[20]

While the health of the Light Division rebounded to a new peak,[21] McClellan moved to Warrenton where he was relieved of his command and superseded by Major General Ambrose E. Burnside. This bewhiskered classmate of Powell Hill's was to leave a greater impress upon the nation's tonsorial habits than upon its military annals. A modest man, he had twice refused the offer to command the Army of the Potomac, declaring himself incompetent for such responsibility. Only his friends' compelling argument that Washington had asserted a similar disbelief in his abilities finally persuaded Burnside to replace his close friend. As one historian subsequently noted, "It was left, however, for

---

[18] S.H.S.P., *19,* 181.
[19] O.R., *19,* Part 1, 982.
[20] S.H.S.P., *19,* 181.
[21] Welch, 34; Chamberlayne, 129.

Burnside to do what Washington never did—to prove his assertion to be true."[22]

Sensitive to his government's desire for swift aggressive action, Burnside quick-stepped his army of 125,000 down the north bank of the Rappahannock to Fredericksburg intent on driving to Richmond before Lee could consolidate his divided forces. But Lee as usual anticipated his adversary's strategy, and immediately ordered his two corps to unite at Fredericksburg. On a rainy November 22, the Light Division struck its tents and proceeded through Winchester to Mt. Jackson. Turning east the column crossed the Blue Ridge at Thornton's Gap. The long line was visible for miles "as it wound up and down and around, with glittering arms and accoutrements, like some long serpent, and with silver scales, dragging its tortuous folds along. At night it was even more pleasant to see a thousand bivouac fires flashing and glowing on the mountain side, while weary soldiers rested and chatted after the labors of the day."[23]

After marching 175 miles in twelve days[24] the Light Division reached Yerbey's, an estate about five miles south of Fredericksburg. Here the men, confined to their campfires by raw, snowy weather, discussed a rumor that their chief was to be promoted and given an independent command. Hill apparently credited the story, for he expressed to Pender the hope that the North Carolinian would soon be promoted to Major General, presumably to succeed him as divisional commander.[25] Hill's veterans welcomed this prospect as it would mean separation from Jackson who they felt had treated Hill unfairly. And at least one brigadier in the division felt that "Old Jack" discriminated against officers of the Light Division because of his feud with Hill.[26]

Speculation regarding the future of Powell Hill and his Light Division was interrupted on Thursday, December 11, by reports

---

[22] H. W. Elson, *History of the United States, IV*, 207.
[23] Caldwell, 55.
[24] *Ibid.*
[25] Pender MSS, Dec. 3, 1862.
[26] *Ibid.*, April 11, 1863. During this period of his feud with Jackson, Hill ironically was counseling Ham Chamberlayne, his youthful artillerist, to avoid being "a soldier and a controversialist at the same time." Chamberlayne, 143, letter of December 5, 1862.

of feverish enemy activity in front of Fredericksburg. As Burnside's three Grand Divisions began crossing pontoon bridges over the Rappahannock, Lee concentrated his 78,000 man command along a seven mile front on the hills behind Fredericksburg. The Light Division moved at dawn on Friday, and by noon Hill was putting his brigades into position covering Lee's right along a wooded ridge which arced parallel to the Rappahannock from Deep River Ravine on the left to Hamilton's Crossing on the right.[27]

Pender's brigade supported Braxton's and Davidson's batteries on low wooded ground next to Longstreet's troops. To Pender's right and some 150 yards in advance of the front line five North Carolina regiments rested on their arms as their new brigadier, James H. Lane, inspected his position. Between Lane's right and Archer's left lay a 600 yard gap through which jutted a tongue of flat, marshy woodland tangled with dense undergrowth. To the right of this coppice and overlooking the Richmond Stage Road, Hill posted Archer's brigade augmented by two of Brockenbrough's regiments. In the timbered covert skirting Prospect Hill, a cleared spur crowning the right, Hill concealed fourteen rifle and Napoleon guns under the personal supervision of Colonel R. Lindsay Walker. Ahead of the front line Hill stationed a line of skirmishers protected by the railroad embankment.[28]

Along a military road to the rear of the first line, Hill stationed his reserves. Brockenbrough's two remaining regiments took position behind Walker's batteries; Gregg's brigade, 500 yards behind the front, overlapped the interval between Archer and Lane; and Thomas' four regiments in turn covered the gap between Lane and Pender with orders to render assistance to any part of the line requiring it.[29] With an unprecedented concentration of eleven muskets per yard, Jackson reinforced Hill's front with the divisions of Early, D. H. Hill, and Taliaferro.

By Friday evening the Light Division had occupied its assigned fringe of woodland without revealing its strength to Federal balloonists. However, as at Second Manassas, Hill had left a sizeable

[27] O.R., *21*, 653.
[28] *Ibid.*, 645, 653, 654, 656, 662.
[29] *Ibid.*, 653.

gap in his front line. Lane was disturbed about this undefended sector on his right, and called it to Hill's attention. No measures were taken, probably because Hill felt reluctant to jeopardize the health of troops in a cold damp bog which he considered impassable. Should the enemy be so foolish as to storm this gulf, Hill would mow them down with Walker's batteries while Gregg moved into the gap to prevent Archer and Lane from being flanked.

Hill's view was shared by Stuart whose attention was called to the unprotected segment by his gargantuan Prussian aide, Major Heros von Borcke. The latter suggested that the timber on the undefended projection be felled, but Stuart did not consider this necessary as he believed the Federals would not be able to advance that far under the sweeping cross-fire of Hill's artillery.[30] Jackson also noted the interval between Lane and Archer, and although he even predicted that the enemy would attack this salient, he did not order Hill to cover it.[31]

Friday night the Light Division shivered under a blanket of fog which the Rappahannock unfurled over the battlefield.[32] As daylight filtered through the fog on Saturday morning, Powell Hill and Jackson together with their staffs assembled on Prospect Hill where they were seen "looking out through the white mists of the morning into the plain below, from which there arose an indistinct murmur like the distinct hum of myriads of bees, vaguely announcing to us its hostile occupation by thousands of human beings."[33] For some undisclosed reason, Jackson had chosen this occasion to array himself in a glittering new braided uniform given him by Stuart. However, Hill's relations with his chief were so strained that he abstained from any recorded participation in the usual amenities and bantering that attended this event.

About 10 o'clock the fog lifted revealing three seemingly interminable rows of enemy infantry drawn up in battle lines on the plain opposite Hill's front. These bluecoats, which proved to be Meade's Pennsylvanians, were accompanied by ten full batteries.

---

[30] H. von Borcke, *Memoirs of the Confederate War for Independence* (cited hereafter as von Borcke), *II*, 107.
[31] Dabney, 610.
[32] O.R., *21*, 588.
[33] von Borcke, *II*, 113.

As if on parade with their glistening bayonets and fluttering regimental banners, the Federal ranks moved forward to the attack. They had advanced but a short distance when two Confederate guns of Pelham's horse-artillery, which had taken a forward position beyond a marshy stream on the right, raked their lines in flank. Surprised and shaken, Meade's advance stalled for half an hour while four Federal batteries attempted to silence Pelham.[34]

With his ammunition almost exhausted Pelham withdrew, whereupon Meade's guns opened "promiscuously" on Hill's front for about an hour.[35] To one defender "the boom of guns, the whiz and explosion of shells, the snapping of trees, was awfully grand,"[36] but it was also costly in both men and horses.[37] Nevertheless Hill's infantry and artillerists held their fire as ordered to avoid disclosing their strength and positions.[38]

At noon the enemy again sounded the advance, and preceded by "clouds of skirmishers," Meade's columns "right gallantly essayed another attempt."[39] Forward they surged to within half a mile of Hill's front before Walker and Pelham opened with shell and canister "from our long silent but now madly aroused batteries."[40] In the face of this devastating fire which drove in Meade's skirmishers and tore wide gaps in his line, the enemy withdrew to the Richmond Stage Road where over twenty-five of his guns concentrated a withering fire on Walker's batteries.[41]

Within an hour Meade had rallied his troops which were reinforced by three fresh divisions. Again the solid blue lines moved forward against the Light Division, and again they were raked by Hill's guns. Though their advance was slowed the Federals crossed the open fields and drove—as Jackson had predicted—toward the gap between Lane and Archer. Lane notified Hill of the threat,[42] and Archer called on Gregg to move forward into the interval.[43]

---

[34] O.R., *21*, 645.
[35] *Ibid.*
[36] Caldwell, 58.
[37] O.R., *21*, 649.
[38] *Ibid.*, 645-46.
[39] *Ibid.*, 646, 649.
[40] *Ibid.*, 646.
[41] *Ibid.*, 649.
[42] *Ibid.*, 654.
[43] *Ibid.*, 657.

Lane's right regiments, the Thirty-Seventh and Twenty-Eighth North Carolina, received the initial onslaught. These troops quickly changed front along the railroad to meet the flanking force, and managed to hold their ground with a furious fire.[44] After the men had emptied their cartridge cases their officers handed them ammunition from the dead and wounded. Meanwhile, Lane sent an urgent appeal to Gregg for reinforcements.[45] When action on this sector waned, the bluecoats assailed Lane's front further to the left. Wedging between the Twenty-Eighth and Thirty-Third regiments, the Federals flanked the split North Carolina brigade which was forced to retire until reinforcements arrived.[46]

While Lane stubbornly contested the Federal thrust on the left of the gap, another Federal brigade pressed through the presumably impenetrable woods on Archer's left and attacked the Nineteenth Georgia and Fourteenth Tennessee regiments in rear and flank. Unprotected by pickets or scouts, these men on the right shoulder of the gap had been lying on the ground with their arms stacked. Surprised, they leaped to their feet and attempted to form a front but soon gave way leaving about 160 prisoners in enemy hands. When the Seventh Tennessee saw its neighbors streaming to the rear it also retired. Archer appealed to Gregg for help, but fearing it might arrive too late, he pulled the Fifth Alabama Battalion from his extreme right and hustled it to his left where the First Tennessee and parts of the Seventh Tennessee changed front and stemmed the advance on that flank. After exhausting their ammunition these regiments charged the enemy and hurled him back across the railroad.[47]

Meanwhile, Meade's determined veterans poured through the gap and forced their way through the interlacing timber. Across their path lay Gregg's brigade along the rough military road. Confident that the bluecoats could not penetrate Hill's first line, Gregg's chief concern was to prevent his men from firing on their comrades, "a thing too often done in our woods-fights".[48] Gregg had taken every precaution to avoid this danger even to the extent of ordering

[44] *Ibid.,* 654.
[45] *Ibid.,* 654-55.
[46] *Ibid.,* 655.
[47] *Ibid.,* 657.
[48] Caldwell, 59.

the men to stack their arms and lay down to take cover from enemy artillery.[49]

With their view obstructed by timber, Gregg's men mistook the advancing enemy for retiring Confederates. As bluecoats fell upon Gregg's right regiment, the South Carolinians dived for their rifles. Gregg, handicapped by deafness, rode up and compounded the confusion by ordering the men to quit the stacks and refrain from firing on their "comrades." It was his last order. In full uniform the "chivalrous gentlemen and gallant soldier," as Hill eulogized him, was shot through the spine and toppled from his horse.[50]

Colonel D. H. Hamilton of the First South Carolina then assumed command of Gregg's brigade, and rode along the lines admonishing the men to "remain quiet and steady".[51] Next he threw back the right wing of his own regiment and checked the onrush. On receiving an order from Hill, he joined the troops concentrating to plug the gap. These forces consisted of the Forty-Seventh and Twenty-Second Virginia regiments of Brockenbrough's brigade plus the division of "that gallant old warrior, General Early" whose assistance Hill had requested. Early's troops crashed through the woods on the double-quick to spearhead a fierce charge which Walker's. guns supported in driving the enemy out of the interval and back across the railroad.[52] The fact that some of the men were fighting within sight of their homes seemed to inspire them "to drive the enemy back at all hazards".[53]

General George Meade, his slouch hat ventilated with two bullet holes, also found it "much too hot for me" on Lane's front.[54] Thomas, in answer to Lane's call, advanced as rapidly as the undergrowth permitted. Encountering the enemy at the edge of the woods he threw forward his Georgians by the flank, and deploying by successive formations squarely met

---

[49] *Ibid.*, 58-9.
[50] *Ibid.*, 59.
[51] O.R., *21*, 651.
[52] *Ibid.*, 647, 649.
[53] *Ibid.*, 651.
[54] *B. and L., III*, 135.

and checked the Pennsylvanians. Then joined by two of Lane's regiments they drove the enemy to their original position.[55]

While the furious struggle was in progress on Hill's center, Gibbon's Federal division opened a devastating fire on Pender's men and guns for which the terrain offered scant protection. Pender was shot in the left arm but insisted on resuming command as soon as his wound was dressed.[56] After Davidson's and Latimer's batteries repulsed two enemy demonstrations on this sector, a third enemy column employed the shelter of Deep Run Ravine to gain the embankment on Pender's left from which it was finally driven by a desperate counterattack.[57]

By mid-afternoon Hill's bent line had sprung back to its original position, and the enemy seemed content merely to bring up reserves to strengthen his lines. On the left, however, Burnside persisted in dashing wave after wave of his dispirited troops against Longstreet's impregnable position on the heights behind shell-ravaged Fredericksburg. With the Federals repulsed on the right and slaughtered on the left, Jackson saw an opportunity to employ his entire corps in a countercharge that would drive the enemy into the Rappahannock. Excitedly he notified Powell Hill to advance his whole line and drive the enemy, but later countermanded this order in the face of an overpowering artillery demonstration.

Burnside, despite appalling casualties, wanted to renew the carnage on Sunday but was dissuaded from this folly by subordinates. Lee thus won a notable defensive victory with less than half the 12,647 losses of his opponent.[58] However, a breakdown of the casualty lists showed that the Light Division had sustained twice as many casualties as any Confederate division engaged.[59]

Although casualties were inevitably high in Hill's division which had absorbed fierce onslaughts against Lee's right, there was some feeling that losses would have been lower had Hill closed the gap between Lane and Archer. Lee refrained from passing judgement, but Jackson left no doubt that he considered Hill negligent.

---

[55] O.R., *21*, 646, 653, 655.
[56] *Ibid.*, 648.
[57] *Ibid.*, 647, 650, 662.
[58] *Ibid.*, 142.
[59] *Ibid.*, 648.

In his report he stated: ". . . before General A. P. Hill closed the interval which he had left between Archer and Lane, it was penetrated, and the enemy, pressing forward in overwhelming numbers through that interval, turned Lane's right and Archer's left."[60]

Unvoiced but also apparent was the lack of Hill's sure hand on his brigades during the critical breakthrough. Customarily in the right place at the right time, Hill had been conspicuously deficient in directing the defense and coordinating the rally. Prearrangements were so faulty that when Lane was assailed he sent an aide to request reinforcements from Gregg, and if that officer was unable to send them, "to apply to Thomas or anybody else whom he might see in command of troops for assistance."[61]

Hill was disinclined to belabor these matters. In his official report he dismissed the matter of the unprotected gap with a statement that he had posted Gregg's brigade across it. Then in a more affirmative vein he concluded by "calling the attention of the lieutenant-general to the admirable manner in which the troops of this division behaved under the most trying of all things to a soldier, viz, inaction under a heavy fire of artillery."[62]

---

[60] *Ibid.*, 632.
[61] *Ibid.*, 655.
[62] *Ibid.*, 647.

CHAPTER XIV

"The Best Soldier Of His Grade"

(Chancellorsville)

S HORTLY AFTER Burnside's defeat at Fredericksburg, President and Mrs. Lincoln visited the bountifully supplied but demoralized Federal army at Falmouth. In honor of the Commander-in-Chief, Burnside staged a grand review during which the President sat bareheaded, seemingly lost in meditation. Suddenly he turned to the braided commander beside him and asked, "General Couch, what do you suppose will become of all these men when the war is over?" The question impressed the despondent commander "as very pleasant indeed that somebody had an idea that the war would sometime end."[1]

By contrast, Lee's supremely confident veterans on the south bank of the Rappahannock were preoccupied with mundane problems of physical comfort. Hill's men, most of whom were accustomed to warmer climes, encamped on the snow-laden terrace above the river near Moss Neck about ten miles southeast of Fredericksburg.[2] Here the soldiers in butternut erected log huts which, though crudely fitted and damp, afforded better protection than the recently captured enemy tents.[3] At Yuletide some artillery officers in the Light Division provided a feast at which Hill and some of his brigadiers "were all as merry as if there were no war."[4]

During this long respite rations gradually diminished.[5] Beef became scarce, and tobacco and coffee were obtained by trading via toy boats with the enemy across the river.[6] Early in January the troops received eight months' pay, but with soap costing $1.25

---

[1] B. and L., *III*, 120.
[2] Caldwell, 65. This encampment was located on the site of what today is Camp A. P. Hill, an active army installation which operates as a maneuver and firing area for both active and reserve components of all services. Communication from Colonel P. L. Burke, Commanding, Camp A. P. Hill, Virginia.
[3] *Ibid.,* 69.
[4] Chamberlayne, 151, Dec. 27, 1862.
[5] Caldwell, 70.
[6] Dunaway, 60.

a cake and apples six for a dollar,[7] "the poor eleven dollars of
Confederate money quickly dwindled."[8] Notwithstanding the un-
usually severe weather and the scant fare, the Light Division
enjoyed generally good health. Many recuperated from ailments
contracted the previous summer, and some even put on weight.[9]

By common consent the picket lines were inactive, except
for the occasional taunting refrain of Yankees singing "O soldiers,
won't you meet us."[10] Only once was the peaceful routine of camp
life disturbed by a major alarum. Late in January, Burnside,
desirous of regaining the confidence of his army, roused his troops
and prepared to cross the Rappahannock a few miles above Fredericksburg with the intention of falling on Lee's flank.[11] However,
a violent storm turned the roads into a quagmire which buried
Burnside's plans in a sea of mud. Thereupon the bewhiskered
Federal commander was supplanted by "Fighting Joe" Hooker,
whom Lincoln admonished: "In your next battle *put all your men
in.*"[12]

After the excitement of the "Mud Campaign" subsided, Hill's
brigades turned to intra-mural snowball battles interspersed with
light picket duty and a minimum of drilling.[13] Despite generally
good morale, Hill found it necessary to employ "psychological pun-
ishments" to enforce discipline. Offenders were marched through
camp with boards on their backs stating, "I am a coward," "I am a
thief," or "I am a shirker from battle."[14] In the case of a deserter
from the Forty-Seventh Virginia, the entire regiment was lined up to
witness his execution.[15]

Early in 1863 Lee's army was divested of considerable man-
power and leaders to meet threats elsewhere. In January, D. H.
Hill was dispatched to rally his native North Carolinians against
a Federal demonstration which threatened to sever communications

---

[7] Douglas, 210.
[8] Caldwell, 71.
[9] *Ibid.*
[10] Dunaway, 60.
[11] B. and L., *III*, 118.
[12] *Ibid.*, 120.
[13] Caldwell, 71.
[14] Welch, 45.
[15] Dunaway, 60.

between Richmond and the South.[16] The following month Burnside, now reinstated as head of his old Ninth Corps, steamed down the Potomac to Newport News. To thwart a Federal advance on Richmond from this direction and also gather huge supplies of salted fish and bacon in eastern North Carolina, Lee detached Longstreet with the divisions of Hood and Pickett.[17]

About this time a group of politicians in Richmond instigated a movement to send Powell Hill west to replace hapless Braxton Bragg, a fellow West Pointer. On March 8, Ewell, recuperating from the loss of his leg, wrote Early of this effort, adding: "A good move if they send troops with him as a Major-General, but I doubt if he would answer to supersede Bragg and the rest 'to the manner born'." Although nothing materialized, this movement is an interesting indication of Hill's peculiar ability to get along with politicians. With Longstreet and Jackson he quarreled heatedly and bitterly, but to President Davis "he was brave and skillful, and always ready to obey orders and to do his duty."[18]

Within Hill's division several important changes now occurred. Command of Gregg's South Carolina brigade was proffered first to Wade Hampton, who declined it, and then to Colonel Samuel McGowan who had compiled a distinguished record as colonel of the Fourteenth South Carolina regiment. McGowan accepted what proved to be a popular appointment.[19] Another vacancy existed in Charles Field's First Brigade which had been in charge of Colonel John M. Brockenbrough, its senior colonel, since its regular brigadier was severely wounded at Second Manassas. With Field indefinitely incapacitated, Lee assigned Brigadier General Harry Heth to command of this brigade. Heth had been the "goat" in Hill's class at West Point, and prior to assuming command of the First Brigade he had served with Kirby Smith in Tennessee.[20] Finally, Major William H. Palmer of the First Virginia Volunteers joined the Adjutant and Inspector General's Department of the

---

[16] O.R., *18*, 819; O.R., *21*, 1093.
[17] O.R., *18*, 926, 933, 876, 883-84.
[18] S.H.S.P., *27*, 452.
[19] O.R., *21*, 1100.
[20] Heth MS, 142.

Light Division following Major Morgan's transfer to the West.[21]

About this time mounting reports of Federal atrocities against the civilian populace of northern Virginia provided inflammatory topics of conversation in Confederate camps. Cadmus Wilcox, Hill's friend and classmate, described some of these depredations in a letter to his sister:

> They steal, rob, enter houses, take many things they want before the eyes of the master and mistress of the house . . . Even what they do not want they destroy . . . actually reducing people to the point of starvation, and then insulting them by telling them that they will sell them what they want if they will take the oath of allegiance. I did not know that any people could be so brutal.[22]

Outraged at such barbarism, Hill vowed to his associates that he would retaliate by burning Washington to the ground.[23]

Although the problems of command kept him busy, Powell Hill managed to find time to fan the flame of his bitter dispute with Jackson. As early as January 8 he reminded Lee of Jackson's charges and requested an early trial. He pointed out that two of his important witnesses, Branch and Gregg, had been killed, and to expedite matters he offered to waive any claims to a trial by peers and accept a court composed of officers of any rank.[24]

Lee, with consummate tact and patience, replied within a week. Skillfully avoiding any inferences which might be construed as prejudicial, the commanding General objectively reviewed the power of an officer to arrest a subordinate, emphasizing its necessity as an instrument of discipline. However, he "did not think that in every case where an officer is arrested there is a necessity for a trial by court-martial . . ." Hopefully, Lee concluded: "Upon examining the charges in question, I am of the opinion that the interests of the service do not require that they be tried, and have, therefore returned them to General Jackson with an indorsement to that effect. I hope that you will concur with me that

---

[21] Letter Book, Light Division, A. P. Hill to S. Cooper, April 6, 1863.
[22] Wilcox MSS, Letter of April 21, 1863 to his sister, Mary.
[23] Pender MSS, Letter to his wife, April 9, 1863.
[24] O.R., *19*, Part 2, 731-32.

further prosecution is unnecessary, so far as you are concerned, and will be of no advantage to the service."[25]

Hill was not appeased by Lee's moderate and sensible suggestions, but persistently resumed his case in a legal "thereto" style liberally punctuated by unseemly venom. In a letter of Army Headquarters dated January 29, he wrote:

> I have the honor to acknowledge the receipt of the letter of January 12 from the commanding general. I beg leave to state that I do not now nor ever have disputed the right of the superior to arrest any officer under him, and to release him whenever he saw fit so to do, or that he might do so and prefer no charges, provided the *party arrested consented thereto*. Otherwise an engine of tyranny is placed in the hands of the commanding officers, to be exercized at their will, to gratify passions or whims, and against which there is no appeal. In my own case the commanding general having returned the charges against me by General Jackson without trial is a rebuke to him, but not as public as was General Jackson's exercize of power toward me. The general must acknowledge that if the charges preferred against me by General Jackson were true, that I do not deserve to command a division in this army; if they are untrue, then General Jackson deserves a rebuke as notorious as my arrest. I beg leave most distinctly to disclaim any credit which General Jackson may have given me for the good results of his punishment, as to my better behavior thereafter, and that its only effect has been to cause me to preserve every scrap of paper received from corps headquarters, to guard myself against any new eruptions from this slumbering volcano. I respectfully forward again my charges against Lieutenant-General Jackson and request that he be tried on them.
>
> As to the indorsement of the commanding general on these charges, I will state that these charges were forwarded by me to General Jackson several *days before* I had any intimation that General Jackson intended to prefer charges against me, and that, so far as I know, his charges grew out of mine, and not mine out of his.[26]

Audacious and scathing to the point of impertinence, Hill in his acrimony divulged here for the first time in writing the nub of his intransigence. Sure of his case, substantiated by what he considered Lee's private reprimand of Jackson, he would be satisfied with nothing less than a rebuke to "this slumbering volcano" as publicly humiliating as the one he had suffered while marching at the rear of his division through Maryland.

Not content with self-vindication, Hill boldly assumed the offen-

[25] *Ibid.*, 732.
[26] *Ibid.*, 732-33; Letter Book, Light Division, January 29, 1863.

sive by requesting that Lee bring the current hero of the army to trial on charges which Hill had framed and submitted after the Maryland campaign. Although the text of Hill's charges has never been found, it presumably dealt with Jackson's alleged abuse of authority.

When Lee showed no disposition to act further in this matter, Hill utilized his report on the battle of Slaughter's Mountain to relight the fuse. By devoting a major portion of the account to a justification of his actions which had precipitated the dispute, he forced Jackson to defend himself. Corps and divisional headquarters bristled with activity as the two principals and their aides gathered testimony relating to the case.[27] In his endorsement of Hill's report which he forwarded to Lee on March 19, Jackson contested his subordinate's version point-by-point.[28]

As the fuse burned shorter events moved quickly. When Hill learned the gist of Jackson's endorsement, he renewed his plea for a trial. Jackson realizing he confronted a foe as relentless as himself, now prepared for a showdown by carefully revising his eight specifications of neglect of duty. By the middle of April the stage was set for a dramatic climax when a new incident complicated the controversy.

Captain R. H. T. Adams, Chief Signal Officer of the Light Division, was found to have disclosed the contents of an intercepted enemy message to persons other than those authorized to receive such information. When Jackson directed Adams to conform to regulations in such matters, the latter refused on the basis that he could not obey orders which did not channel through Hill. Thereupon, Jackson summarily removed Adams whose case was immediately championed by Hill.

On April 23 Hill angrily complained in a note to Major "Sandie" Pendleton, Jackson's Adjutant General:

Captain R. H. T. Adams, my Signal Officer, was relieved from duty and ordered to report to Genl R. E. Lee.

He has done so, and now returns and reports that Genl Lee is ignorant

---

[27] Douglas, 215. Also, letter of March 13, 1863 from A. P. Hill to Major A. S. Pendleton.

[28] O.R., *12*, Part 2, 216.

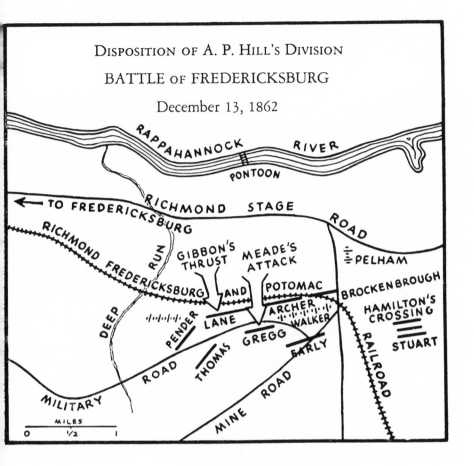

DISPOSITION OF A. P. HILL'S DIVISION

BATTLE OF FREDERICKSBURG

December 13, 1862

RAPPAHANNOCK   RIVER

PONTOON

← TO FREDERICKSBURG   RICHMOND   STAGE   ROAD

RICHMOND FREDERICKSBURG

GIBBON'S
THRUST

MEADE'S
ATTACK

PELHAM

DEEP RUN

POTOMAC

BROCKENBROUGH

PENDER   LANE   AND   ARCHER   WALKER

HAMILTON'S
CROSSING

THOMAS   GREGG   EARLY

STUART

ROAD

MILITARY

MINE   ROAD

RAILROAD

MILES
0   ½   1

Divisional Commanders of the Third Corps

MAJ. GEN. R. H. ANDERSON
From an original negative in
The Meserve Collection

MAJ. GEN. HARRY HETH
Photo National Archives

MAJ. GEN.
WILLIAM MAHONE
Photo National Archives

MAJ. GEN. W. DORSEY PENDER
Photo courtesy Library of Congress

MAJ. GEN. CADMUS M. WILCOX
Photo National Archives

of any such order. I request to know why Capt. Adams, a most capable and the *most efficient* Signal Officer, was relieved from duty on my staff. I say nothing of the discourtesy of relieving thus summarily an Officer of my Staff, without any explanation to myself.[29]

The same day Hill dashed off a dispatch to Army Headquarters reiterating an earlier request for clarification as to "how far my authority extends in my own division."[30] Hill took the position that, "the unity of my command is entirely destroyed if my superior can give orders direct to my Staff Officers, and my knowledge of these orders made entirely dependent upon the will of the Staff Officer."[31] However, his insistence that, "all orders affecting to organization or efficiency of my Division should pass through me"[32] was aggravating such enmity between Hill and Jackson that Lee referred the question of its propriety to the Adjutant General for a ruling. Hill, of course, had employed this system consistently and openly, having notified Jackson's Adjutant General five months previously that he had ordered Adams to ignore any order coming directly from Jackson.[33]

Weary of parrying Hill's unremitting jabs, Jackson decided that the time had come for a parting of the ways. In endorsing Hill's letter to Lee concerning the Adams affair, Jackson wrote: "When an officer orders in his command such disregard for the orders of his superiors, I am of the opinion that he should be relieved from duty with his command, and I respectfully request that Genl. Hill be relieved from duty in my Corps."[34]

How Lee would have unravelled this Gordian knot is an intriguing conjecture. The commanding General had no desire to contravene Jackson's expressed desire in this matter, but to separate Hill from the Second Corps would leave Jackson without an experienced divisional commander. Lee certainly did not relish this prospect when D. H. Hill, Hood, Pickett, and Longstreet were detached, and the enemy showed increasing signs of restiveness.

---

[29] Letter Book, Light Division, A. P. Hill to Major A. S. Pendleton, April 23, 1863.
[30] *Ibid.* A. P. Hill to Brig. Gen. Chilton, April 23, 1863.
[31] *Ibid.* A. P. Hill to R. H. Chilton, March 11, 1863.
[32] *Ibid.*
[33] Letter from A. P. Hill to Capt. A. S. Pendleton, November 13, 1862.
[34] Jackson MSS. April 24, 1863.

Hill's services were sorely needed, but to whom could he be assigned? The possibility of transferring him to the West had already been explored and rejected. Returning him to Longstreet was inadvisable despite an easing of relations between the two.[35] Lee's most probable solution would have been the one he had considered for some time, and which he was soon to adopt under tragically altered circumstances, namely, the creation of a third corps with Hill as commander.[36]

For the present, however, Lee was spared this fateful decision by ominous activity across the Rappahannock. As the Federal camps came to life, Lee wrote his wife, "Mr. Hooker looms very large over the river. He has two balloons up in the day and one at night. I hope he is gratified at what he sees . . ."[37] "Fighting Joe" apparently did like what he saw, for the end of April he activated his well conceived plan to envelop Lee's reduced command. He dispatched Stoneman with 10,000 cavalry to harass Lee's line of communications and threaten Richmond, while Sedgwick's 40,000 men crossed on pontoons to pin down the Army of Northern Virginia at Fredericksburg. Hooker then marched three corps of his 138,000 man army[38] by the north bank of the river which they crossed at Germanna Ford and Ely's Ford. Thence the three converging columns proceeded southeastward to fall on Lee's left flank and rear.

When the vigilant Stuart reported Hooker's movements, Lee correctly discerned the underlying strategy of his new adversary. Leaving Early with about 10,000 men and part of the reserve artillery to detain Sedgwick,[39] Lee rushed Longstreet's two remaining divisions and Jackson's corps westward to confront Hooker.[40]

Before dawn on Friday, May 1, the Light Division broke camp and followed Rodes' division of Jackson's corps along the

---

[35] Sorrel, 88.
[36] O.R., *25*, Part 2, 810.
[37] C.M.H., *III*, 372. Letter from R. E. Lee to his wife, March 3, 1863.
[38] O.R., *25*, Part 2, 320.
[39] Jubal A. Early, *Autobiographical Sketch and Narrative of the War Between the States*, (cited hereafter as Early), 197-98.
[40] O.R., *25*, Part 2, 759, 797.

military road to the Plank Road where the column turned left toward Chancellorsville.[41] A heavy fog concealed the column for awhile from Hooker's observation balloons and observatories on the heights across the river.[42]

When within four miles of a large brick tavern and outbuildings adorning the intersection bearing the pretentious name of Chancellorsville,[43] Hill formed his line of battle preparatory to joining the general advance Jackson had ordered. Upon learning that the Federals were retiring toward Chancellorsville, Hill directed Heth, his new senior brigadier, to take his own brigade together with McGowan's and Lane's by a northerly cross road to the Old Turnpike and feel his way toward the enemy lines.[44] Heth disposed Orr's rifles and the Fourteenth South Carolina regiment as skirmishers who were uncovering strong enemy resistance when Jackson and Hill rode up to study the situation. Jackson was soon convinced that the enemy position was too formidable to storm in the fading light, and he ordered the men to halt and hold their line.[45] Then he joined Lee in a pine thicket to ponder the next move.[46]

Hooker manifestly was too firmly entrenched in the entangling wilderness for Lee to hazard a frontal attack with his pitifully inferior numbers. Although Jackson maintained that Hooker would retire under cover of darkness, Lee was convinced that the Federal commander would make a stand in his present position. As the two commanders explored various means of assuming the offensive, Stuart rode into camp with news from Fitz Lee that the Federal right to the west of Chancellorsville was completely in the air. This inviting flank, unprotected by any natural barrier and weakly fortified with breastworks which faced only south, instantly kindled the imagination of the commanding General and his "supremest flanker and rearer."[47] Both agreed upon a flank attack in force.

---

[41] O.R., *25*, Part 1, 885, 901, 939.
[42] C.M.H., *III*, 375.
[43] O.R., *25*, Part 1, 885; Dunaway, 65.
[44] O.R., *25*, Part 1, 890.
[45] *Ibid.*
[46] Henderson, 663.
[47] Douglas, 220. Douglas' quote of a Federal officer wounded at Chancellorsville.

Saturday broke cloudless and sunny, a typical May morn. Leaving Lee with only 14,000 men of Longstreet's corps to confront Hooker, Jackson in full uniform started his 28,000 veterans on their fateful mission. Hill's men rolled up their blankets, gulped cold rations,[48] and fell in behind Rodes' and Colston's divisions.[49]

Westward the long butternut line quick-stepped along an unfrequented tree-lined road which concealed the column almost along its entire length from enemy observation. Happily, the ground was just damp enough to soften the tread and blanket the dust.[50] On approaching Catharine Furnace the men crossed a clearing where they were espied by Federals who opened fire. However, the enemy construed Jackson's movement as a retreat toward Gordonsville, and even the careless boast of a captured veteran of the Twenty-Third Georgia to "wait till Jackson gets round on your right" was dismissed as harmless bravado.[51]

Early in the afternoon the enemy attacked Hill's wagon train near Catharine Furnace, whereupon Archer countermarched his own and Thomas' brigade to beat it off.[52] Meanwhile the head of the column proceeded north on Brock Road to the Orange Plank Road where Jackson intended to turn eastward. While the parched infantrymen enjoyed one of their three respites on this twelve mile trek, Jackson rode further north at Fitz Lee's request. Arriving at an eminence near the Old Turnpike, Jackson flushed with excitement as he surveyed Hooker's right. To the east stretched a long line of unmanned breastworks and abatis behind which arms were stacked. Oblivious of danger, crescent insigniad soldiers of Howard's Eleventh Corps lolled in groups while awaiting a supper of dressed beeves being readied for distribution.[53]

Jackson immediately perceived that by attacking down the Old Turnpike he could assail the unsuspecting foe in reverse. Abruptly he ordered the column to continue northward to the turnpike where the men then wheeled right for a mile and formed their

---

48 Caldwell, 74.
49 O.R., *25*, Part 1, 885.
50 Caldwell, 76.
51 B. and L., *III*, 183.
52 O.R., *25*, Part 1, 924.
53 Dunaway, 67.

battle lines. Rodes' division took the lead, supported by Colston—both commanders disposing two brigades on each side of the road. Hill closed the rear, placing Heth's and Pender's brigades north of the road with Lane's and McGowan's ready to follow in column. Meanwhile Archer and Thomas, having repulsed the attack on the wagon train, were hastening to rejoin the division.[54]

As a magnificent rainbow spread its colorful bands across the late afternoon sky,[55] brigade buglers sounded the charge. Forward rushed the long lines of cheering veterans—their weariness evaporating in an eagerness to surprise the enemy they had not engaged for almost five months. In what seemed "an incredibly short time,"[56] Rodes' division drove in Howard's pickets, brushed aside road barricades, and fell on the unprotected right. The German regiments, gripped by panic, divested themselves of all accoutrements which hampered their flight.[57]

While Rodes' men flushed the bluecoats, Powell Hill and his staff rode along the turnpike, turning off at intervals to check the progress of each brigade and to restrain "our poverty-stricken soldiers from a general pillage" of abandoned Federal knapsacks.[58] Further ahead Stuart's horse artillery galloped along the road, pouring canister into the bluecoats who offered only token resistance as they fled three miles across the fields of Talley's Farm, over the ridge at Rev. Melzi Chancellor's farm, and past the Wilderness Church in the vale to take refuge behind a line of log breastworks and abatis along a cross road about a mile west of Chancellorsville.[59]

As Jackson's front lines pursued the enemy through the woods to these fortifications, men and officers became separated and scrambled, and the offensive ground to a halt in the growing darkness. Rodes, realizing Jackson's desire to maintain the momentum gained in crumpling up Hooker's flank, requested his chief to push Hill's troops forward to take over the front.

---

[54] O.R., *25*, Part 1, 915-16, 925.
[55] C.M.H., *III*, 384.
[56] *Ibid.*
[57] S.H.S.P., *6*, 231.
[58] *Ibid.;* Caldwell, 77.
[59] O.R., *25*, Part 1, 885, 940; S.H.S.P., *43*, 48-49; C.M.H., *III*, 384-85.

Hill had anticipated that Jackson would call up the Light Division for a night attack, and he had already begun passing his brigades by moonlight through the disordered front lines to form a new line of battle.[60] Jackson, impatient to storm the enemy's works at Chancellorsville and at the same time cut off Hooker's line of retreat, exhorted his senior divisional commander; "Press them. Cut them off from the United States Ford, Hill. Press them."[61]

However, as Lane began to dispose the leading brigade in accordance with Hill's orders, an artillery duel broke out on his front. Unwilling to maneuver his troops in the darkness under this barrage, the North Carolinian ordered his men to lie down. Noting this inactivity, Hill sent W. H. Palmer, his Chief-of-Staff, to ascertain why "the little General"[62] had not moved forward. Lane replied that his men were pinned down by a raking fire, and he suggested that Hill order Moorman's battery of Stuart's Horse Artillery to cease firing in the hope the enemy would follow suit. Hill stopped Moorman whereupon the enemy also ceased firing.[63] Lane then formed his battle line—the Seventh and Thirty-Fifth North Carolina regiments taking position on the right of the turnpike while the Eighteenth and Twenty-Eighth formed on the left, Lieutenant Colonel Forney's Eighteenth North Carolina occupying a dense patch of scrub oaks bordering the road.[64] Lane deployed the Thirty-Third North Carolina as a skirmish line.[65]

Lane now rode back to ask Hill if he should advance or await further instructions. On reaching the turnpike he encountered Jackson busily dispatching couriers with orders for Hill to hurry.[66]

---

[60] O.R., *25*, Part 1, 885.

[61] S.H.S.P., *6*, 266; C.M.H., *III*, 385.

[62] *Lee's Dispatches*, ed. D. S. Freeman, (cited hereafter as Lee's Dispatches), 115.

[63] S.H.S.P., *8*, 494.

[64] *Ibid.*

[65] O.R., *25*, Part 1, 916. The existence of a skirmish line at the time Jackson rode ahead of Lane's line is a matter of dispute. Captain Wilbourn, who accompanied Jackson, stated: "There proved to be no such line—not even a picket or a vidette—and hence the wounding of Jackson." (S.H.S.P., *6*, 274). On the other hand, Lane reported: "As soon as this (cannonading) was over, I deployed the 33 N. Carolina troops forward as skirmishers . . ." (O.R., *25*, Part 1, 916.) And Major Leigh, who accompanied Hill, referred to passing "our most advanced line," presumably Lane's skirmishers. (S.H.S.P., *6*, 232.)

[66] S.H.S.P., *6*, 266.

To avoid further delay, Lane explained his situation to Jackson, who with a pushing gesture toward the enemy, replied, "Push right ahead, Lane."[67] It was now about 8 o'clock,[68] and Jackson decided to ride forward along the turnpike and reconnoiter. Hill, riding up with his staff, caught sight of his chief sallying forth into the darkness and spurred his horse to remain within call.[69]

While the two chieftains rode toward the enemy's lines Lane started to advance his regiments. Suddenly a Federal officer waving a white handkerchief emerged from shadows on the right and inquired whether Lane's troops were Union or Confederate. Lane considered this an illegitimate use of the truce flag and held the officer while he sent to Hill for instructions.[70] Thus alerted to the enemy's presence in that sector, Lane's kneeling veterans scanned the front for moving silhouettes.[71]

Unaware of this activity in their rear Jackson and Hill, in separate groups but within earshot, rode forward several hundred yards before the "melancholy cries of the 'whippowil' "[72] were drowned by the ringing of axes which signalled the bluecoats' frenzied attempt to barricade themselves against further assaults. Captain Conway Howard, Hill's engineer, skirted too close to a Federal battery and was captured.[73] After pausing to estimate the extent of Hooker's defenses, Hill and Jackson, still within sight of each other, trotted back toward Lane's position.[74]

Suddenly the discharge of a single musket rang out ahead, followed almost instantly by a volley.[75] Nervous skirmishers on Lane's right were firing on a small party of Federal cavalry and had drawn the fire of an enemy battery which swept the road with a storm of canister and grape.[76] Hill's party spurred forward, but when within fifty yards of their lines they were mistaken for

---

[67] S.H.S.P., *8*, 494.
[68] *N. C. Regts., II*, 559.
[69] C.V., *13*, 233; S.H.S.P., *6*, 231-32.
[70] The Federal officer was Lt.-Col. Levi Smith of the 128th Pennsylvania regiment which soon threw down its arms and surrendered to Lane. O.R., *25*, Part 1, 916.
[71] S.H.S.P., *6*, 267; O.R., *25*, Part 1, 916; *N. C. Regts., II*, 37.
[72] S.H.S.P., *6*, 279.
[73] C.M.H., *III*, 385-86.
[74] *Ibid.*, 386.
[75] S.H.S.P., *6*, 267.
[76] *Ibid.*, 232, 278; O. R., *25*, Part 1, 916.

Federal cavalry and fired upon by the Eighteenth North Carolina.[77] Hill instinctively threw himself upon the ground until the firing subsided, then arose and called at the top of his voice to the men to cease shooting.[78] Around him lay a number of wounded and dying, among whom was Captain Murray Taylor, his Aide-de-Camp, pinned under a fallen horse. Hill hastened to extricate his youthful aide,[79] but immediately abandoned this effort when informed that Jackson was wounded. Mounting his horse he rode along the turnpike with several of his staff until he espied his disabled chief lying under a little pine tree near the road.[80] Hill dismounted and directed Captain Leigh to accompany him while the others remained on guard in the turnpike.[81] Hill found that Captain Wilbourne, Jackson's Chief Signal Officer, had just finished putting Jackson's arm, splintered to the elbow by a couple of ounce minie balls, in a sling improvised from a handkerchief.[82]

Hill expressed deep regret at the accidental wounding which Jackson described as "very painful,"[83] and explained that he had been trying to make the men cease firing. As Jackson obviously was in a critical condition, Hill dispatched Leigh to procure a surgeon and an ambulance.[84] Then kneeling beside the officer with whom he had carried on a relentless feud, Powell Hill unbuckled Jackson's belt and sabre, and gently removed his blood-drenched gauntlets to relieve the painful pressure. Resting his chief's blood-stained head and shoulders against his chest,[85] Hill offered him brandy from a flask which Captain R. H. T. Adams (the same signal officer recently involved in the Hill-Jackson dispute) had relieved from a captured Federal officer.[86] Jackson at first hesitated, then reluctantly drank a little when Wilbourne told him it would sustain him until he could be transferred to the rear.[87]

---

[77] O.R., *25*, Part 1, 919; S.H.S.P., *6*, 232.
[78] S.H.S.P., *6*, 267.
[79] C.V., *13*, 233.
[80] S.H.S.P., *6*, 232-33.
[81] *Ibid.*, 271-72.
[82] *Ibid.*, 268, 272; C.M.H., *III*, 386.
[83] S.H.S.P., *6*, 269.
[84] *Ibid.*, 233.
[85] S.H.S.P., *43*, 51.
[86] S.H.S.P., *6*, 278.
[87] *Ibid.*, 273.

While Hill contemplated how Jackson could be moved to safety, he heard Captain Adams demand the surrender of two Federal skirmishers who had wandered toward the Confederate lines.[88] This increasing activity in the vicinity prompted Hill to transfer Jackson carefully to other hands with a considerate promise to keep news of the accident from the men.[89]

With drawn pistol Hill, now in command of the Second Corps, mounted his horse and returned to his lines.[90] After exhorting Lane's troops to repel any attempt to retake their rifle pits, Hill returned on foot to search for something where Jackson had been wounded. Possibly he was concerned lest the advancing foe recover Jackson's telltale fieldglasses, and haversack containing papers and dispatches which Wilbourne had removed from Jackson's person.[91] He was thus engaged when the enemy opened with musketry and thirty-two guns on the head of the Light Division.[92] A minie ball wounded Hill in the calves of his legs, painfully crippling him. After hobbling back to the lines he vented his anger on the Eighteenth North Carolina for firing at a noise, but regained his composure when a back-woodsman of Company B laconically opined: "Everybody knows the Yankee army can't run the Light Division and one little general needn't try it."[93] Amused, Hill limped down the road to the rear of his lines where he laid down on a litter. As he was unable to walk or take the saddle without suffering excruciating pain, command of the corps devolved upon Rodes until Stuart arrived about midnight in response to Hill's summons.[94] Hill, lying unceremoniously upon the litter, formally turned over his command to Stuart with Rodes' acquiescence. A brief council of war was then held at which "it was thought best, under all circumstances, not to push the pursuit any farther that night."[95]

Hill was still paralyzed below the knees when daylight permitted

---

[88] *Ibid.*, 270.
[89] *Ibid.*
[90] *Ibid.*
[91] *Ibid.*, 269.
[92] O.R., *25*, Part 1, 885.
[93] *N. C. Regts., II*, 38.
[94] O.R., *25*, Part 1, 885-87, 942-43.
[95] *Ibid.*, 886.

a resumption of the battle. Resignedly he followed the progress of Sunday's engagement by ear and dispatch from his position behind the lines. Commencing at dawn, Confederate artillery, including Pegram's redoubtable battery, decisively paved the way for Stuart's pulsating infantry lines to move forward and link up with the two divisions advancing under General Lee. Late in the morning Chancellorsville was in Southern hands.[96]

Despite the Light Division's irregular performance this day, Harry Heth, Hill's senior brigadier, overlooked its shortcomings and paid tribute to Hill in his report as he wrote: "Although deprived of the presence of their gallant commander, [Hill's men] showed on this day that the spirit with which he had inspired them by successes on so many battle-fields was still present, and each and all did their duty."[97]

Unfortunately, Lee's opportunity to crush Hooker was forestalled by the necessity of dispatching troops to bolster Early's force against Sedgwick who was advancing from Fredericksburg. After Sedgwick was repulsed and driven across the river, Hooker took advantage of a deluge to withdraw the remainder of his army to the hills above Fredericksburg.[98] When Powell Hill resumed command of the Second Corps on May 6,[99] no Federals were to be found south of the Rappahannock.[100] Lee thereupon ordered his army to retrace its steps to the previous encampment near Fredericksburg. The Light Division reached Moss Neck on Thursday, May 7 to find the camp denuded of shelters, "and nobody to blame."[101]

On Friday, Hill composed what he termed a "very imperfect sketch of our operations"[102] during the recent campaign. Lacking in detail it definitely was, but certainly not in eulogies. With characteristic generosity, Hill stated: "Brigadier-General Rodes distinguished himself much, and won a proud name for himself

---

[96] *Ibid.*, 800.
[97] *Ibid.*, 892.
[98] *Ibid.*, 801, 826, 830, 851-52, 945.
[99] O.R., *25,* Part 2, 782.
[100] O.R., *25,* Part 1, 802, 852, 945.
[101] Caldwell, 87.
[102] O.R., *25,* Part 1, 885.

and his division." And of Stuart, a potential rival for corps command in the event of Jackson's death, Hill wrote: "Major-General Stuart is deserving of great commendation for his admirable management of the troops. Called suddenly late at night to a new sphere of action, and entirely ignorant of the positions of the brigades, with indomitable energy he surmounted all difficulties and achieved a glorious result."[103]

While unsparing in his praise of valorous conduct, Hill was impatiently contemptuous of inglorious behavior. In reading Early's report of operations around Fredericksburg, he noted that the Fifty-Eighth Virginia had ignominiously lost its colors while retiring from an exposed position. When the color-bearer was shot and dropped the colors, neither he nor the standard was retrieved by the color-guard. Hill was completely unsympathetic to the regimental commander's request for a new standard, and forwarded the report to Lee with an indorsement that "this regiment be not allowed to carry a color until it has redeemed its own by capturing one in battle."[104]

However, the problems and rejoicings which followed in the immediate wake of Chancellorsville were all overshadowed by anxiety as to the fate of Jackson, who lay fighting for his life at Guiney's Station. Hope rose and then faded while the whole army prayed for his recovery. On May 10, a warm, sunny Sabbath, Dr. Lacy, Jackson's chaplain, preached a reassuring sermon at Hill's headquarters on the text: "We know that all things work together for good to them that fear God."[105] But in the afternoon tragic news of Jackson's death shrouded the camps in gloom. The grievances of those, including Powell Hill, who felt themselves wronged by Jackson's stern and sometimes unorthodox concept of justice, melted in a realization of the irreplaceable loss sustained by his passing. Hill could take some comfort in the knowledge that against a macabre background he had thrust aside the issues separating them to embrace his chief in final, tender solicitude. There was satisfaction, too, in reports that Jackson had called

---

[103] *Ibid.,* 886.
[104] *Ibid.,* 1002.
[105] Douglas, 227.

on A. P. Hill "to prepare for action" just before the great commander crossed the river to rest in the shade of the trees forever.[106]

Grief over Jackson's death was soon blended with speculation
regarding his successor. Ewell, Powell Hill, and Stuart were regarded as the strongest and most likely contenders for promotion
to corps command. Modest, capable Dick Ewell, now recovered
from his wound at Groveton and sporting a wooden leg, was
universally liked and respected. Stuart, though ambitious and
vainglorious, did not aspire as was rumored to Jackson's post.
In a letter to his wife, "Jeb" confided: "There has been a great
deal of talk of my succeeding General Jackson, but I think it
without foundation in fact."[107] Hill was very fond of Stuart, his
only plaint being the jocular one that every visit of the cavalry
leader and his banjo player, Sweeney, demoralized the Light
Division by making the foot-soldiers want to "jine the cavalry."[108]

The Middle of May, General Lee reviewed the Second Corps.[109]
As he galloped along the lines at a gait that only Hill and a staff
member could match,[110] proud veterans of the Light Division
wondered whether their dashing, young commander would be appointed to the corps command they firmly believed he deserved.
Lee himself was formulating the answer, which he outlined in a
letter to Davis on May 20:

> I have for the past year felt that the corps of this army were too large
> for one commander. Nothing prevented my proposing to you to reduce
> their size and increase their number but my inability to recommend com-
> manders. Each corps contains, when in fighting condition, about 30,000
> men. These are more than one man can properly handle and keep under
> his eye in battle in the country that we have to operate in. They are always
> beyond the range of his vision, and frequently beyond his reach. The loss
> of Jackson from one-half the army seems to me a good opportunity to
> remedy this evil. If, therefore, you think Ewell is able to do field duty,
> I submit to your better judgement whether the most advantageous arrange-
> ment would not be to put him in command of three divisions of Jackson's
> corps, to take one of Longstreet's divisions, A. P. Hill's division, and form

---

[106] Dabney, 719: Dr. Hunter McGuire, "Stonewall Jackson, an Address" in
McGuire and Christian, *The Confederate Cause and Conduct in the War Between
the States* (cited hereafter as McGuire), 229.
[107] Thomason, 392.
[108] S.H.S.P., *8,* 451.
[109] Caldwell, 89.
[110] E. A. Moore, *The Story of a Cannoneer Under Stonewall Jackson,* 177-78.

a division of Ransom's, Cooke's, and Pettigrew's brigades, and give the corps formed to A. P. Hill. In this event I also submit to you whether it would not be well to promote Ewell and A. P. Hill. The former is an honest, brave soldier who has always done his duty well. The latter, I think upon the whole, is the best soldier of his grade with me.[111]

President Davis concurred, and on Sunday, May 24, Lee summoned Powell Hill to his tent to notify him of his promotion to Lieutenant General in command of the newly created Third Corps. Lee explained that the new command would comprise three divisions: R. H. Anderson's division of Longstreet's corps, the Light Division reduced by two brigades, and a new division to be formed from two brigades of the old Light Division plus two new ones.[112]

Although naturally gratified at receiving this long coveted promotion, Hill lost little time reflecting on his new status other than to invite his wife to visit him and share the good news together. As he retired to his quarters that afternoon his first concern was the selection of a successor to command the Light Division. Having organized, christened, and directed the division which had distinguished itself on many a fateful field, he naturally evinced a fatherly solicitude in its future. He was especially anxious to preserve the command's "pride in its name, . . . its 'shoulder to shoulder feeling,' and good feeling between the different brigades."[113] He feared that unless the new commander was carefully selected, this esprit de corps—probably the finest of any division in the army—would disintegrate.

Powell Hill's unqualified choice to command the Light Division was twenty-nine year old William Dorsey Pender, whose consistently fine record as a brigadier had gained him recognition as one of the staunchest and most aggressive officers in the Army of Northern Virginia.[114] Earlier in the year Hill had unreservedly commended Pender as the best brigadier in the Second Corps with a recommendation that he be promoted to Major General.[115] However, Heth had subsequently joined the division at Lee's behest

[111] O.R., *25*, Part 2, 810.
[112] *Lee's Dispatches*, 91.
[113] Wilkins MSS, Letter from A. P. Hill to R. E. Lee, May 24, 1863.
[114] *Lee's Dispatches*, 115.
[115] Pender MSS, Letters to his wife, April 8, 1863 and April 11, 1863; Letter Book, Light Division, A. P. Hill to R. E. Lee, January 31, 1863.

and automatically superseded Pender as its senior brigadier. Hill, fully aware of the sensibilities involved, forcefully set forth his views in the following letter which he wrote and delivered to the commanding General the afternoon of his own appointment:

> Of General Heth I have but to say that I consider him a most excellent officer and gallant soldier, and had he been with the Division through all its hardships, and acquired the confidence of the men, there is no man I had rather see promoted than he. On the other hand Gen. Pender has fought with the Division in every battle, has been four times wounded, and never left the field, . . . has the best drilled and disciplined Brigade in the Division, and more than all, possesses the unbounded confidence of the Division. At the battle of Chancellorsville he seized the color, and on horseback led his brigade up to and into the Federal intrenchments.
>
> The effect of such examples of daring gallantry at critical moments is incalculable. I am very earnest in this matter, for I know that 10,000 men led by a Commander whom they know, and have fought with, may turn the tide of battle, and I do not think the Confederacy can afford to have this Army defeated. Hence, as much as I admire and respect Gen. Heth, I am conscientiously of opinion that in the opening campaign my Division under him, will not be half as effective as under Gen. Pender.[116]

As Lee had indicated that a new division was to be formed and attached to the Third Corps, Hill proposed that Heth be placed in command of it. Hill's letter was so cogent that Lee inclosed it with his own on May 25 to Davis urging the promotion of both Heth and Pender.[117] This recommendation was subsequently adopted, and the end of May the two new Major Generals assumed command of their divisions.[118] Pender's Light Division included his old brigade—henceforth commanded by Alfred M. Scales—[119] McGowan's, Thomas', and Lane's. Heth's division comprised Archer's and Heth's brigades of the old Light Division plus Johnston Pettigrew's North Carolina Brigade and Joseph Davis' Mississippi Brigade.[120] J. R. Cooke's North Carolina Brigade also was assigned to Heth, but it did not join the Corps until early in October.[121] Anderson's division, comprising the brigades of

---

[116] Wilkins MSS, Letter from A. P. Hill to R. E. Lee, May 24, 1863.
[117] *Lee's Dispatches*, 91-92.
[118] O.R., *25*, Part 2, 840.
[119] O.R., *27*, Part 3, 909.
[120] O.R., *25*, Part 2, 840.
[121] *N. C. Regts., II*, 440.

Mahone, Perry, Posey, Wilcox, and Wright,[122] brought the Corps' strength well above 20,000.[123]

Hill competently handled these major organizational changes together with minor ones such as that involving the appointment of Lawrence B. Taylor, a refugee from Alexandria, to his military court. In endorsing Taylor, Hill wrote:

> From Mr. Taylor's reputation as a conscientious gentleman and one of a high order of ability, I respectfully recommend him for the position. I have made but one recommendation and I desire this to be understood as my second choice.

Spirits soared high in the new corps. The men were in excellent health and better equipped "than at any period prior or subsequent."[124] One veteran boldly prophesied that the army "will fight better than they have ever done, if such a thing is possible."[125] In their thirty-seven year old Lieutenant General the officers and men placed unbounded confidence based on his distinguished record. Pender confidently averred that Hill "would give as much satisfaction as he had in divisional command."[126] Kyd Douglas reviewed Hill's career in these admiring terms: "As a division commander he had few equals. He was quick, bold, skillful, and tenacious when the battle had begun; as at Mechanicsville he did his work dashingly and well."[127] And Porter Alexander, Longstreet's able artillerist, reflected that "he had been an excellent division commander, and done conspicuous fighting and marching in previous campaigns."[128]

Would the larger sphere of corps command spell even greater glory?

---

122 S.H.S.P., *6*, 35.
123 O.R., *27*, Part 2, 292; Welch, 54.
124 Caldwell, 95.
125 Welch, 55.
126 Pender MSS, Letter to his wife, June 28, 1863.
127 Douglas, 147.
128 Alexander, 367.

CHAPTER XV

"If Hell Can't Be Taken. . ."

(Gettysburg)

Wвith the north dispirited
by Hooker's stunning defeat at Chancellorsville, Lee felt that the
time was ripe for the long contemplated invasion of Pennsylvania.
The first week in June he started Ewell and Longstreet north-
westward toward the Potomac[1] while Hill screened their movement by erecting earthworks along the line occupied by the Army
during the battle of Fredericksburg.[2]

Hooker soon became suspicious and thrust a force across the
Rappahannock to probe Hill's position, which a diarist in Pender's
division considered impregnable against "any Yankee force which
may come at us."[3] After brief skirmishing the Federals concurred
in this estimate, and the opposing camps settled down to a quiet,
friendly routine. Newspapers were exchanged,[4] and joint concerts
were held nightly during which the rival bands on opposite sides
of the river played Yankee Doodle, Star Spangled Banner, Dixie,
Bonnie Blue Flag and concluded with a nostalgic rendition of
Home Sweet Home. Thereupon a shout would arise from both
shores "showing there was one tie held in common by these two
grand armies."[5]

Before Lee left to accompany Ewell and Longstreet, he drafted
detailed instructions for the Third Corps. Hill was to contest any
advance of Hooker's, calling up forces from Hanover Junction or
retiring as he deemed advisable. The commanding General also
established a line of couriers which would enable Hill to "keep
me informed of everything material relative to yourself, position,
and of the enemy." In the event Hooker withdrew, the Third Corps

---

[1] O.R., 27, Part 2, 293.
[2] Caldwell, 89.
[3] Welch, 54.
[4] Caldwell, 90; Welch, 53.
[5] *N. C. Regts., IV*, 175-76.

was to keep tabs on his movements. Hill's eyes then read with gratification Lee's final paragraph directing him "to open any official communications sent to me, and, if necessary, act upon them according to the dictates of your good judgement."[6]

Lee's selection of Powell Hill for this responsible autonomous post clothed with broad discretionary authority is interesting in view of the Lieutenant General's oft-demonstrated impulsive tendencies. Doubtless it was dictated in a large measure by the alternatives. Thus, Longstreet as usual was unenthusiastic about an offensive,[7] and in the Chancellorsville campaign he had been indisposed to rejoin Lee with his sorely needed divisions. Ewell, another possible choice, enjoyed a high reputation among his troops, but Lee had worked with him only briefly during the Seven Days. Hence the commanding General decided to rely upon Hill whose zeal and skill he had seen demonstrated repeatedly.

Scrupulously following Lee's orders, Hill observed the enemy closely for evidence of his intentions. Ere long he became suspicious that Hooker was copying Lee's stratagem, viz., masking his withdrawal with the visible holding force opposite the Third Corps. Hill decided to test the enemy's strength, and ordered a demonstration at Moss Neck which resulted in the enemy's withdrawal of four regiments to the north bank of the river.[8] By Sunday, May 14, all the Federal rifle pits lining the southern shore were empty.[9]

Hill dispatched several scouts to trail Hooker,[10] and bade affectionate but anxious farewell to Dolly who had insisted on staying with her "General" as long as possible.[11] In obedience to Lee's orders[12] he then started the corps toward the Valley which Ewell was gaily clearing of Milroy's bluecoats.[13] Averaging about fifteen miles a day,[14] Hill's newly shod troops[15] passed through the Blue

---

[6] O.R., *27*, Part 3, 859.
[7] B. and L., *III*, 248-49.
[8] O.R., *27*, Part 2, 294.
[9] Caldwell, 91; O.R., *27*, Part 2, 306.
[10] O.R., *51*, Part 2, 723.
[11] Pender MSS, Letter to his wife, June 7, 1863.
[12] O.R., *27*, Part 2, 306.
[13] *Ibid.*
[14] Welch, 57.
[15] A. J. L. Fremantle, *Three Months in the Southern States* (cited hereafter as Fremantle), 180.

Ridge at Chester Gap and then headed north along the invasion route toward Maryland and Pennsylvania. "Shouting and hurrahing as usual"[16] the motley uniformed veterans forded the Potomac at Shepherdstown on June 25.[17] Nary a soldier doubted the ability of this invading force "to drive the Federal army into the Atlantic Ocean."[18]

The conquerors presented a marked contrast to their haggard appearance the previous fall. Although much of their equipment and wagons bore the telltale second-hand "U.S." imprint, the men were comfortably supplied.[19] Straggling, which had shorn 2,000 men from the Light Division in three days during the Maryland campaign, was now under better control.[20] Regiments were well closed, each followed by its retinue of colored servants and slaves together with stretcher bearers wearing red badges on their hats.[21]

Nowhere was the change more evident than in Powell Hill. Instead of walking grimly at the rear of his division while under arrest, he now rode proudly at the head of his corps where he frequently enjoyed the company of the commanding General. In deference to his new position he wore a black felt hat adorned with gold cord, and usually carried his sword.[22]

With the exception of a few sympathizers such as the woman who cheered Hill's column with "Go it boys! I'm glad to see you coming here again,"[23] most Marylanders received them with the same restraint as previously. However, this wait-and-see attitude did not permeate the youngsters, who found in the friendly invaders "a dash . . . which Northern men lacked."[24] On learning that General Lee and his generals were observing the Army from a grove atop a hill near Williamsport, young Leighton Parks hustled thence with a pail of raspberries. His token of hospitality was gratefully accepted, in return for which he was invited to snack with Lee, Longstreet, and Hill.

---

[16] Caldwell, 92.
[17] *Ibid.*
[18] S.H.S.P., *4*, 151.
[19] Fremantle, 186-87.
[20] *Ibid.*, 292.
[21] *Ibid*, 186-87.
[22] *Ibid.*, 198.
[23] Caldwell, 92; O.R., *27*, Part 2, 324.
[24] Century Magazine, Vol. 70, 259.

During lunch Master Leighton's ingenuous opinions provided the officers a refreshing diversion from the burdens of command. Afterward, Lee held the boy on his knee. When the commanding General's attention was distracted by another matter, Hill beckoned the lad to his lap where the two enjoyed a chat. Finally, Longstreet said, "Come, Hill, you've had him long enough; pass him over." Whereupon the massive Dutchman, who had lost his three children in a scarlet fever epidemic the previous year, affectionately rubbed his great brown beard against the boy's tender face.[25]

The end of June, Hill's divisions appropriately entered the beautiful Canaan of Pennsylvania via comfortable macadam roads. The superabundance of "everything that administers to comfort"[26] bewildered the eyes of veterans by now long accustomed to the sight of devastated and untended farmland. One marcher wrote glowingly to his wife: "I have never yet seen any country in such a high state of cultivation. Such wheat I never dreamed of, and so much of it."[27] Luscious ripe cherries proved particularly inviting to Hill's men who stripped the trees along the roads to Fayetteville, a village about ten miles east of Chambersburg.[28] Here the corps encamped on Saturday, June 27.[29]

Lee planned to push northward and take Harrisburg, having already started Ewell's column toward the state capital when he received information that Major General George G. Meade had replaced Hooker and was advancing the Federal Army toward South Mountains.[30] With the enemy thus threatening his line to the Potomac, and lacking the eyes of Stuart whose cavalry was capturing a Federal wagon train on the outskirts of Washington,[31] Lee cancelled plans for the envelopment of Harrisburg and ordered the Army to concentrate east of Chambersburg.[32]

Accordingly, Lee directed Longstreet and Hill "to proceed

---

25 *Ibid.*, 262.
26 Welch, 58.
27 *Ibid.*
28 Casler, 247.
29 S.H.S.P., 2, 39.
30 B. and L., *III*, 250.
31 O.R., 27, Part 2, 694.
32 *Ibid.*, 307.

from Chambersburg to Gettysburg."[33] and recalled Ewell from Carlisle "to join the army at Cashtown or Gettysburg as circumstances might require."[34] Then with apparent unconcern the commanding General told his attending officers: "Tomorrow, gentlemen, we will not move to Harrisburg as we expected, but will go over to Gettysburg to see what General Meade is after."[35]

The Third Corps led the eastward procession. Hill set Heth's division in motion on Monday, followed by the Light Division on Tuesday. As the column plodded through the rain it passed the smoldering ruins of Thaddeus Stevens' Caledonia iron factory which Early's troops had recently burned on their way to the Susquehanna.[36] Soon the hard roads wound steeply through the rugged, towering terrain to Cashtown Pass, a village eight miles northwest of Gettysburg that derived its name from a local tavern-keeper's insistence on cash payment.

Unaware of the enemy's proximity, Heth sent Pettigrew's brigade—"the largest, best equipped, finest looking brigade of the whole army"—on Tuesday morning to Gettysburg where a supply of shoes reportedly was obtainable.[37] This was a welcome prospect to marchers whose soles were worn thin or through on the macadam turnpike roads.[38] Heth himself shopped nearby for a hat—a necessity his men frequently procured by the simple device of a "long arm" exchange with well-dressed citizens encountered along the line of march.[39] Heth chose one from the stock his Quartermaster had requisitioned from local merchants. As the chapeau fitted loosely, the clerk adjusted it by inserting paper wadding

---

[33] *Ibid.*

[34] *Ibid.*, 317.

[35] J. A. Longstreet, *From Manassas to Appomattox* (cited hereafter as Longstreet), 383.

[36] Anderson's division did not start until Wednesday, when it marched to within two miles of Gettysburg. Welch, 61, 66; O.R., *27*, Part 2, 607.

[37] Meade likewise lacked information regarding Lee's position. As late as June 30 he wrote to Couch, "The enemy (A. P. Hill) hold Cashtown Pass . . . I am without definite and positive information as to the whereabouts of Longstreet and Ewell." O.R., *27*, Part 3, 1084; W. T. Poague, "Gunner With Stonewall," Ed., M. F. Cockrell, 70; S.H.S.P., *4*, 157.

[38] Welch, 77.

[39] Fremantle, 196.

between the felt and sweat band—a simple fitting that was to save Heth's life.[40]

Early that evening Pettigrew returned and reported to Heth that he had not entered Gettysburg and purchased the shoes because enemy cavalry occupied the town. He added that the sound of drums rolling ominously on the far side of town indicated the arrival of infantry. At Heth's insistance, Pettigrew related his findings to Hill who had just ridden up with Pender's division.[41] After hearing the news Hill commented: "The only force at Gettysburg is cavalry, probably a detachment of observation. I am just from General Lee, and the information he has from scouts corroborates that I have received from mine—that is, the enemy are still at Middleburg, and have not yet struck their tents." As Middleburg was sixteen miles south of Gettysburg, Heth inquired: "If there is no objection, I will take my division to-morrow, and go to Gettysburg, and get those shoes!" Hill replied without hesitation, "Do so."[42]

Although Hill discounted the possibility of an enemy concentration at Gettysburg, he prudently dispatched a courier to Lee with Pettigrew's information together with a request that the commanding General start Anderson from Fayetteville early the next morning. At the same time he notified Ewell of his intention to advance Wednesday morning and ascertain what was on his front.[43]

That night Hill's two leading divisions bivouacked on the slopes around Cashtown. Here many hungry veterans packed neighboring farmhouses, where for a half dollar in Confederate money they gorged their stomachs with fried ham, stewed chicken, biscuits, buckwheat cakes, preserves, coffee and cold, rich milk.[44]

On returning to camp the men discovered that an order had been issued to cook one day's rations, have it in their haversacks, and be ready to march at 5 o'clock the next morning.[45] Whatever suspicions this directive may have aroused were tempered by a

---

[40] Heth MS, 146-47.
[41] S.H.S.P., *4*, 40; O.R., *27*, Part 2, 317.
[42] S.H.S.P., *4*, 157; Heth MS, 145.
[43] O.R., *27*, Part 2, 607.
[44] Welch, 63.
[45] *Ibid.;* O.R., *27*, Part 2, 607.

rare issuance of whiskey[46] coupled with the return of Major "Willie" Pegram.[47] This "incomparable young man" who had been stricken with fever after Chancellorsville, rode ninety miles in an ambulance to join his artillerists when he learned of an impending engagement. Notified of his arrival, Hill said, "Yes, that is good news," and hastened to greet his youthful gunner.[48]

Shortly after daybreak on a cloudy, muggy July 1, Heth's division was roused by the order to fall in. Hastily his 7,000 sleepy-eyed men[49] rolled up their blankets and tents, shouldered their Enfield rifles and formed in line.[50] Pender's division followed at 8 o'clock.[51] Hill awoke feeling miserable,[52] and decided to remain at Cashtown until Anderson's division arrived. He had carefully instructed Heth to report immediately the presence of any appreciable enemy force and to avoid forcing an engagement.[53]

As Heth's column moved along the rolling Chambersburg Turnpike there were no signs of the enemy until mid-morning when blue videttes were sighted about three miles west of Gettysburg.[54] These mounted sentinels quickly withdrew after one fired a warning shot from his carbine,[55] whereupon Heth continued a couple of miles further to a range of hills overlooking Willoughby Run. Before ordering his troops to cross this stream and advance up the wooded hill toward Gettysburg, Heth placed several of Pegram's batteries in position on an eminence and ordered Pegram to shell the woods to see if he could get a response. When none was obtained, Heth deployed Archer's and Davis' brigades astride an unfinished railroad leading into Gettysburg, and directed them to reconnoiter and occupy the town.[56]

Heth's mile long line[57] moved forward rapidly and pushed in

[46] Caldwell, 94.
[47] S.H.S.P., *8*, 427.
[48] S.H.S.P., *14*, 6, 15-16.
[49] S.H.S.P., *4*, 158.
[50] Caldwell, 96.
[51] S.H.S.P., *8*, 515.
[52] Fremantle, 203.
[53] S.H.S.P., *4*, 126.
[54] O.R., *27*, Part 2, 317.
[55] *N. C. Regts., II*, 343.
[56] Heth MS, 146; O.R., *27*, Part 2, 317; S.H.S.P., *4*, 158.
[57] Welch, 64.

Buford's dismounted cavalry. But Archer and Davis had scarcely gained the opposite bank of Willoughby Run when they struck the stubborn Iron Brigade of General John Reynolds' First Corps.[58] This rugged mid-Western unit which had earned its cognomen from McClellan for its intrepid performance at South Mountain prior to the battle of Antietam,[59] defiantly wore tall, bell-crowned black hats which made the men conspicuous in line.[60] In the fast and furious engagement which ensued two of Davis' regiments were captured as was Archer with sixty to seventy of his men.[61] Both brigades retired with considerable losses.[62]

This surprisingly vigorous reception clearly demonstrated the presence of an enemy force far greater than the detachment of cavalry which Lee and Hill had anticipated.[63] Heth, knowing that Pender was coming up, formed his brigades into line in a wooded ravine to the right of the railroad[64] where the men nervously joked and officers offered words of encouragement.[65] Soon McIntosh's battery of Pender's division arrived and took position on the crest of a hill behind Heth's line.[66] Then for two hours the combined fire of Pegram's and McIntosh's guns kept the enemy at range's length.[67]

Meantime Hill at Cashtown was puzzled by the distant roar of artillery, and he was unable to enlighten Lee who rode up to inquire anxiously what it meant.[68] Without further delay Hill decided to ride to Gettysburg and learn first-hand the state of affairs. Lee followed shortly.[69]

Early in the afternoon the two commanders met again among Pegram's smoking guns where they learned what had transpired[70] during the morning. Hill was mystified by the Yankees' spirited

---

[58] O.R., *27*, Part 2, 317; Heth MS, 146.
[59] *N. C. Regts., II,* 348.
[60] *Ibid,* 351.
[61] O.R., *27*, Part 2, 638.
[62] *Ibid.,* 317, 638, 646, 649; S.H.S.P., *4,* 158.
[63] O.R., *27*, Part 2, 317, 637.
[64] S.H.S.P., *4,* 158.
[65] *N. C. Regts., II,* 350.
[66] O.R., *27*, Part 2, 607.
[67] S.H.S.P., *8,* 427.
[68] W. H. Taylor, *Four Years with General Lee,* 92.
[69] S.H.S.P., *4,* 126.
[70] Heth MS, 147.

resistance,[71] and he ordered Pender to form behind Heth's right to support the latter should the engagement be resumed.[72] Lee, however, was reluctant to renew the battle in the absence of information as to the strength of the enemy on his front.[73]

About 2:30 the decision was resolved by the arrival of Rodes' division of Ewell's corps which crashed out of the woods north of Gettysburg and fell upon the Federal flank. But again the bluecoats, freshly reinforced,[74] retained their poise and re-formed quickly to meet this new assault. Rodes' line, perpendicular to Heth's, became snarled in the heavy fighting, whereupon Heth rode to Lee and suggested he be permitted to join the attack in order to relieve some of the pressure on Rodes. But Lee replied, "No; I am not prepared to bring on a general engagement to-day— Longstreet is not up."[75]

Heth returned to his division where he soon discovered that the enemy was removing troops from his front and throwing them against Rodes. Again he pressed Lee for permission to attack, and this time he was told: "Wait awhile and I will send you word when to go in."[76] Shortly, Early's troops arrived on Rodes' left, and together they began pressing the bluecoats back toward the town. Sensing a rout, Lee told Hill to advance Heth.[77]

In what one onlooker described as a "really magnificent sight,"[78] Heth's brigades pressed forward irresistibly against Meredith's Iron Brigade. This time the yelling Southerners pushed back the stubborn Yankee farmers. Along one sector of the enemy's front fifty fallen bluecoats lay in a straight line as mute testimony to their stiff resistance.[79] In another field Hill saw a zealous bluecoat purposefully plant a color round which his regiment fought obstinately. When it was finally obliged to retire, the color-bearer left last, turning around at intervals to shake his fist at the advancing

---

[71] Fremantle, 203-04.
[72] O.R., *27*, Part 2, 638.
[73] S.H.S.P., *5*, 41; S.H.S.P., *8*, 516.
[74] O.R., *27*, Part 2, 317.
[75] S.H.S.P., *4*, 158.
[76] Heth MS, 147.
[77] O.R., *27*, Part 2, 317.
[78] Welch, 64.
[79] Dunaway, 84.

column. Hill admired such spirit, even in the enemy, and he expressed regret when this gallant Yankee fell.[80]

After overwhelming the enemy's skirmishers, Heth's men broke the first line of battle and proceeded to assail the second. In the full tide of this successful sweep Heth was rendered unconscious by a minie ball which spent its lethal force in passing through the improvised padding in his hat.[81] As Pettigrew took over Heth's command, Hill ordered Pender to relieve Heth's weary line,[82] which had lost 2,700 men in 25 minutes.[83]

It was about 4 o'clock when the Light Division began its advance.[84] Hill held Thomas' brigade in reserve to the left of the Turnpike,[85] while Scales, Perrin, and Lane unleashed their fury on the enemy who had taken position behind temporary breastworks on a ridge less than half a mile west of the town.[86] Lane's brigade was detained by a force of dismounted enemy cavalry,[87] but Scales and Perrin maintained their alignment as they ascended the hill held by the bluecoats. Reserving their fire, these two brigades pressed forward in the face of a storm of musketry and grape. By the time Scales had advanced to within seventy-five yards of the enemy's fortifications, every field officer in the brigade except one was either killed or wounded. Although suffering from a leg wound, Scales assisted Pender in rallying the men and then joined Perrin in the pursuit.[88] Perrin's South Carolinians readily dislodged the enemy on their front, and raced ahead of adjoining brigades to drive the foe from successive positions through the town to Cemetery Hill.[89]

Hill, who with Lee had been watching the action from the west side of Willoughby Run, now rode slowly with his staff over

---

[80] Fremantle, 204.
[81] Heth MS, 147.
[82] S.H.S.P., *8*, 516.
[83] S.H.S.P., *4*, 158.
[84] S.H.S.P., *8*, 516.
[85] O.R., *27*, Part 2, 607.
[86] Colonel A. Perrin of the Fourteenth South Carolina Volunteers commanded McGowan's brigade while its regular brigadier recuperated from a leg wound received at Chancellorsville. Welch, 51-52; S.H.S.P., *8*, 515.
[87] *Ibid.*, 516; S.H.S.P., *5*, 41-42.
[88] S.H.S.P., *8*, 517-18.
[89] *Ibid.*, 517.

the bitterly won ground to the Seminary on the outskirts of the town.[90] He lamented the absence of cavalry with which to press the pursuit and gain information concerning the enemy's numbers and dispositions. Therefore, "under the impression that the enemy were entirely routed—my own two divisions, exhausted by some six hours hard fighting—prudence led me to be content with what had been gained, and not push forward troops exhausted and necessarily disordered, probably to encounter fresh troops of the enemy. These two divisions bivouacked in the positions won, and Anderson, who had just come up, was also bivouacked some two miles in rear of the battle-ground."[91] While Hill thus concluded his action for the day, Ewell nearby pondered instructions from Lee to carry Cemetery Hill, "if he found it practicable."[92]

Although Powell Hill regarded the first day's engagement as "a brilliant victory",[93] there were those who did not share his estimate. In the protracted and unseemly scuffle to affix responsibility for the army's overall failure at Gettysburg, Hill shared the bitter criticism heaped upon Stuart, Ewell, Longstreet, and Lee. Hill's critics accused him of recklessly precipitating a battle which Lee desired to avoid and then of failing to press a routed enemy.

Within the Third Corps, Hill's conduct inevitably was compared with what Old Jack probably would have done in the same circumstances. Heth voiced the universal speculation as to "whether, if Stonewall Jackson had been in command of Hill's corps on the first day—July 1st—a different result would have been obtained."[94] A despondent South Carolina surgeon in McGowan's brigade frankly lamented Hill's failure to employ Anderson's fresh reserve division against the enemy on Cemetery Hill. "If 'Old Stonewall' had been alive and there," he wrote his wife, "it no doubt would have been done. Hill was a good division commander, but he is not a superior corps commander. He lacks the mind and sagacity of Jackson."[95]

---

[90] C.V., *21*, 433.
[91] O.R., *27*, Part 2, 607.
[92] *Ibid.*, 317.
[93] O.R., *51*, Part 2, 811.
[94] S.H.S.P., *4*, 155.
[95] Welch, 67.

Colonel John S. Mosby in his memoirs minimized the importance of Stuart's absence, and contended that all the Army had to do was live off the country and await the enemy at Cashtown. "General Lee," he wrote, "was surprised by A. P. Hill—not by the enemy."[96] Wise indicted both Stuart and Hill, claiming that the latter's "unquenchable thirst for battle" had led him to take "control of the situation out of the hands of the commander-in-chief."[97]

More recently, Eckenrode and Conrad in their biography of Longstreet state: "of all the three corps commanders Hill was probably the most blameworthy. It was his precipitancy and incaution that committed the Confederates to battle under such disadvantageous circumstances. He should have held off from advancing on Gettysburg until Lee came up."[98]

However, the following review of events as they unfolded at the time, shows clearly that the usually impulsive and impatient Powell Hill, in this instance displayed a full appreciation of his responsibilities as commander of a third of Lee's army:

1. When Lee learned that the enemy had crossed the Potomac and was heading for South Mountains, he ordered the Army to concentrate east of the mountains to protect the line of communication with Virginia. Ewell was directed "to join the army at Cashtown or Gettysburg as circumstances might require." Lee had no predisposition against an advance to Gettysburg, as both he and Hill believed that Meade was still encamped in Maryland.

2. Upon learning that Pettigrew had ascertained the presence of Federals in Gettysburg, Hill notified Lee and Ewell, adding that he intended to advance the following day. Although he was convinced that the force on his front was only a detachment of cavalry, he instructed Heth to avoid bringing on a general engagement. Significantly, he did not accompany the leading division the morning of July 1, which, although ill, he most certainly would have

---

[96] J. S. Mosby, *The Memoirs of Colonel John S. Mosby*, 246, 251.
[97] Wise, *II*, 615.
[98] H. J. Eckenrode and B. Conrad, *James Longstreet, Lee's War Horse*, 211.

    done had he even remotely considered a major engagement in the offing.

3. Heth advanced as cautiously as circumstances, including the absence of cavalry, permitted; and after the initial clash he formed his lines and waited. Lee did not regard this action as one which committed the entire army to battle, for when Heth asked permission to renew the attack, he replied, "No, I am not prepared to bring on a general engagement today—Longstreet is not up." And when the order was finally given for Heth to attack, it was done at Lee's—not Hill's—instance.

Lee with his customary perspective and eminent fairness, summarized the situation in his report as follows:

> It had not been intended to deliver a general battle so far from our base unless attacked, but coming unexpectedly upon the whole Federal army, to withdraw through the mountains with our extensive trains would have been difficult and dangerous. At the same time we were unable to await an attack, as the country was unfavorable for collecting supplies in the presence of an enemy, who could restrain our foraging parties with local and other troops. A battle therefore had become, in a measure, unavoidable, and the success already gained gave hope of a favorable issue.[99]

At the close of the first day's engagement Lee informed his corps commanders that he intended to resume the offensive the next day. Details of the attack were formulated at a conference held on Seminary Ridge shortly after daybreak on Thursday. Lee, seated on a log and holding a map on his knee, was flanked on one side by Hill and on the other by Longstreet, who meditatively whittled a stick.[100] The commanding General directed "Old Pete" to bring up the divisions of Hood and McLaws and place them obliquely to the right of Hill's men on Seminary Ridge. When these troops were in position Longstreet was to sweep up the Emmitsburg road and envelop the enemy's left flank. When the action reached Hill's sector Anderson's division was to attack frontally. Meanwhile, both Ewell and Hill were to demonstrate

---

[99] O.R., *27*, Part 2, 318. E. P. Alexander, Longstreet's distinguished artillerist, contended that "Even after the second day's battle . . . it was possible to have withdrawn from the offensive and taken the defensive . . ." S.H.S.P., *4*, 100.

[100] Fremantle, 205-06.

against the Federal center and right to prevent Meade from transferring reinforcements to resist Longstreet's assault.[101]

Longstreet energetically opposed this offensive tactic but Lee
held fast. As the commanding General folded his map Hill left to
dispose his troops which occupied a line roughly parallel to the
Federal position on Cemetery Ridge. Pender's division on the left
made a sharp angle with Ewell's line which described a semicircle
around the Union right. On Pender's right, Hill brought forward
Anderson's division to relieve Heth's battered troops which were
placed in reserve.[102] Here the bandage-swathed veterans were
cheered by the sprightly tunes of Captain Mickey's blaring band.[103]
Hill also directed that his artillery comprising 55 guns, be placed
in eligible positions along the line from which to engage the enemy
at long range.[104]

Hill completed his arrangements with dispatch, but Longstreet,
sulky and dilatory, was slow in getting his divisions into position.
While Lee prodded Longstreet, Hill must have wondered whether
another well-conceived plan for successive assaults was to be frustrated by tardiness born of obstinacy. In mid-afternoon he was.
joined by Lee beneath a tree which shaded them from the July
sun.[105] From this observation post the nervous commanders[106] enjoyed a full view of the field from Gettysburg on the left to Big
Round Top on the right.

About 4 P.M. the suspenseful silence was broken by "Old Pete's"
batteries. Soon afterward Hood's division on the extreme right
moved to the attack. McLaws joined in the assault somewhat
later whereupon both divisions became hotly engaged as they advanced against stubborn resistance.

As the action reached Anderson's right shortly after 6 P.M.
the brigades of Wilcox, Perry, Wright, and Posey advanced
successively in echelon from right to left in the face of a cruel
fire of grape, canister, and musketry.[107] Posey's advance faltered,

---

[101] S.H.S.P., *2*, 41-42; O.R., *27*, Part 2, 318, 608.
[102] S.H.S.P., *2*, 224; O.R., *27*, Part 2, 608.
[103] *N. C. Regts., II*, 362.
[104] Alexander, 409; S.H.S.P., *8*, 427-28.
[105] Fremantle, 208.
[106] Heth MS, 148.
[107] Alexander, 401.

but the three right brigades quickly drove the enemy from the Emmitsburg Road to the cover of a ravine and a line of stone fences in his rear. Anderson's men pursued them and after a severe struggle dislodged the bluecoats from their position and captured a number of batteries.[108]

Anderson's uneven line now swept forward toward the strong Federal position on the ridge. Wilcox reached its foot and Wright gained the crest itself before coordination was lost. But Perry withdrew and thereby exposed Wilcox's left and Wright's right. This forced Wilcox to retire under heavy enemy pressure as did Wright upon whom the enemy converged from all directions. Shortly after dark the disheartened and depleted brigades had fallen back to the positions they had occupied before the attack was launched.[109]

Who was responsible for the failure of this charge, which if properly supported most probably would have obviated its costly and unsuccessful repetition the following day? Immediate responsibility rested on R. H. Anderson, who, as divisional commander of the troops engaged, displayed an inauspicious lack of diligence in his initial action with the Third Corps. Wilcox, writing to Lee after the war, claimed, "I am quite certain that Gen'l A. (Anderson) never saw a foot of the ground on which his three brigades fought on the 2nd of July . . . I may be wrong Gen'l A, but I always believed that he was too indifferent to his duties at Gettysburg."[110]

Wilcox's indictment was strongly supported by the faulty disposition and coordination of Anderson's troops. Each brigade had formed in a single line without support, and each advanced with its left flank in the air with intervals of space and time separating each attack.[111] Although Hill intended Anderson to employ his entire division,[112] Mahone's brigade had not been thrown in to

---

108 S.H.S.P., *2*, 42.
109 S.H.S.P., *8*, 317-18. Wilcox's brigade of 1,600 sustained 577 casualties; Perry lost 300 of his 700 who started; and Wright's brigade suffered a loss of 684 out of 1,800. Alexander, 400-02; S.H.S.P., *8*, 318; S.H.S.P., *4*, 116.
110 Lee MSS, Addendum to Wilcox's report of the Battle of Gettysburg.
111 Alexander, 400.
112 S.H.S.P., *8*, 315.

support the assault at the critical juncture because of a confusion in Anderson's orders.[113]

Hill also was culpable to a lesser degree. Before the attack Lee had enjoined him to develop the assault into a major action should the opportunity arise. The successful penetration of the Federal front by Wilcox and Wright certainly offered just such an advantage, but Hill failed to support it by throwing in Heth's reserve division or by advancing Pender. At this critical juncture he was observing the action with Lee, who apparently also felt it unnecessary or inadvisable to commit more troops with nightfall approaching.

In addition to Anderson's repulse, Hill suffered his greatest individual loss as corps commander in the mortal wounding of William Dorsey Pender. During Anderson's attack Pender rode to the extreme right of his line to ready his division for an advance. While thus engaged near sunset he was severely wounded in the leg by a fragment from a bursting artillery shell.[114] Although the resolute and exacting little North Carolinian had been wounded in almost every engagement he had always shrugged off the effects and insisted on retaining command of his troops. However, this time his wound was so serious that he reluctantly relinquished command of the Light Division to Brigadier General Jim Lane and allowed himself to be taken to the rear. The next day as he was unable to mount his horse,[115] plans were made to move him by ambulance to Staunton, Virginia. There his infected leg was amputated, but he failed to rally.[116]

Pender's loss was irreparable. Hill regarded him as the best officer of his grade he had ever known, and in his official report, he wrote: "On this day, also, the Confederacy lost the invaluable services of Maj. Gen. W. D. Pender, wounded by a shell and since dead. No man fell during this bloody battle of Gettysburg

---

[113] Lee MSS, Addendum to Wilcox's report on the Battle of Gettysburg.

[114] Lee probably was referring to this instance, rather than to Pickett's charge the following day (as reported by Heth in 1877), when he said: "I shall ever believe if General Pender had remained on his horse half an hour longer we would have carried the enemy's position." S.H.S.P., *4*, 154; S.H.S.P., *5*, 38; S.H.S.P., *8*, 519.

[115] S.H.S.P., *5*, 38.

[116] Welch, 72; *N. C. Regts., IV*, 180.

more regretted than he, nor around whose youthful brow were clustered brighter rays of glory."[117] Hill would keenly miss his unassuming lieutenant for whom he had a fraternal affection, and who like himself was renowned for zeal, skill, and gallantry.[118] Lee considered Pender the most promising young officer in the army,[119] an estimate universally endorsed by veterans in the Light Division, one of whom went so far as to opine that "Pender was an officer evidently superior even to Hill."[120]

Despite discouraging losses during the second day's engagement, Lee was confident "that with proper concert of action and with increased support that the positions gained on the right would enable the artillery to render the assaulting column, we should ultimately succeed."[121] Accordingly, he ordered Longstreet to resume the attack on Friday morning with his entire First Corps, now reinforced by the arrival of Pickett's fresh division from Chambersburg.[122]

However, "Old Pete" still was unreconciled to Lee's plan for an offensive. With vigor bordering on insubordination he endeavored to persuade his chief to interpose the army between the Federal army and Washington, thereby maneuvering Meade into attacking him. Failing in this, Longstreet then insisted that his weakened divisions employed the previous day would be taken in reverse if they attempted to storm the strongly defended ridge.[123] Undeterred by his subordinate's objections, Lee decided to make the attack with Pickett's division augmented by Heth's and half of Pender's divisions. This combination constituted a striking force of about 15,000 which Longstreet could hurl across the open fields to pierce the Federal center about a mile distant on Cemetery Ridge.[124]

Later in the morning Lee, Longstreet, and Hill discussed details of the projected assault while seated on the trunk of a fallen tree

---

117 O.R., *27*, Part 2, 608.
118 S.H.S.P., *8*, 519.
119 Pender MSS, Letter of Gen. G. C. Wharton, MS Sept. 5, 1893.
120 Welch, 74.
121 S.H.S.P., *8*, 519.
122 O.R., *27*, Part 2, 320.
123 *Ibid.*
124 S.H.S.P., *8*, 520; *R. E. Lee, III*, 117.

in front of Heth's division.[125] In sharp contrast to his sullen col-
league, Powell Hill enthusiastically endorsed Lee's offensive plan
and "begged General Lee to let me take in my whole Army
Corps."[126] Although Lee admired and appreciated such spirit he
had to refuse, stating: "What remains of your corps will be my
only reserve, and it will be needed if General Longstreet's attack
should fail."[127] On the other hand, if the attack developed according
to plan, Hill was to place Anderson's division at "Old Pete's"
disposal.[128]

With the die cast, Hill directed Heth's 4,300 bruised effectives[129]
under inexperienced brigadiers, together with Lane's and Scales'
brigades of Pender's division to report to Longstreet. As the six
brigades filed off to take their positions, Major General Isaac
Trimble, who had arrived at Gettysburg without a command, reported to Hill that Lee had assigned him command of Pender's
two brigades which were to be used in the assault.[130] Hill immediately told him to relieve Lane who was then executing Longstreet's order to form these brigades to the rear and right of Heth's
division which was still under the temporary command of Pettigrew. This deployment resulted in the second line being shorter
than the first leaving Pettigrew's left unsupported. It was not in
accordance with Lee's intention that Pender's brigades should form
en echelon on Pettigrew's left. If Hill spotted this faulty disposition
of his troops he failed to correct it or report the situation to
Longstreet on whose shoulders he doubtless felt the responsibility
now lay.

To the right of Pettigrew and Trimble, George Pickett confidently disposed his three brigades in two lines behind which
Wilcox's brigade of Anderson's division formed a flank guard.[131]
The infantry were ordered to remain out of sight until the artillery
silenced the enemy's batteries. Then the two wings of the assaulting

---

[125] S.H.S.P., *7*, 92.
[126] S.H.S.P., *41*, 40.
[127] S.H.S.P., *4*, 140.
[128] *Ibid.*, 84; O.R. *27*, Part 2, 608.
[129] S.H.S.P., *4*, 159.
[130] O.R., *27*, Part 2, 608.
[131] S.H.S.P., *4*, 116.

force were to charge along converging lines upon a little clump of trees on Cemetery Ridge.[132]

While these preparations were in progress violent cannonading broke out along the front of the Third Corps. There a swarm of bluecoats, exasperated by a telling fire from Hill's sharpshooters ensconced in a house and barn between the lines, resolutely advanced to eliminate this annoyance. Thereupon Hill ordered his artillerists to cover the riflemen. Federal batteries took up the challenge, and for half an hour Hill's guns expended precious ammunition in an aimless duel.[133]

After the din of Hill's guns subsided, the troops massing for the attack reclined on the ground in the woods behind Longstreet's batteries. As they waited impatiently some grumbled, "If we had Jackson, we would move and do something."[134] Finally at 1 o'clock Longstreet's guns began a furious bombardment of the Federal position. Two hours later the waiting troops formed and advanced "with the deliberation and accuracy of men on drill."[135]

Soon the Federal batteries opened sharply upon the obliquely advancing line. Pettigrew's horse was shot under him and he was wounded in the left hand by grape shot.[136] Trimble received a wound in the leg,[137] but both commanders remained with their men who closed ranks and "in imposing order that . . . drew admiration of its wonderful army,"[138] gained the plank fences along the Emmitsburg Road.[139] As the thinned lines swept up the hill Davis' and Brockenbrough's brigades (the latter temporarily commanded by Colonel Mayo) on the extreme left of the front line fell behind. Unsupported, they turned and fled without orders under the withering fire of Federal batteries.[140]

Undeterred by the loss of these two brigades, the remaining

---

[132] O.R., *27*, Part 2, 447-48, 504-05.

[133] Porter Alexander estimated that Hill's batteries spent about one-third of their available rounds, excluding the reserve which was not readily accessible. This fight broke out about 11 A.M. S.H.S.P., *4*, 103.

[134] *N. C. Regts., IV*, 179.

[135] S.H.S.P., *5*, 44. Description by Maj. Gen. I. R. Trimble.

[136] *N. C. Regts., II*, 366.

[137] S.H.S.P., *8*, 321.

[138] S.H.S.P., *41*, 46.

[139] S.H.S.P., *32*, 191.

[140] Dunaway, 91.

troops converged on the clump of trees where they too were decimated by a murderous fire in front and flank. Trimble's handful of North Carolinians overran Pettigrew's line and with a fierce yell hurdled the last stone fence only to fall back when no support was forthcoming.[141] Fifty minutes after the charge had started, a sullen, disorganized procession threaded its way back to Seminary Ridge. Some of the men grumbled, "If Old Jack had been here it wouldn't have been like this."[142] But Trimble told Hill, "If hell can't be taken by the troops I had the honor to command to-day it can't be done at all."[143]

Whether the outcome of Pickett's charge, as history was to label this action, would have been different under the direction of a more enthusiastic commander than Longstreet is questionable in view of Meade's formidable strength and position. Nevertheless, Lee's choice of Longstreet to direct the assault constitutes one of the baffling aspects of this fiasco. Obdurate "Old Pete," always a proponent of defensive tactics, himself felt that Lee "should have put an officer in charge who had more confidence in his plan."[144]

Lee may have hesitated for reasons of military courtesy to change commanders with plans when he decided to substitute half of Hill's corps for the divisions of Hood and McLaws. Dr. D. S. Freeman believed that Lee's choice was dictated by the fact that "with Jackson dead (Lee) had no other subordinate of the same experience or military grasp as Longstreet."[145] However, "Old Pete" vitiated these attributes at Gettysburg by his stubborn refusal to employ them in the execution of his chief's plan.

Powell Hill, with all of his acknowledged shortcomings, would seem in retrospect to have been the logical choice for this task. Two-thirds of the troops engaged on July 3 were his; the action occurred on his front; and he had complete confidence in Lee's plan. Furthermore, he had shown the commanding General at Gaines' Mill and Sharpsburg that he was entirely capable of

---

[141] S.H.S.P., *5*, 43-44.
[142] Dunaway, 91.
[143] *N. C. Regts., IV*, 180.
[144] Longstreet, 388.
[145] *Lee's Lieutenants, III*, 146.

directing a major offensive operation. Perhaps Lee anticipated such ex post facto judgements as this when he told General Heth after Gettysburg: "I notice, however, my mistakes are never told me until it is too late."[146]

---

[146] S.H.S.P., *4*, 160.

CHAPTER XVI

"I Made The Attack Too Hastily"

(Bristoe Station)

BY THE flickering light of a lone candle in Hill's tent, Lee and Hill planned the army's retreat from Gettysburg. After studying a map spread between their camp-stools the two commanders agreed that unless Meade assumed the offensive, the Third Corps, which had suffered most heavily,[1] should lead the retreat after dark on Saturday, July 4. As the Federals showed no signs of stirring the next day, Lane's brigade led the long procession through a driving rain along the short route to Hagerstown via Fairfield and Waynesboro.[2] Much of the way Lee and Hill rode together at the head of the column.[3]

Unfortunately this road was not macadamized and the wagons and artillery carved deep ruts in the muddy surface rendering it almost impassable.[4] Veterans plodding through the dense mud acquired a coat of mire which completely obscured the color of their clothing.[5] Added to these woes was the disheartening news that the enemy had partially destroyed the pontoon bridge at Falling Waters over which Hill had crossed into Maryland and over which the army now intended to retreat.[6] As the Potomac was swollen to swimming depth[7] which precluded fording, Hill's Corps erected breastworks at Hagerstown where the troops engaged in skirmishing and artillery duels with the enemy.[8]

By Monday, July 13 the waters had subsided sufficiently for Hill to pull his famished men out of the trenches and start them

---

[1] Allan listed Lee's losses at Gettysburg as follows: Longstreet's Corps—7,659; Ewell's Corps—6,087; and Hill's Corps—8,982. S.H.S.P., *4, 34.
[2] O.R., *27*, Part 2, 322, 608; Welch, 69; S.H.S.P., *2, 46.
[3] *N. C. Regts., II,* 662.
[4] Welch, 69.
[5] *N. C. Regts., II,* 587.
[6] S.H.S.P., *2, 46.
[7] Caldwell, 105.
[8] *N. C. Regts., II,* 478, 587; *Ibid., IV,* 183; S.H.S.P., *5, 45.

toward the repaired bridge at Falling Waters[9] where Lee anxiously awaited the withdrawal of his army in the face of Meade's threatening advance. While Ewell's men shouldered the receding waters farther upstream at Williamsport, Longstreet's Corps and the division of R. H. Anderson crossed the pontoons at Falling Waters.[10] Heth's and Pender's divisions at the rear of the infantry column trudged all night through ankle-deep mud to reach the heights bordering the Potomac early Tuesday morning.[11]

Here Hill halted the two divisions and ordered Heth to form in line of battle facing northward "to let the wagons and artillery get over the river."[12] No skirmishers were posted as friendly cavalry presumably screened the retiring column from the enemy, and after stacking their arms the exhausted footsoldiers dropped off to sleep on the wet ground.[13]

Later in the morning Hill directed Heth to move both divisions across the river. Pender's division had just started to cross when a squadron of Federal cavalry suddenly debouched from the woods into an open field about half a mile from Heth's line.[14] This group of about forty-five horsemen, which Heth and his staff mistook for a unit of Confederate cavalry passed earlier in the morning, nonchalantly advanced to within 175 yards before halting. Some of Heth's men became nervously suspicious of the blue-coated cavalry, but Heth cautioned them, "No, don't fire."[15] Then at the command, "Draw sabers, charge!" the mounted force quickly overran Heth's epaulements crying "Surrender you damn rebels, surrender." An enemy sergeant interposed between Heth and Pettigrew, and in the ensuing melee Pettigrew was unhorsed. As he started to rise the sergeant shot him in the groin.[16]

As the rudely awakened defenders scrambled for their muskets, Heth rode rapidly along the line excitedly exhorting his troops

---

[9] O.R., *27*, Part 2, 609, 639; S.H.S.P., *2*, 225; Caldwell, 106; *N. C. Regts., II*, 587.
[10] S.H.S.P., *2*, 46, 225.
[11] Welch, 70; O.R., *27*, Part 2, 639.
[12] *N. C. Regts., II*, 375, 662; S.H.S.P., *2*, 47; Dunaway, 97.
[13] Dunaway, 97.
[14] *N. C. Regts., II*, 375
[15] *Ibid., IV*, 560.
[16] Heth MS, 150; Dunaway, 98.

to "Keep cool, men, keep cool!"[17] A color-bearer in Brockenbrough's brigade exclaimed, "Come on boys; it's nothing but cavalry," and ran forward with his bullet-ridden flag. Others followed and within five minutes the entire Federal squad of Illinois cavalrymen was killed, wounded or captured.[18] Only two Confederates were killed in this brief scuffle, but as Hill lamented, "Unfortunately for the service, one of these was the gallant and accomplished Pettigrew,"[19] beloved by his men as "the Sir Philip Sidney of the South."[20]

Soon another enemy force appeared and demonstrated vigorously, whereupon Hill ordered Heth to retire his troops across the river. This was accomplished with the loss of about 500 men and two pieces of artillery which had to be abandoned.[21] After the last soldier had crossed, the bridge was swung loose from the Virginia shore.[22]

Safe on Virginia soil, the Third Corps slowly threaded a circuitous route to Culpeper Court House and thence to Orange Court House where Hill proceeded to rehabilitate his shattered and disheartened command.[23] Shortly after establishing headquarters at Orange Court House, he called on Cadmus Wilcox, his old friend and classmate to inform him of his probable promotion to Major General to succeed Pender as commander of the Light Division. Wilcox, in his short round jacket and battered straw hat,[24] resignedly dissented. When Hill asked why, he answered that there was no particular reason other than his past disappointments at being passed over following his performance at Williamsburg, Gaines' Mill, and Salem Church. Consequently, he was now one of the oldest brigadiers in the service, his commission at that rank antedating Hill's.[25] However, he said he had ceased to dwell upon his situation as he hoped to be relieved soon from the army.

---

17 Dunaway, 98.
18 *Ibid.;* Heth MS, 150.
19 O.R., *27*, Part 2, 609.
20 *N. C. Regts., II,* 568.
21 O.R., *27*, Part 2, 609.
22 O.R., *27*, Part 2, 310; *N. C. Regts., II,* 478.
23 Caldwell, 109.
24 Fremantle, 215.
25 Cullum, No. 1325.

Hill expressed regret at this possibility and said he hoped Wilcox would remain in the service.[26] A week after this interview Wilcox received his promotion as Hill had predicted, and he stayed with his new command until Appomattox.[27]

Despite numerous desertions which reached nine one day in Wilcox's division,[28] Hill managed to restore the morale of his troops. With the cooperation of Major J. G. Field, his Chief Commissary, the Third Corps was better supplied than any in the army.[29] Lean bodies fattened on plentiful rations of beef, bacon, flour, sugar, potatoes, and vegetables.[30] Provision for care of the sick and wounded improved so markedly that hospitalized patients no longer were considered hopeless.[31] One veteran later recalled the cheerful spirit in Hill's Corps during this period when "our elastic spirits revived from the depression of July, and satisfaction with the present and confidence of the future was almost unanimously expressed."[32]

Morale in the Third Corps was further strengthened by a widespread surge of religious fervor. The hitherto perfunctory attitude of battle-jaded veterans toward religious observances was now supplanted by genuine interest and concern in spiritual matters. Even the dullest preachers drew large, attentive congregations in crude chapels built by the men.[33] Services were held almost every day[34] followed at night by hymn singing and prayer services. Professions of faith increased as did formal church membership, "and many more evinced from this time a seriousness in beautiful contrast with former immorality."[35]

Hill welcomed this spiritual revival as a force which elevated the moral tone of his command by diminishing gambling, intoxication, and carousing—vices which he felt impaired a soldier's verve and

---

[26] Wilcox MSS, no date.
[27] M. J. Wright, *General Officers of the Confederate Army, Officers of the Executive Departments of the Confederate States,* 35.
[28] Welch, 78-79; Caldwell, 112.
[29] "Sketches of Southern Generals," Part IV.
[30] Welch, 73-75; Caldwell, 111.
[31] Welch, 74-75.
[32] Caldwell, 112.
[33] C.M.H., *III,* 429.
[34] Welch, 78.
[35] Caldwell, 112-13.

efficiency. In so far as Hill personally was concerned, there is no evidence that he was affected by this movement. The few extant references to his religious life portray an undemonstrative, highly principled Episcopalian who confined the outward observances of his faith to Sunday worship. His wife averred that before the war he never missed a service, and during the conflict he attended church whenever possible.[36]

In contrast to Jackson and Lee, Hill never invoked or acknowledged divine aid in battle. On the other hand, an incident at Mine Run in the fall of 1863 illustrates his sensitivity to the spiritual appeal. While riding with Lee to the shell-raked front, Hill came upon a group of ragged soldiers holding a prayer meeting at the end of the Light Division. Both commanders dismounted, removed their hats, and stood quietly until the last prayer was finished. Those who observed Hill at this scene noted that he was visibly touched.[37]

Two additional sidelights on Hill's attitude toward religion have been preserved by Rev. J. Wm. Jones who served as chaplain under Hill in the Thirteenth Virginia and later became Chaplain of the Army of Northern Virginia. In his book *Christ in Camp* Jones significantly omitted any reference to Powell Hill in the chapter on "Influence of Christian Officers," although he had the highest personal regard and affection for Hill. Jones also recorded a revealing episode which occurred shortly before the evacuation of Petersburg. While distributing tracts and religious newsletters to a throng of veterans, Jones noticed the approach of a distinguished cavalcade that included Lee, Gordon, and Powell Hill. As the officers drew rein Gordon eagerly inquired about Jones' work, and Lee said he had several prayer books for the chaplain to distribute. As for Powell Hill, Jones stated: "My old colonel,

---

[36] The Times-Dispatch, Richmond, June 11, 1905—An interview with the General's wife. Before the Maryland campaign, Captain C. M. Blackford described a service he attended at Green Springs where "I found a very distinguished party gathered at the church. General Jackson was there, and Generals Winder, Pender, and A. P. Hill . . . all like myself, dressed in their best." *Letters from Lee's Army,* compiled by S. L. Blackford, letter dated August 4, 1862. Dr. Welch, a surgeon in Hill's Corps, reported seeing Hill in attendance at an Episcopal church in Petersburg a few weeks before the latter's death. Welch, 124.

[37] Robertson, Part IV, 8, Nov. 4, 1934.

now Lieutenant General A. P. Hill, and one of the most accomplished soldiers, as well as one of the most high-toned gentlemen whom the war produced, pleasantly asked of me, as he gave me a hearty greeting, 'John' (As he always familiarly called me), 'don't you think the boys would prefer hard-tack to tracts just now?' 'I have no doubt that many of them would,' I replied, 'but they crowd around and take the tracts as eagerly as they surround the commissary when he has anything to issue, and besides other advantages, the tracts certainly help them to bear the lack of hard-tack'. 'I have no doubt of it', he said, 'and I am glad you are able to supply the tracts more abundantly than we can the rations'."[38]

By fall "the tone of the whole command was all that could be desired,"[39] whereupon Hill decided to stage a grand review for the commanding General. Word of the forthcoming pageant spread quickly, and on a balmy Friday early in September[40] the local populace and soldiers from other commands gathered on the plain at Orange Court House to watch Marse Robert review the Third Corps.

Hill's twenty-thousand veterans—their bright muskets glittering in the sun as their tattered but proud banners fluttered in the breeze—were drawn up by divisions in a long column. At the appointed time Hill mounted Prince, his favorite jet black steed, and rode up to Lee who as usual was astride Traveller. After exchanging greetings the two generals and their staffs galloped around each division, Anderson, Heth, and Wilcox joining the cavalcade as it reached their respective commands. After traveling the nine mile route at a rapid gait, Lee and Hill drew rein at the reviewing stand where they gazed admiringly as the troops broke by companies and paraded before them in review.[41]

None witnessing or participating in this imposing spectacle doubted that the Army of Northern Virginia, even stripped of Longstreet's Corps recently sent West to reinforce Bragg, could

---

[38] W. J. Jones, *Christ in Camp*, 52-53.
[39] Caldwell, 113.
[40] O.R., *51*, Part 1, 1088. This review was held Sept. 11, 1863.
[41] Captain R. E. Lee, *Recollections and Letters of Robert E. Lee*, (cited hereafter as *Recollections and Letters of Robert E. Lee*) 106-07.

whip the Army of the Potomac which Meade was concentrating on a front extending from Culpeper to the Rapidan.[42] When Lee learned later in the month that the Federal commander also was detaching troops to the West,[43] he decided to prevent the transfer of additional enemy reinforcements by clearing Virginia of the Army of the Potomac.

On Friday, October 9, Ewell and Hill broke camp, crossed the Rapidan, and started along the circuitous route to the enemy's left in accordance with Lee's plan to turn Meade's strong position at Culpeper and strike him as he retreated. However, the element of surprise was lost when a Federal signal station on Pony Mountain read Confederate signal flags communicating intelligence that a "formidable movement" was afoot.[44] When Meade retreated along the Orange and Alexandria Railroad, Lee sent his two corps northward on a wide sweep in the hope of intercepting the Federal army before it reached the Washington defenses.

On Tuesday evening, October 13, Hill's column reached Warrenton where it rejoined Ewell's corps which had traversed a more direct route.[45] That night the veterans were in high spirits as they partook of white cabbage and "anticipated a pleasant affair if we should succeed in catching him (Meade)."[46]

In accordance with Lee's orders, Hill roused his troops before sunrise on Wednesday and started them moving along the Warrenton and Alexandria turnpike. At Broad Run Church he learned from various reports and the rumbling of distant wagons that the enemy were moving northward along a parallel road. Hill directed Anderson to take the leading division and attempt to strike the retreating column. When Anderson soon ascertained that the enemy force consisting of cavalry had been driven back by Fitz Lee, he turned his division toward Greenwich which Hill had reached about 10 A.M.[47]

Here Heth's men captured a number of stragglers from a

---

[42] O.R., *29*, Part I, 410; *Ibid.*, Part 2, 706.
[43] O.R., *29*, Part 2, 754.
[44] B. and L., *IV*, 83.
[45] O.R., *29*, Part 1, 410.
[46] Caldwell, 114.
[47] O.R., *29*, Part 1, 426; *N. C. Regts., II*, 440.

Federal force which had encamped nearby the previous night and hastily departed only two hours before Hill's arrival.[48] With the strong scent of the enemy dilating his battle-hungry nostrils, Hill prepared to move in for the kill. While Heth's and Wilcox's divisions, flanked on the right by Ewell's troops, advanced in the direction of Bristoe Station, Hill passed his skirmish line and galloped ahead to stalk the enemy and plan his destruction.

Picking his way between discarded guns, knapsacks, and blankets which had been strewn along the road by fleeing Federals,[49] Prince bore his rider to the hills overlooking Bristoe Station, Broad Run, and the plain to the north. Drawing rein, Hill espied swarms of bluecoats—those in the foreground were catching their breath while their comrades and wagons on the far side of the run appeared to be scurrying toward Manassas.[50] Hill, flushed with excitement at the prospect of a smashing victory, attributed the enemy's precipitate retreat to the approach of the Third Corps.[51]

"Determined that no time must be lost,"[52] Hill immediately notified Heth to hurry. Cooke's brigade, at the head of Heth's column, responded on the double—desirous of proving itself in its first battle under Powell Hill. Sensing a fight which might soil their newly issued gray coats and blue pants, the North Carolinians had just changed into their old clothes.[53]

On reaching a crest of wooded hill, Heth formed his line of battle perpendicular to the road and parallel to Broad Run.[54] As Cooke's troops filed to the right and Kirkland's and Walker's (formerly Brockenbrough's) brigades took position on the left, Hill glued his eyes on the retreating Yankees. Impatient lest his quarry escape before he could strike a blow, he ordered Heth to push forward with the troops already in line. While Heth's advance units started toward the front, Hill sent a courier to direct Poague's

[48] O.R., *29*, Part 1, 430; *N. C. Regts., II,* 440.
[49] *N. C. Regts., II,* 440.
[50] O.R., *29*, Part 1, 426. The troops Hill saw consisted of about two Federal brigades. *N. C. Regts., II,* 441.
[51] Heth MS, 151.
[52] O.R., *29*, Part 1, 426.
[53] *N. C. Regts., II,* 444.
[54] O.R., *29*, Part 1, 426, 430.

batteries to take position upon a hill on the extreme left.[55] When the guns were ready, Hill directed them to open—whereupon a few shots sufficed to send all the bluecoats in sight scurrying across Broad Run in confusion.[56]

Having scratched the enemy, Hill ordered Heth, whose troops were now in position, to cross the run and overwhelm the enemy.[57] Heth pushed forward his brigades, but as the front line emerged from the thick undergrowth into the clearing, the men halted a few moments to correct their faulty alignment. During this interval Hill shifted his gaze to the right where he viewed with concern two enemy columns busily engaged in getting into position on the right and rear of Cooke's brigade.[58] Realizing the danger to his flank, Hill told Heth to suspend the general advance. As further precautions he dispatched a courier to Cooke with orders to keep an eye on his right and hurried another aide to notify Anderson to advance McIntosh's artillery battalion and two brigades to protect Cooke's flank.[59]

When enemy skirmishers shortly began firing on Cooke's right regiment, the Twenty-Seventh North Carolina, its regimental commander espied behind the railroad embankment a solid line of bluecoats as far as his eyes could see.[60] This disconcerting information was sent to Heth who in turn relayed it to Hill. At the same time Captain S. R. Johnston, an engineer of Lee's staff, having examined the ground on the right volunteered to ride to Hill and explain the unforeseen peril.[61] After receiving Heth's report but before Johnston's arrival, Hill ordered Heth to "advance at once,"[62] with the reassurance that Anderson's troops now coming into view would cover his right.[63]

Under the admiring but anxious eyes of their corps commander, Heth's three advance brigades resumed the pursuit "in beautiful

---

[55] *N. C. Regts., II,* 441.
[56] *Ibid.;* O.R., *29,* Part 1, 426, 430.
[57] O.R., *29,* Part 1, 426.
[58] *Ibid.,* 426, 430, 435.
[59] *Ibid.,* 426, 428.
[60] *Ibid.,* 438.
[61] *N. C. Regts., II,* 441.
[62] *Ibid.*
[63] O.R., *29,* Part 1, 426, 431.

order and quite steadily."[64] Cooke's brigade advancing at a quick-step passed the crest of a pine-domed hill and began the descent toward Broad Run when the front line perceived the enemy drawn up behind the railroad embankment and supported by batteries on rising ground to the rear. At that moment Hill heard this force "of whose presence I was unaware,"[65] fire a destructive volley which raked Cooke's line and severely wounded its scrappy commander.[66] While Cooke's troops rushed toward the railroad, Kirkland abandoned his advance on the left and swung around to assist them.[67] As Kirkland's troops wheeled to the right, the left of the line struck the enemy in the railroad cut near Broad Run. Fiercely the North Carolinians drove the enemy lining the embankment, but their charge faltered at the second line when a well-placed Federal battery north of the run opened a withering enfilading fire.[68] Kirkland was wounded and the brigade fell back leaving a number in the cut where they were captured.[69] Meantime, Walker's brigade, which had crossed Broad Run in accordance with Hill's original orders, recrossed to extend Kirkland's left; but Kirkland had been driven back before this movement was completed.[70]

On the right Cooke fared no better. His gaping line charged to within forty yards of the railroad when the bluecoats rose and delivered a volley that more than halved one regiment. Undeterred, the leading Twenty-Seventh North Carolina regiment pushed ahead several more steps only to find itself alone, whereupon survivors began the "murderous trip" back up the hill.[71]

Cooke's broken brigade retired through McIntosh's battery which Hill had posted in an exposed position on a hill between

---

[64] *Ibid.*, 426-27.

[65] *Ibid.*, 427. This Federal force was General Gouverneur Warren's II Corps, about 3,000 strong, which had been marching northward along the railroad from Catlett's Station. Warren, who was familiar with this locality, galloped up after the cannonading began and ordered his men to face left and run for the railroad cut. After repulsing Hill's advance Warren resumed his march toward Manassas. O.R. *29*, Part 1, 241-42.

[66] *N. C. Regts., II*, 442.

[67] O.R., *29*, Part 1, 427.

[68] *Ibid.*, 431.

[69] *Ibid.*, 427, 431.

[70] *Ibid.*, 432.

[71] *N. C. Regts., II*, 443.

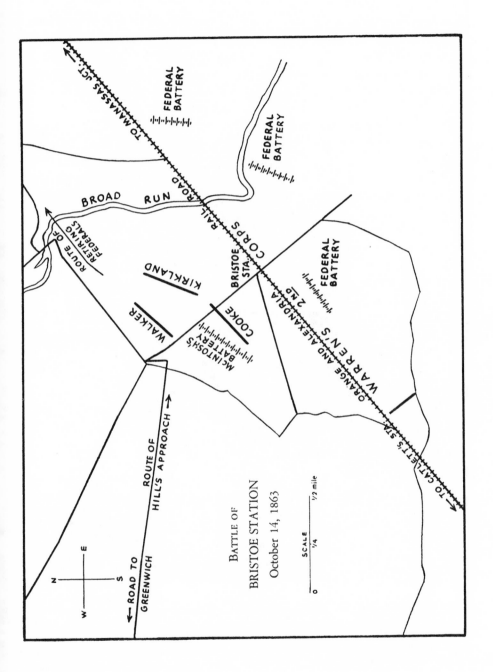

BATTLE OF
BRISTOE STATION
October 14, 1863

SCALE
0   ¼   ½ mile

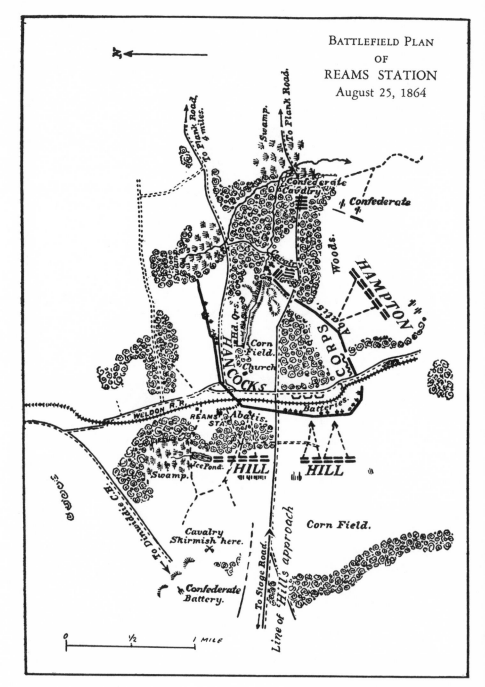

BATTLEFIELD PLAN
OF
REAMS STATION
August 25, 1864

Adapted from *North Carolina Regiments.*

two pine thickets opposite the railroad station.[72] However, Hill had failed to notify Heth of this disposition and the battery had been left without support.[73] With Cooke's troops in full flight the enemy now rushed forward and seized five of the guns which they quickly ran down the hill under the protection of their own batteries.[74]

Far more serious than the loss of these guns was the tragic plight of Heth's two valiant North Carolina brigades which together sustained almost 1,300 casualties.[75] Reaction to this costly and humiliating defeat was quick and sharp throughout the ranks, press, and official circles. Veterans branded the engagement a "slaughter pen,"[76] "bloody massacre,"[77] and "rash enterprise,"[78] while a surgeon in Wilcox's division—which arrived too late to see action—reported to his wife that the repulse "was all due to the miserable mismanagement of General Hill or General Heth, or possibly both of them."[79]

Hill, fully cognizant of the barrage of criticism leveled against him for this unreconnoitered, headlong attack, assumed full responsibility for the fiasco.[80] His apologia, which he confined to a few brief references in his correspondence and official report, set forth his outlook on that fateful afternoon. He admitted his failure to reconnoiter beyond the railroad embankment, "as I supposed that other troops (Ewell's) were taking care of them."[81] With utter frankness he concluded, "I am convinced that I made the attack too hastily, and at the same time that a delay of half an hour, and there would have been no enemy to attack. In that event I believe I should equally have blamed myself for not attacking at once."[82] President Davis succinctly annotated Hill's report with the comment: "There was a want of vigilance."[83]

---

[72] O.R., *29*, Part 1, 431, 436.
[73] *Ibid.*, 431.
[74] *Ibid.*, 426, 437.
[75] *Ibid.*, 427, 433; *N. C. Regts., II*, 443.
[76] *N. C. Regts., II*, 45.
[77] *Ibid.*, 773.
[78] *Ibid., IV.*, 562.
[79] Welch, 81.
[80] Heth MS, 152.
[81] O.R., *51*, Part 2, 811. Letter from A. P. Hill to H. Heth, June 13, 1864.
[82] O.R., *29*, Part 1, 427.
[83] *Ibid.*, 427-28.

Lee characteristically refrained from direct criticism of Hill, preferring instead to express his disapprobation of the proud, sensitive commander's precipitate action in a far more poignant manner. The morning after the battle he rode with Hill over the corpse-strewn field. After listening gravely to Hill's account of the affair, he commented tersely, "Well, well, General, bury these poor dead men and let us say no more about it."[84]

---

[84] Long, 311. Hotchkiss stated that "Lee met Hill with stern rebuke for his imprudence, then sadly directed him to gather his wounded and bury his dead." C.M.H., *III*, 426. However, the "stern rebuke" was not corroborated by the ear-witness account reported above.

CHAPTER XVII

"I Will Not Have The Men Disturbed"

(The Wilderness)

HAVING FAILED to crush Meade, Hill's troops discouraged his return by destroying a stretch of track on the Orange and Alexandria Railroad between Manassas and the Rappahannock.[1] This accomplished, the Third Corps returned to its old camps at Orange Court House.[2] Here the men erected winter quarters and rested.[3]

In nearby Culpeper one of Hill's admiring neighbors volunteered to recruit sixty able-bodied men to act as an escort for the county's most distinguished son. Although Hill appreciated the sentiment, he abhorred any proposal smacking of pomp and sinecures. He therefore promptly declined the offer with this comment: "I have no use for an escort; besides, sir, I think that your sixty able-bodied men could render better service to the country by joining the ranks of some infantry regiment than by acting as bodyguard to any general."[4]

The men had scarcely begun to hibernate in their crude shelters when Hill ordered them to break camp and move eastward. On the bitterly cold Friday after Thanksgiving, a long column of shivering veterans plodded along Plank Road to Mine Run, a stream which meandered into the Rapidan.[5] While Meade approached this stream from the east, Lee formed his line of battle on the opposite bank. General Early, now commanding ailing Dick Ewell's Second Corps, entrenched on the left as Hill dug in on the right. Heth's men finding themselves opposite Warren's recently enlarged command, undertook the erection of rifle-pits with redoubled zest in anticipation of an opportunity to square

---

[1] Welch, 81; *N. C. Regts., II,* 479, 663.
[2] Heth MS, 152.
[3] Caldwell, 118.
[4] "Sketches of Southern Generals," Part V.
[5] B. and L., *IV,* 88.

accounts for their humiliating reception at Bristoe Station.[6]

After waiting in vain for Meade to attack, Lee decided to take the offensive on Wednesday, December 2. Early was directed to pin down the enemy in front while Hill put Anderson's and Wilcox's divisions on Warren's flank with orders to attack at daybreak. Great was the chagrin, therefore, when Wednesday's dawn revealed that the enemy had decamped during the night.[7]

Disappointed, the half-frozen troops "marched like cavalry."[8] back to Orange Court House to endure a long, severe winter.[9] As inclement weather curtailed drilling and guard duty, Hill confined military exercises chiefly to picket duty and roll calls at reveille and tattoo.[10] The men occupied themselves with religious services and snowball fights. One such sham battle between Cooke's and Kirkland's brigades developed into a bruising fray when some of the more determined combatants cored their snowballs with stones and other hard objects. By mutual agreement the exhausted opponents finally called the battle a draw, but the bitterness engendered was softened only after several engagements against the common foe.[11]

Early in January Hill visited the capital which he found full of Kentuckians and convalescing comrades-in-arms. The gallant Hood, recuperating from the loss of a leg shattered at Chickamauga, hobbled on crutches to Mrs. Ives' theatricals and taffy pulls as he paid leap-year court to lovely Sally Preston.[12] Heros von Borcke, recovering from a shot through his throat, found it embarrassingly difficult to vocally express his appreciation for Congress' recent vote of thanks for his support of the cause.[13]

With paper money depreciating so rapidly that even the Davis family found it difficult to live within the President's income.[14]

---

[6] Heth MS, 152.
[7] O.R., *29*, Part 1, 896; B. and L., *IV*, 90-91.
[8] *N. C. Regts., IV*, 188.
[9] Welch, 87; Caldwell, 121.
[10] Caldwell, 121.
[11] *N. C. Regts., II*, 379-80.
[12] Mrs. M. B. Chesnut, *A Diary from Dixie* (cited hereafter as Chesnut), 280, 331, 345, 355, 368-71, 385.
[13] *Ibid.*, 340, 350.
[14] *Ibid.*, 395.

Powell Hill readily appreciated the hardships and privations of his own little family. Oranges cost $5 apiece, turkeys $23, flannel $70 a yard, and forlorn second-hand shoes $85 a pair.[15] Dolly doubtless repeated to her husband the housewives' popular quip then current: "You take your money to market in the market basket, and bring home what you buy in your pocketbook."[16]

Beneath the capital's distractive mask of revelry and frivolity Hill noted with apprehension a growing mood of pessimism. President Davis, whose suicide was rumored daily,[17] discussed the outlook to intimates in melancholy cadences.[18] *The Examiner* frankly announced in its columns that the army would not be ready until spring,[19] and news from North Carolina disclosed that state's intention to offer peace terms.[20] As a prominent war-time resident of Richmond stated: "Everybody who comes in brings a little bad news, not much in itself, but the cumulative effect is very depressing indeed . . . Hope and fear are gone, and it is distraction or death with us."[21]

Hill deprecated any sentiments which savored of defeatism, and he therefore eagerly welcomed the stimulating effect of General John Hunt Morgan's arrival in the capital on a snowy Thursday, January 7, 1864.[22] Dolly's dashing brother had recently effected a spectacular escape from Columbus penitentiary where he had been held prisoner after being captured on his dramatic cavalry raid into Ohio. The visit of this debonair adventurer stirred the imagination and hopes of a capital which was finding it difficult to accustom itself to adversity.[23]

On his arrival in Richmond, Morgan was greeted by Hill and John B. Gordon at the Ballard House where a reception and dinner were held, followed by a convivial wassail around a capacious ten gallon bowl of swirling apple toddy. Late in the festivities

---

[15] *Ibid.*, 352, 368, 382.
[16] *Ibid.*, 368.
[17] Swiggett, 192.
[18] Chesnut, 355.
[19] *Ibid.*, 346.
[20] *Ibid.*, 348.
[21] *Ibid.*, 355, 357.
[22] Swiggett, 199.
[23] *Ibid.*, 199; Chesnut, 353n.

teetotaler Jeb Stuart arrived to meet his western counterpart for the first time.[24]

On Friday Hill and Stuart rode with Morgan in a carriage through cheering throngs to Mayor Mayo's reception on the south portico of city hall.[25] Here the Rebel Raider was hailed as the "Marion of the Second Revolution."[26] Morgan modestly responded, and when Hill declined to speak because of an ailing voice,[27] Stuart took the speaker's stand to fervently dispel rumors that he and Morgan were bitter rivals.[28]

By mid-January Hill had returned to the front. Probably as a result of comments heard during his visit to Richmond, he turned his attention to bolstering the morale of his good friend and devoted lieutenant, Harry Heth. Since Heth's appointment to divisional command after Chancellorsville he had been the unfortunate victim of a series of reverses for which he was widely criticized. With accustomed loyalty and solicitude, Hill thoughtfully composed the following letter to Heth:

General:

Having been informed that it was probable some misapprehension existed in regard to your management of your division at Gettysburg, Falling Waters and Bristow, it is but simple justice to you that I say your conduct on all these occasions met with my approbation. At Gettysburg, the first days fight, mainly fought by your Division was a brilliant victory—you were wounded that day, and not again in command of your division until the retreat commenced. At Falling Waters the enemy were kept at bay until the army had crossed the Potomac and the prisoners taken by the enemy were stragglers, and not due to any fault of yours. At Bristow the attack was ordered by me and most gallantly made by your division—another Corps of the enemy coming up on your right was unforseen, as I had supposed that other troops were taking care of them. I write you this letter that you may make such use of it as may be deemed advisable by you.

Very Respectfully
A. P. Hill[29]

By such considerate acts together with his usual organizational skill, Hill managed to maintain excellent morale throughout the

---

[24] Swiggett, 199-200.
[25] C. F. Holland, *Morgan and His Raiders*, 293.
[26] Swiggett, 200.
[27] Chesnut, 353.
[28] *Ibid.;* Swiggett, 200.
[29] O.R., *51*, Part 2, 811.

Third Corps during this discouraging winter. His three divisional commanders continued in good health at their posts. Returning absentees plus older conscripts netted by a tightened conscription act swelled the Corps to 22,000.[30] One of Hill's veterans who had served with the Army of Northern Virginia since its organization, wrote optimistically to his wife: "I believe if we whip the Yankees good again this spring they will quit in disgust. Their course is not just, like ours, and they are sure to become discouraged more readily."[31]

Aside from sporadic enemy cavalry forays which were easily repulsed,[32] the remainder of the winter passed uneventfully in the camps around Orange Court House. However, with the coming of spring both sides of the Rapidan bristled with preparations for the campaign all knew was coming. Across the river at Culpeper Court House, Lieutenant General U. S. Grant established his headquarters on March 26.[33] Lincoln had plucked this "vigilant and self-reliant"[34] hero of Vicksburg from the Western theater and placed him in command of all the Union armies.[35]

Anticipating that this new opponent would lose no time in assuming the offensive now that the rain-drenched roads had dried,[36] Lee met his commanders on Monday, May 2 at the signal station on Clark's Mountain. In addition to the commanding General this distinguished coterie included Powell Hill and his divisional commanders, Ewell and his staff, and "Old Pete" Longstreet who had just returned from his fruitless Tennessee campaign.

Through their field-glasses the high command studied the white-canvassed landscape north of the Rapidan. As the group concluded its examination, Lee pointed toward Chancellorsville and expressed the opinion that Grant would move southward across the Rapidan at Germanna or Ely's fords. Before disbanding he bade his lieu-

---

[30] C.M.H., *III*, 432; B. and L., *IV*, 153. The April 20, 1864 returns of the Army of Northern Virginia reported the strength of Hill's Corps as 22,199. Alexander, 497.
[31] Welch, 86.
[32] *Ibid.*, 89; Caldwell, 122-23.
[33] B. and L., *IV*, 100.
[34] *Ibid.*, 113. Letter from Lincoln to Grant, April 30, 1864.
[35] *Ibid.*, 98.
[36] Welch, 91; *Recollections and Letters of Robert E. Lee*, 122-23.

tenants ready their commands to move as soon as the signal station crew flagged news that the Federal army had broken camp.[37]

At 9 A. M. Wednesday morning, May 4 a signal officer on Clark's Mountain spelled out the news that blue columns were moving toward Lee's right.[38] Two hours later Hill's men were cooking their rations and preparing to march. With the numerical odds stacked almost two-to-one in Grant's favor, Hill released all of his men who were under sentence of court-martial or under any arrest.[39] Before the bread was all baked, bugles and kettle-drums summoned the troops to fall in and march eastward along the Orange Plank Road toward Chancellorsville. Heth's division led the column at a rapid gait,[40] followed by Wilcox's four brigades. Hill left Anderson's division at Rapidan Heights to guard the rear and then follow the next day.[41] Parallel and to the left of Hill's line of march, Ewell's 17,000 veterans[42] advanced along the Orange Turnpike with orders to regulate their march by Hill's. Lee urged Ewell if possible to avoid bringing on a general engagement until Longstreet arrived with his two divisions from Gordonsville.[43]

Lee rode with Powell Hill at the head of the Third Corps[44] probably with a view to keeping a rein on his most impulsive Lieutenant General. As the two commanders trotted ahead of the confident troops on this beautiful and calm May day, they doubtless discussed Grant's southward thrust at the points predicted by Lee with the apparent intention of advancing directly on Richmond. Lee's strategy was to assail the Federal army in the dense, tangling Wilderness which would conceal his inferior numbers and at the same time immobilize Grant's vastly superior ordnance.[45] Almost exactly a year previously Jackson had rolled up Hooker's flank in this locality. Could Old Jack's successors repeat?

---

[37] C.M.H., *III*, 431-32; B. and L., *IV*, 118.
[38] C.M.H., *III*, 433.
[39] Caldwell, 126. Grant started the Wilderness campaign with 118,000 troops (B. and L., *IV*, 152), against which Lee could muster only 62,000 (B. and L., *IV*, 152; C.M.H., *III*, 432).
[40] *Ibid.*
[41] C.M.H., *III*, 433; S.H.S.P., *14*, 523.
[42] C.M.H., *III*, 432; B. and L., *IV*, 153.
[43] O.R., *36*, Part 1, 1070.
[44] C.M.H., *III*, 434; S.H.S.P., *14*, 523-24.
[45] B. and L., *IV*, 122.

About sunset Hill halted his column at Verdiersville where the men bivouacked.[46] The next morning, preceded by Stuart and some of his cavalry, Hill's troops eagerly resumed the march despite the fact that Grant's order barring sutlers from accompanying his army[47] robbed the Confederates of their customary anticipation of material rewards. Favorable weather, "a more beautiful day never dawned,"[48] kept spirits high; and as the marchers passed the lines erected the previous winter at Mine Run they cheered and exclaimed, "Marse Bob is going for them this time."[49]

Lee certainly seemed to confirm this sentiment as he again rode cheerfully and confidently with Hill at the head of the column.[50] Pre-battle anticipation heightened late in the morning when one of Ewell's staff-officers galloped up to Lee and reported that the Second Corps, now almost three miles north of Hill's column, had encountered a strong line of Federals moving southeasterly toward the Orange Plank Road. Lee reiterated his earlier orders for Ewell to regulate his march by Hill's progress and to avoid a general engagement until Longstreet was up. However, the disturbing sound of heavy firing on the left soon indicated that Ewell had made contact with the enemy. Lee and Hill subsequently learned that the Second Corps had been assailed by a strong force which Ewell's veterans quickly repulsed with a bold and vigorous counterstroke.[51]

Meanwhile Hill's troops, flanked by forest fires on both sides of the Orange Plank Road,[52] proceeded to Parker's store where skirmishers encountered a heavy line of dismounted cavalry. Stubbornly the bluecoats contested Hill's advance units before retiring slowly to the main Federal column on Brock road.[53] During this brush George Tucker, chief of couriers in the Third Corps, implored Hill's permission to join the skirmishers in order to shoot

---

[46] O.R., *36* Part 2, 948.
[47] O.R., *33*, 817.
[48] John B. Gordon, *Reminiscences of the Civil War* (cited hereafter as Gordon), 234.
[49] W. L. Royall, *Some Reminiscences* (cited hereafter as Royall), 28. Letter from Colonel W. H. Palmer to Royall.
[50] B. and L., *IV*, 240-41.
[51] O.R., *36*, Part 1, 1028.
[52] Caldwell, 126.
[53] Royall, 28; B. and L., *IV*, 122, 155; *N. C. Regts., II*, 446.

a Yankee and appropriate the steed to replace his own which had died during the winter. Hill acquiesced, whereupon Tucker in his ardor imprudently exposed himself and was wounded in the thigh.[54]

While awaiting the arrival of Heth's division, Lee, Hill, and Stuart together with their staff-officers turned off to the left of the Orange Plank Road and after riding a short distance dismounted in the shade of some trees in a large field near the Tapp farm. While resting at this vantage point they peered down the open valley of Wilderness Run at the long lines of bluecoats already in line of battle. They were thus engrossed when a party of enemy skirmishers emerged from pine thickets on the left and advanced to within pistol shot of the surprised Confederate commanders. Lee walked rapidly toward Heth's oncoming troops to give orders to Colonel Taylor, his Adjutant-General; Stuart rose to his full height and defiantly faced the enemy; while Hill remained seated, feeling that his apparent unconcern would allay enemy suspicions. After a tense pause the Federal officer, himself alarmed at finding himself in the presence of gray-clad officers, ordered his men to "right about," whereupon they disappeared into the timber.[55]

It was now mid-afternoon and Heth's division was up, followed closely by Wilcox's troops. Lee halted the latter column about a mile from the Brock road and directed Wilcox to file to the left and plug the inviting gap between Ewell's right and Heth's left.[56] Meantime, Hill directed the deployment of Heth's division on the right. Skirmishers spread out along a wide front ahead of Heth's brigades which were forming their line of battle perpendicular to the Orange Plank Road—one brigade on the left and three on the right.[57] Hill also posted sixteen guns of Poague's and McIntosh's battalions in a clearing on the Tapp farm where they could closely support the infantry. When a staff officer called Hill's attention to the absence of any road over which the guns could be withdrawn in case the infantry were driven back, Hill answered

[54] S.H.S.P., *12*, 187.
[55] Royall, 28; C.M.H., *III*, 435; B. and L., *IV*, 241.
[56] Heth MS, 155.
[57] Alexander, 501.

that he was fully aware of this but that in battle the guns must risk capture as the price of holding the line against enemy thrusts.[58]

Shortly after the line on the right had formed, Lee sent a staff officer to Heth with orders to move forward and occupy Brock Road if he could accomplish it without precipitating a general engagement. Heth replied that the enemy held the road with a strong force which would require at least his entire division to dislodge. He added that it was impossible to foretell whether the proposed attack could be confined to his sector, but that he was ready to move if Lee gave the order.[59]

Before this message reached Lee, Heth's line was furiously assailed by a strong Federal line which had advanced through concealing undergrowth to within ninety yards of Heth's position.[60] Finally catching sight of the bluecoats, Heth's men poured a destructive volley which forced them back to the Brock road where they re-formed, entrenched, and brought up strong reinforcements.[61]

On the left, Wilcox formed Scales' and McGowan's brigades into a line oblique to Heth's front. At the command "Forward!" these brigades swept ahead through tangled thickets of pine, scrub oak, and cedar which rendered it impossible to keep alignments to say nothing of glimpsing the foe.[62] After proceeding about two hundred yards and capturing two hundred prisoners, Wilcox withdrew this force in compliance with orders from Lee that it was now imperative to support Heth.[63]

While Wilcox countermarched his troops and shoved them into position on Heth's left, the enemy charged Heth repeatedly in an effort to drive him back to Parker's store.[64] However, Heth had skillfully drawn his line just below the crest of a slight elevation atop which his men placed a row of logs that screened the defenders from enemy view and fire.[65] Behind this simple but

---

[58] Royall, 29.
[59] Heth MS, 154-55.
[60] *Ibid.*
[61] C.M.H., *III*, 437; B. and L., *IV*, 157.
[62] B. and L., *IV*, 154.
[63] *N. C. Regts., II*, 665; Heth MS, 155.
[64] B. and L., *IV*, 155; Heth MS, 155.
[65] B. and L., *IV*, 157n.

effective defense Heth's division stoutly repulsed seven separate assaults delivered at close range.[66]

During this desperate struggle in the impenetrable Wilderness officers lost contact with their men, commands became scrambled, and soldiers strayed into enemy lines. Movements were adjudged by ear in this battle which of necessity was fought fragmentarily by regiments and brigades rather than by divisions.[67] One Federal participant described the engagement as "bushwhacking on a grand scale in brush."[68]

Late in the day an enemy attempt to turn Hill's right succeeded in driving back part of Scales' brigade.[69] Hill tried to rally the weary men by conspicuously exposing himself to enemy fire, and sent for Lane's brigade—his last reserve. Raising their rebel yell as usual,[70] the North Carolinians moved forward in perfect order and drove the bluecoats back through a swamp at the point of the bayonet.[71] As Lane stayed this threat another Confederate officer voiced the hope of all when he said: "If night would only come!"[72]

But the fighting was not yet over. Wilcox astride his white mount[73] reported to Heth who told him that the enemy had been "awfully punished" in seven separate assaults. Heth felt that the time had come for their two divisions to counterattack, but as he subsequently lamented: "This proved to be a mistake. I should have left well enough alone."[74] For as the men in butternut moved forward "the whole Wilderness roared like fire in a canebreak."[75] The center of the attacking line overran part of the Federal breastworks and captured a battery,[76] but the enemy then rallied, evicted the Confederates, and drove them back about half a mile.[77]

Added to this reverse was a report at sunset that the bluecoats

---

[66] *Ibid.*, 122, 157; Heth MS, 155; C.M.H., *III*, 436, 438.
[67] B. and L., *IV*, 122.
[68] A. Buell, "The Cannoneer," an article in "The National Tribune," 167-69, 1890.
[69] S.H.S.P., *9*, 125.
[70] *Ibid.*
[71] *N. C. Regts.*, *II*, 569.
[72] Royall, 29.
[73] *N. C. Regts.*, *II*, 47; Ibid., *IV*, 194.
[74] Heth MS, 155.
[75] *N. C. Regts.*, *II*, 665.
[76] C.M.H., *III*, 438.
[77] Heth MS, 155.

were pushing into the interval between the Second and Third Corps. As Powell Hill had committed his last reserve, he called on Major Vandergraff's Fifth Alabama Battalion, which had been guarding prisoners, to rush to this threatened sector. With a cheer which magnified their scant 125 muskets, the Alabamians hurled back the intruders and thereby staved off the last enemy thrust of the day as darkness settled over a field on which both man and nature had been savagely ravaged.[78]

Before the deafening roar and roll of musketry died away in the shadows, Lee had formulated his plans for Friday. Longstreet had been ordered up to relieve Hill during the night, and at daybreak Lee would hurl "Old Pete's" two divisions together with Anderson's division of Hill's Corps against Grant's left while Ewell tightened the vise on the opposite flank. In the event Ewell was unable to operate against the Federal right, or if the enemy shifted to the Confederate right as Wilcox reported they were doing, Lee wanted Ewell to move the Second Corps to the Orange Plank Road and support Longstreet's offensive.[79]

Cognizant of Lee's intentions, Powell Hill decided to let his exhausted men rest where they dropped until Longstreet arrived. Hill had been ill during the day, and he welcomed an opportunity to relax on a camp stool in front of a small fire which had been kindled near Poague's guns just behind the lines.[80] His discomfort was assuaged somewhat by the realization that his two divisions numbering about 15,000 had fought an estimated 40,000 Federals to a standstill. Lee warmly commended the valiant defense of the Third Corps, and magnanimous Dick Ewell sent word that he had heard Hill's battle and wished to congratulate him on his success.[81]

Heth and Wilcox, however, were too disturbed about the precarious condition of their lines to share these plaudits with Hill. Their ragged front resembling a "worm fence"[82] remained as it

---

[78] Royall, 30.
[79] O.R., *36*, Part 2, 953.
[80] Royall, 30; Heth MS, 155; J. W. Jones, *Army of Northern Virginia Memorial Volume* (cited hereafter as *Army of Northern Virginia Memorial Volume*), 221, an address by Private Leigh Robinson of the Richmond Howitzers.
[81] Royall, 30.
[82] *Ibid.*

was at the end of the day's fighting.[83] In some sectors the opposing lines were only fifty yards apart.[84] Lane's men "could almost hear the Federals breathing."[85] and all along Hill's line the sounds of enemy movements and preparations were disquietingly audible.[86] Squads sent to straighten the lines fell into enemy hands.[87]

When Heth rode up to report this situation at corps head-quarters, Hill rose and warmly greeted his disturbed lieutenant:

"Your division," he lauded, "has done splendidly today; its magnificent fighting is the theme of the entire Army."

Heth curtly agreed that the men had fought heroically and then proceeded to discuss the problem which worried him. He explained that because of the confused alignment in which the men were lying at every conceivable angle, "we cannot fire shot without firing into each other. A thin skirmish line would drive both my division and Wilcox's, situated as we now are. We shall certainly be attacked early in the morning."[88]

Hill replied that General Lee's orders were to rest the men as they were, and added:

"No, I will not have the men disturbed. Let them rest as they are. It is not intended that they shall fight tomorrow. Longstreet is now at Mine Run. General Lee has ordered him to move . . . He has only eight miles to march. He will be here long before day. He will form in line back of you and Wilcox. Your divisions will fall back through Longstreet's."[89]

Although Heth was far from reassured by Hill's estimate of the situation, he left without pressing the issue further at this time. Meantime, Wilcox boldly ignored Hill's fetish for protocol and went directly to Lee who gave him substantially the same answer Hill had offered Heth. Still concerned, Wilcox later called on Hill to second Heth's alarm but Hill remained adamant.[90]

After midnight Hill rode back to Parker's store to inquire whether any news had been received from Longstreet. About the

---

[83] B. and L., *IV*, 123; *N. C. Regts., II*, 48, 665.
[84] B. and L., *IV*, 123.
[85] *N. C. Regts., II*, 570.
[86] B. and L., *IV*, 123.
[87] Royall, 30.
[88] Heth MS, 156.
[89] *Army of Northern Virginia Memorial Volume*, 221.
[90] Heth MS, 156.

same time one of Lane's men who had wandered into enemy lines and back again reported the absence of a single picket between Wilcox's line and the Federal skirmishers.[91] Still Hill did not consider it practicable to re-form his lines, construct a fire trench, or even to serve ammunition.[92]

With a gnawing concern that surmounted all other considerations, Heth appealed twice more to Hill for permission to re-form his lines. He proposed to take one side of the road and Wilcox the other. But by the third visitation, Hill's patience—thinner than usual in his ill condition—snapped. Peremptorily he announced:

"Damn it Heth, I don't want to hear any more about it; I don't want them disturbed."[93]

Still "agitated by an anxiety such as he never felt before or afterwards,"[94] Heth finally determined to go over Hill's head and lay matters before Lee. But after searching two hours for him in vain, he was forced to vent his anxiety in solitude while pacing up and down behind his troops until daybreak.[95] Bound by orders he knew would result in needless casualties, he wondered why Lee and Hill had permitted their solicitude for the troops' immediate comfort prevent them from taking sensible routine defensive measures. He concluded, "The only excuse I can make for Hill is that he was sick."[96]

Wilcox also spent the night in anguish. As daybreak approached and the First Corps still had not arrived, he ordered the pioneers to fell trees for an abatis to protect his serried line of defenders. However, even this last-minute effort was promptly thwarted by enemy fire which forced the choppers to desist.[97]

Despite Powell Hill's assurances that Longstreet's divisions would arrive in time, there was considerable apprehension at the campfire headquarters of the Third Corps. Major William H. Palmer, Hill's youthful Chief-of-Staff, described the general anxiety that night in a letter to a compatriot: "We could not sleep," he

---

[91] *N. C. Regts., II,* 47.
[92] *Army of Northern Virginia Memorial Volume,* 221; Sorrel, 240.
[93] Heth MS, 155.
[94] *Army of Northern Virginia Memorial Volume,* 228.
[95] *Ibid.*
[96] Heth MS, 156.
[97] *Army of Northern Virginia Memorial Volume,* 228.

wrote, " but waited for news of Longstreet; for we knew that at the first flush of the morning the turning attack on our right would open with overwhelming numbers, and, unsupported, the men must give way."[98]

As gray dawn pierced nature's budding labyrinth in the surrounding Wilderness, Hill and his aides rode to the left to examine the undefended stretch of ground along the half mile interval between the Second and Third Corps. Major Palmer dutifully stayed beside the smoldering campfire where he soon descried the familiar form of General Longstreet loping his horse across the open field. As "Old Pete" drew rein near the embers, Palmer warmly grasped his hand and said, "Ah, General, we have been looking for you since 12 o'clock last night. We expect to be attacked at any moment and are not in any shape to resist."[99]

Longstreet started to reply, "My troops are not up, I have ridden ahead . . ." when his voice was drowned in a roar of musketry, whereupon "Old Pete" immediately spurred his horse toward Parker's store to hurry his troops.[100] Hill returned a moment later and galloped forward along the Orange Plank Road to rally his men who were unmistakably streaming to the rear.[101] These front-line troops under exposure to a withering fire on both flanks had resisted as best they could before breaking in what one officer described as "confusion worse confounded."[102]

Concerned lest the right wing of his army melt away, Lee also took a hand in staying the rout. As Wilcox's men rushed past the low temporary breastworks in front of Poague's batteries about 200 yards behind the original battle line, Lee rode up to General McGowan and chided, "My God! General McGowan, is this splendid brigade of yours running like a flock of geese?"[103]

While the troops halted and re-formed, Hill excitedly ordered the guns to fire obliquely into the mass of bluecoats advancing

---

[98] Royall, 30.
[99] *Ibid.*, 28 ff.; *Army of Northern Virginia Memorial Volume*, 228; B. and L., *IV*, 242.
[100] Royall, 31 ff.; *Army of Northern Virginia Memorial Volume*, 228.
[101] Royal, 31 ff.
[102] *N. C. Regts.*, *II*, 48, 665.
[103] Caldwell, 133.

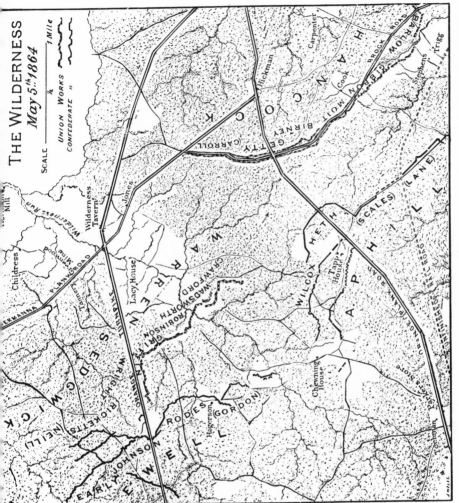

THE WILDERNESS
May 5th 1864

SCALE
½ · · · 1 Mile

UNION WORKS
CONFEDERATE "

From *Battles and Leaders of the Civil War.*

Major General Gouverneur K. Warren, U. S. Army. Hill battled this
redoubtable opponent at Bristoe Station, Jericho Mills,
and Petersburg.

along the broad highway.[104] Impatiently, he endeavored to expedite the action by helping man the guns himself.[105] As only one of these pieces had seen action the previous day, the surprised enemy was momentarily stunned by the hail of grape and canister which belched forth at close range from all sixteen guns.[106] But on both sides of the road retreating troops continued to pour back, pursued closely by the enemy[107] who reportedly was also moving in force toward the gap between Hill and Ewell. Wilcox rode up to report that the hardest enemy blows had caught his line out of joint along the jagged front and collapsed it.[108] With little semblance of order left in his division, Wilcox was ordered to find and guide Longstreet to the front.[109]

At this critical juncture Powell Hill—usually the rescuer—was rescued by the timely arrival of Longstreet's Corps. Trotting down the Orange Plank Road in well-closed double columns,[110] "Old Pete's" steady veterans filed behind Poague's guns. The leading troops proved to be Hood's old division now commanded by Charles Field, recently recovered from a wound received while a brigadier in the Light Division. As the Texans moved into position they could not resist the opportunity to taunt Hill's obviously embarrassed veterans with mock queries such as, "Do you belong to General Lee's army?"[111] In the midst of the surrounding confusion "Old Pete," always imperturbable in the heat of battle, walked his horse along the line and calmly exhorted each company: "Keep cool men, we will straighten this out in short time—keep cool."[112]

While Heth's and Wilcox's divisions re-formed and rested a short distance north of the road,[113] Longstreet's men checked the

---

104 C.M.H., *III*, 439.
105 "Sketches of Southern Generals," Part IV.
106 Royall, 32; C.M.H., *III*, 439.
107 *N. C. Regts.*, *II*, 48.
108 *Ibid.*, B. and L., *IV*, 123.
109 *Annals of the War*, 496.
110 B. and L., *IV*, 124, 241; C.M.H., *III*, 439.
111 *N. C. Regts.*, *II*, 665.
112 Royall, 32.
113 C.M.H., *III*, 440. Davis' Mississippi brigade of Heth's division refused to be withdrawn from this crucial engagement and continued to fight with Longstreet's men. For the spirit and gallantry thus displayed, the brigade which fought this day under Colonel Stone was "complimented and thanked with earnestness and emotion by General A. P. Hill." S.H.S.P., *14*, 526; Royall, 35.

Federal force under Hancock and hurled it back to the Federal entrenchments on Brock road.[114] Later in the morning Longstreet launched a bold counterstroke against the enemy left and succeeded in rolling Hancock's II Corps up "like a wet blanket"[115] until "Old Pete" was severely wounded by a volley from Mahone's flanking force which mistook him for a Federal officer.[116]

Meantime, ailing Powell Hill moved those units of the Third Corps not used to support Longstreet to the left to meet a Federal thrust toward Lee's gaping center. As Hill and his staff rode ahead of these troops they entered a large field at the eastern end of which stood the house and outbuildings of the Chewning farm. The party had dismounted and rested only a short time when it was startled by the breaking of a nearby fence over which a long line of enemy infantry was preparing to advance. In a firm, low voice Hill instantly directed his aides: "Mount, walk your horses, and don't look back." Casually, the little group withdrew from sight, whereupon Hill ordered Major Palmer to ride to Lee and request that a brigade of Anderson's division be sent him. Thus reinforced, Hill met Burnside's advance, reeled the bluecoats back to the main Federal line, and captured many prisoners.[117] Among the Yankee prisoners filing to the rear was an officer who asked Major Palmer: "Were you not at the house a short time ago?" When Palmer replied, "Yes," the prisoner lamented, "I wanted to fire on you but my colonel said you were farmers riding from the house."[118]

Hill now joined up with Ewell[119] to consolidate Lee's line along a front extending from the Orange Turnpike to the Orange Plank Road. After a fierce two-day struggle including a temporary collapse of the right wing, the Army of Northern Virginia now held a position nearer the enemy lines than at the outset of the battle.[120] Even Grant, who reportedly calmed his nerves on twenty Havana

[114] B. and L., *IV*, 124, 241.
[115] C.M.H., *III*, 440.
[116] *Ibid.*, 441.
[117] *Ibid.*, B. and L., *IV*, 161.
[118] Royall, 33-34.
[119] B. and L., *IV*, 126.
[120] *Ibid.*, 128.

cigars during Friday's engagement,[121] conceded in a telegram to Washington: "At present we can claim no victory over the enemy . . ."[122]

Shortly before sunset Ewell attempted to deliver the coup de grace by attacking Grant's carelessly exposed right flank. Although the movement surprised the Federals and resulted in the capture of 600 prisoners plus a portion of the enemy's works, darkness aborted this promising drive.[123]

Haunted by the previous evening's nightmare, Hill's men now threw up formidable earthworks which they supported with well-placed artillery.[124] But the enemy was in no condition to repeat the demoralizing rout of the morning, and on Saturday the opposing lines rested behind their works, cared for the wounded, and buried their dead.[125]

Late Saturday afternoon Lee called at Third Corps head-quarters, now established in a farmhouse, to confer with Hill regarding indications that Grant was moving by the flank to Spotsylvania. As the two commanders discussed the situation while seated on the porch, Hill's staff officers observed activities at Grant's headquarters through a hole punched through shingles on the roof of corps headquarters. When Major Palmer observed and reported that a large park of heavy guns was being moved from a field near Grant's headquarters at Wilderness Tavern to the road running along the Confederate right, Lee quickly decided to dispatch the First Corps, now under R. H. Anderson, to head off the Federals at Spotsylvania. Ewell would follow Anderson, and Hill's Third Corps was to guard the rear.[126]

Thus ended the Army's first of a series of ordeals against a new antagonist whose "grinding principle", Wilcox stated, "was to endeavor to strike the enemy with superior numbers."[127]

---

121 Gordon, 263.
122 C.M.H., *III*, 443.
123 *Ibid.*, 441; B. and L., *IV*, 127.
124 Royall, 34; C.M.H., *III*, 443.
125 C.M.H., *III*, 443.
126 *Ibid.*, 445.
127 Wilcox MSS. No date but written appropriately in red ink.

CHAPTER XVIII

"When A Man Makes A Mistake. . ."

(Spotsylvania to Cold Harbor)

SINCE THE beginning of the Wilderness campaign Powell Hill had been so indisposed that he could scarcely ride. Although army surgeons and colleagues urged him to relinquish the heavy responsibilities of his command he had insisted on directing his troops in this crucial engagement.[1] However, when he found himself unable to sit up on Sunday, May 8, he reluctantly notified Lee who immediately placed Early in temporary command of the Third Corps.[2]

As his men moved southward along a newly cut road, Hill followed in a jouncing ambulance.[3] By Monday morning[4] the column reached Spotsylvania Court House where the Corps, thinned by the previous week's fighting to 13,000 muskets, took position on the right edge of Lee's arrowhead front which jutted toward the gathering foe.[5] Hill ordered his ambulance be drawn up immediately behind the lines[6] where he could counsel with Early and his divisional commanders including "Billy" Mahone, a "mere atom with little flesh,"[7] who henceforth would command R. H. Anderson's old division.[8]

Although Hill was unable to witness the kaleidoscopic movements of his troops, he was highly gratified at the reports of their exploits under Early's vigilant and steady leadership. On Tuesday, "Old Jube" ordered Mahone to extend Lee's left while he moved

---

[1] "The Land We Love," 289, April, 1866-67; "Sketches of Southern Generals," Part V.
[2] O.R., *36*, Part 2, 974; O.R., *51*, Part 2, 827. Letter from Lee to Ewell, May 8, 1864.
[3] Caldwell, 137.
[4] B. and L., *IV*, 128.
[5] Early, 352.
[6] S.H.S.P., *14*, 532.
[7] Sorrel, 276.
[8] O.R., *36*, Part 2, 967.

still further westward with Heth's division to block a Federal advance which threatened to cut Lee's communications.[9]

The next day, May 11, Early shuttled his forces through the rain to counter what proved to be a Federal feint on the left.[10] That evening Hill felt able to attend a conference at Heth's headquarters in a church half a mile south of the Court House. At this meeting the high command discussed reconnaisance reports which indicated that the enemy were retiring from Spotsylvania. Lee believed Grant would head for Fredericksburg, and he instructed his lieutenants prepare to pursue. Powell Hill differed with his chief and voiced the opinion that Grant would continue hammering along the present line. In a rare advocacy of defensive tactics he urged Lee: "Let them continue to attack our breastworks; we can stand that very well."[11]

Just as dawn was breaking the following morning,[12] Thursday, May 12, Grant renewed the attack as Hill had predicted but in a manner which almost spelled disaster for the Army of Northern Virginia. From the pines in front of Ewell's "Mule Shoe" salient emerged a solid mass of bluecoats which advanced, pierced the apex, and quickly overran the defenders in their trenches.[13] Within an hour the exultant Federals captured Generals Johnson and Steuart, 2,800 men, and twenty field pieces.[14]

Having split Lee's army the enemy hastily re-formed his jumbled horde and resumed the southward advance through dense fog.[15] Hancock's II Corps pouring through the gap progressed but a short distance before its left met a rapid, unerring fire from Lane's brigade which the redoubtable North Carolinian had shrewdly wheeled back from its position astride Ewell's right to an unfinished second line of entrenchments in the path of the enemy.[16] Grasping the full import of this crisis, Lane exhorted his men: "You must

[9] B. and L., *IV*, 128; Early, 353-54; C.M.H., *III*, 448.
[10] B. and L., *IV*, 129; Early, 355.
[11] Heth MS, 158 ff.
[12] B. and L., *IV.*, 170.
[13] S.H.S.P., *14*, 529.
[14] B. and L., *IV*, 132.
[15] S.H.S.P., *9*, 146.
[16] S.H.S.P., *9*, 146-47; *N. C. Regts., II*, 666.

hold your ground; the honor and safety of the army demand it."[17]

Wilcox quickly dispatched Scales' and Thomas' brigades to Lane's assistance, and together with Gordon's division of Ewell's corps they checked and reeled back Hancock's center and left.[18] After driving the enemy several hundred yards over fallen timbers, Lane's brigade was ordered back to the Court House on the right.[19] With understandably biased pride Lane later claimed "for this brigade *alone* the honor of not only successfully stemming, but rolling back 'this tide of Federal victory which came surging furiously to our right' ."[20]

Meanwhile on the left, Ewell's outnumbered defenders were reinforced by Harris'[21] and Perrin's brigades of Mahone's division plus McGowan's South Carolina brigade of Wilcox's division. Perrin was killed and McGowan severely wounded in the arm as they led their troops into action.[22] While opposing troops in the salient snatched muskets from each other across breastworks in the war's fiercest hand-to-hand fighting, an unidentified white flag suddenly interrupted the carnage. When the firing ceased, soldiers on each side jumped over the barricades and claimed the others as prisoners. This bizarre impasse was settled by both parties agreeing to return to their own sides whereupon the struggle was resumed.[23]

During the afternoon Hill had an opportunity to observe his men in action on the right side of Lee's arrowhead front.[24] Desirous of relieving pressure on Ewell's salient, Lee decided to hurl units of the Third Corps against Grant's left which was manned by Burnside's IX Corps. Accordingly, Mahone led his former brigade, now commanded by Colonel Weisiger, and Lane's dependable North Carolinians beyond a spur on Heth's front to concealing oak woods just beyond the end of Burnside's line. Lane's cheering

[17] *N. C. Regts.,* II, 571.
[18] B. and L., *IV,* 132; C.M.H., *III,* 451; S.H.S.P., *14,* 530; *N. C. Regts.,* II, 571.
[19] *N. C. Regts.,* II, 571, 666.
[20] S.H.S.P., *9,* 147.
[21] Brigadier General Nathaniel H. Harris succeeded Posey who died of a wound received at Bristoe Station. O.R., *33,* 1207.
[22] Welch, 97; Early, 355.
[23] *N. C. Regts.,* II, 51.
[24] *Ibid.*

regiments pushed through trees, charged across an open field, captured an obstreperous six-gun battery, and wheeled left where they encountered Burnside's column advancing through pine thickets to assail Heth. Surprised by Lane's flank attack and subjected to withering musketry and artillery fire from Heth's front, Burnside withdrew his men with considerable loss to strong entrenchments.[25]

As the flanking force returned to the lines near the Court House with over 300 prisoners and three battle flags, Mahone rode up and claimed the flags.[26] When his request was refused he vigorously contested Wilcox's claim that Lane's men deserved credit for their capture. Lee was notified of the dispute and referred the matter to Hill, who, disliking incidents which promoted factionalism within his command, found the opposing claims "irreconcilable."[27]

More pleasing to Hill was the report of Jim Lane's escape from an enemy marksman. During the mêlée with Burnside's troops a bluecoat only ten paces away had leveled a gun at Hill's capable brigadier when young Private Parker at Lane's side spotted and instantly shot the Yankee.[28]

The immeasurable relief which swept Lee's lines after the repulse of Grant's savagely sustained assaults was tempered on Friday morning by news of Stuart's death. After covering the advance of Hill's Corps to the Wilderness, "Jeb" had assisted R. H. Anderson in his successful footrace with Grant to Spotsylvania. That mission accomplished, he had then hastened south to intercept Sheridan from reaching Richmond. At Yellow Tavern, an intersection seven miles north of the capital, Lee's indefatigable chief-of-cavalry overtook the enemy. In the ensuing engagement he was mortally wounded while rallying his men against a charge of George A. Custer's troopers.[29]

During the rainy period following Thursday's gory slaughter

---

[25] *Ibid.,* 51, 666-67; S.H.S.P., 9, 147-49; Early, 355-57.
[26] *N. C. Regts., II,* 52.
[27] O.R., *36,* Part 3, 802-07.
[28] S.H.S.P., *9,* 150.
[29] B. and L., *IV,* 194.

at Spotsylvania, the attenuated forces caught their breaths and licked their wounds. Behind earthworks drenched soldiers clasped guns with numbed fingers and listened to the moaning wounded who had to remain unattended between the lines because Grant refused to grant a truce.[30] One wounded Maryland veteran who had suffered four days without succor finally raised himself to a sitting position and tried to end his misery by clubbing his head with the butt of his musket.[31]

While Grant awaited reinforcements from Washington and shifted troops from the salient to extend his line along the Ny Valley toward Fredericksburg,[32] Lee transferred the First Corps from its position on the left to the right along a line reaching from Hill's right to Snell's Bridge across the Po.[33] Preparatory to this movement Lee ordered Ambrose Wright's Georgia brigade of the Third Corps to seize an eminence opposite Heth's headquarters from which enemy batteries could enfilade Anderson's new line.

While Lee and Hill watched Wright's operation from the rear of a nearby church, the Georgian bunglingly sustained needless casualties, and finally had to be extricated from his predicament by Harris' Mississippi brigade. Hill, unable to contain his wrath, swore he would call for a court of inquiry. But Lee, with calm, mature judgement, replied:

These men are not an army, they are citizens defending their country. General Wright is not a soldier; he's a lawyer. I cannot do many things that I could do with a trained army. The soldiers know their duties better than the general officers do, and they have fought magnificently. Sometimes I would like to mask troops and then deploy them, but if I were to give the proper order, the general officers would not understand it; so I have to make the best of what I have and lose much time in making dispositions. You understand all this, but if you humiliated General Wright, the people of Georgia would not understand. Besides, whom could you put in his place? You'll have to do what I do: When a man makes a mistake, I call him to my tent, talk to him, and use the authority of my position to make him do the right thing the next time.[34]

---

[30] Gordon, 289.
[31] Alexander, 526.
[32] *Lee's Dispatches*, 183.
[33] Alexander, 526-27. This movement was executed May 14-15.
[34] *R. E. Lee, III*, 330-31. Communication from Col. W. H. Palmer to D. S. Freeman, June 25, 1920.

What more pregnant lesson could the commanding General have used to temper the impulsive reaction of the commander who had misdirected the engagement at Bristoe Station?

On Monday, May 16, the weather finally cleared,[35] and the following night Grant stealthily massed a heavy force opposite the Second Corps for another attempt to seize "Hell's Half Acre" as the salient was now dubbed.[36] This time, however, Ewell's artillery and musketry punished the initial assault so severely that the discouraged enemy desisted from further attacks and withdrew[37]

Lee was now convinced that Grant soon would abandon the Spotsylvania front, and he ordered his commanders to demonstrate against the enemy lines to ascertain when they were being weakened. By Saturday, May 21, Lee deduced that Grant was undertaking another "sidling" movement designed to interpose the Federal Army between the Army of Northern Virginia and Richmond.[38] Although he would have preferred to contest Grant's advance "inch by inch," his solicitude for the capital induced him instead to order the army to concentrate along a strong defensive position on the North Anna.[39]

With another engagement brewing Hill was anxious to rejoin his command, and on Saturday afternoon he reported to Lee at the Southworth house south of the Po River that he was sufficiently recovered to resume command.[40] Lee promptly sent word instructing Early to turn over command of the Third Corps to Hill. "Old Jube" received this order as Wilcox was briskly engaging the enemy whom he had caught in the act of withdrawing.[41]

During Early's short association with the Third Corps he won the respect and confidence of Hill's hard-bitten veterans. In turn, "Old Jube" in his autobiography subsequently paid tribute to "The officers and men of the corps (who) had all behaved well, and contributed in no small degree to the result by which Grant was

---

[35] Alexander, 527.
[36] Gordon, 289.
[37] Alexander, 527-28.
[38] *Lee's Dispatches,* 191-92.
[39] *Ibid.,* 192.
[40] O.R., *36,* Part 3, 813-14.
[41] Early, 357; B. and L., *IV,* 135.

compelled to wait six days for reinforcements from Washington, before he could resume the offensive or make another of his flank movements to get between General Lee's army and Richmond."[42]

On assuming command of his corps, Hill received instructions from Lee to move southward not later than 9 o'clock Saturday night over roads parallel to Telegraph Road along which the First and Second Corps already were marching.[43] By forced marches the Third Corps reached the North Anna which it crossed and proceeded on Monday to Anderson's Station just west of Hanover Junction where Lee had established headquarters.

Lee disposed his forces along a strong, strategic line on the south bank of the North Anna. Ewell manned the right, Anderson the center, and Hill the left. This front covered the approaches to Richmond as well as the vital railway arteries supplying the army from the Valley and the South.[44] In this position Lee could blunt a direct thrust by the Federal army, or harass another "sidling" movement toward the capital. As Lee wrote Davis on May 23, "I am in a position to move against him (Grant), and shall endeavor to engage him while in motion."[45]

As Grant's legions assembled on the north bank of the river, Hill's men bivouacked in the oak woods astride the Virginia Central Railroad.[46] Nearby some of Jim Lane's overzealous canteeners found in addition to an abundant supply of refreshing water a flock of sheep which they promptly "captured."[47]

In mid-afternoon the sound of enemy artillery far upstream prompted Lee to reconnoiter that sector in person. After examining the enemy's dispositions across the river, he notified Hill to antici-pate a crossing in the vicinity of Jericho Mills. Upon receipt of this information, Hill dispatched Wilcox to study the ground in-dicated by Lee while he disposed the troops perpendicularly across the railroad to protect the flank.[48] When the straw-hatted com-

---

[42] Early, 357.
[43] O.R., *36*, Part 1, 1058.
[44] C.M.H., *III*, 458-59.
[45] *Lee's Dispatches*, 194-97.
[46] *N. C. Regts.*, *II*, 54.
[47] *Ibid.*, 54-55.
[48] S.H.S.P., *9*, 241.

mander of the Light Division returned from his reconnaissance
he reported that enemy troops (subsequently ascertained to be
Warren's V Corps[49]) had crossed the river and were moving southward from the ford at Jericho Mills. The left of this Federal
force was anchored on the river while artillery commanded the
open ground on the right.[50] Despite these formidable dispositions,
Hill could not resist the prospect of overwhelming an isolated,
unintrenched corps. Confidently, he immediately ordered Wilcox
to move his division up the railroad to Noel's Station, change
front, and charge the enemy.[51]

By 6 o'clock Wilcox had thrown out his skirmish line and
formed his brigades in line of battle parallel to the railroad. At
the command "Forward!" the front three brigades dashed northward followed closely by Scales' North Carolinians. In the front
line Thomas on the left and McGowan in the center soon met
and routed the bluecoats who had not fully formed their lines
in the dense woods. Meanwhile, Scales' brigade moved around
Thomas' left to get on the enemy's flank, forcing the Yankees to
retire to the shelter of their guns which opened with telling effect
on the advancing troops. Thomas' line broke first thereby exposing
McGowan and Scales who in turn retired.[52]

While this see-saw affair was in progress, Lane's brigade, which
formed the right of the first line, advanced four hundred yards
over an open field and entered the woods to engage the enemy
who had taken position on a commanding ridge. When McGowan
fell back and exposed Lane's left, Lane notified Wilcox of his
plight and received orders to push on. As he did so one of his
right regiments broke, whereupon the neighboring regiments who
were fighting fiercely to prevent being outflanked, began bleating
like the "captured" sheep as a grimly humorous gibe at their
fleeing comrades.[53] Lane rallied his men, re-formed the broken line,
and resumed the attack. But alone and unsupported his brigade

---

[49] C.M.H., *III*, 460.
[50] Alexander, 531.
[51] S.H.S.P., *9*, 241; S.H.S.P., *14*, 535.
[52] N. C. Regts., *IV*, 196; Alexander, 531; Caldwell, 153 ff.; Wilcox MS, 45 ff.;
R. E. Lee, *III*, 355.
[53] N. C. Regts., *II*, 55.

made little progress, and he was soon forced to retire to an open field beside the railroad.[54]

Late that evening Heth's division relieved Wilcox's battered command which had sustained 642 casualties to no avail. Early the following morning Lee, although ill, rode to Hill's headquarters to learn the details of Monday's fiasco. Exasperated by the inept handling of this costly action which not only failed to crush the enemy but also enabled him to disrupt westward transportation on the Virginia Central, Lee sternly rebuked Hill by demanding: "Why did you not do as Jackson would have done—thrown your whole force upon these people and driven them back?"[55] Hill's performance at Jericho Mills also raised eyebrows in Richmond where Josiah Gorgas, Chief of Ordnance, noted in his diary: "A. P. Hill does not sustain himself."[56]

Although hypersensitive to such sharp criticism, especially when seasoned with an allusion to Jackson, Powell Hill said nothing, nor is there any evidence that he subsequently harbored any resentment against Lee for this rebuke. Without further ado he simply withdrew his men to Anderson's Station and set them to work digging trenches through the beautiful gardens that stretched from Little River to Ox Ford.[57] Although Hill's men eagerly awaited the opportunity to wreak revenge on their familiar foe, Warren refrained from attacking their formidable defenses.[58]

The Third Corps' front now constituted the left arm of a wedged defensive line Lee drew to prevent Grant from consolidating his forces opposite Hill with those arrayed against Anderson and Ewell.[59] It was a line similar to that at Spotsylvania except that this salient rested securely on the North Anna. In addition to enjoying the excellent defensive protection afforded by this well-chosen position, Lee hoped to mount an offensive against Grant's split front. Over 8,000 fresh troops had just arrived to support

---

[54] S.H.S.P., *9*, 241-42.
[55] C.M.H., *III*, 460.
[56] J. Gorgas, *The Civil War Diary of General Josiah Gorgas*, entry for June 1, 1864.
[57] S.H.S.P., *9*, 242.
[58] Alexander, 531.
[59] B. and L., *IV*, 135.

such a blow, but Lee became too ill to direct field operations. Hence two days were spent merely deflecting Grant's efforts to dent Lee's lines. In one such attempt Warren sent a detachment to reinforce Burnside in a projected assault on the salient defended by Anderson, but Mahone's division attacked the supporting force and drove it back with heavy loss in a fight which reminded one witness, "not a little of some of Jackson's attacks in days gone by."[60]

Unable to penetrate Lee's ingenious defensive line on the North Anna, Grant broke camp Thursday night, May 26,[61] to undertake another encircling movement toward Richmond. Lee withdrew the next day along his short interior lines to a position behind Totopotomoy creek where he could again block either a direct thrust or encircling movement toward the capital. Hill disposed his corps on the left of Lee's line and then wrote army headquarters: "I have a good line and would like to fight it."[62] Grant also recognized Lee's formidable position, and confined his infantry to brisk three-day skirmishing[63] climaxed Wednesday afternoon, June 1, by an attack on Heth's line which Cooke's and Kirkland's brigades repulsed.[64]

Grant meanwhile had begun shifting troops from Hill's front to the Federal left which he was extending southeastward toward Cold Harbor.[65] Lee countered by dispatching Anderson from the center to the right to join Hoke's division arriving from Drewry's Bluff in an attack on Grant's left flank. Early Wednesday morning Anderson made two assaults on the intrenched enemy, but for some inexplicable reason he threw in only two brigades, one of which was under an inexperienced commander. As this inadequate force advanced, the line faltered and then broke under a murderous

---

[60] Caldwell, 165.
[61] Alexander, 532-33.
[62] O.R., *51*, Part 2, 969.
[63] Alexander, 531; S.H.S.P., *9*, 243.
[64] O.R., *36*, Part 1, 1031.
[65] Cold Harbor is the old English name for a tavern where travellers could obtain lodging without food, S.H.S.P., *14*, 535. This hamlet was located just a mile east of Gaines' Mill where Hill had assailed McClellan almost two years previously, Alexander, 535.

hail of bullets discharged from the enemy's new magazine carbines.[66]

After the disappointing failure of this turning movement, Lee ordered Hill to pull out Mahone's and Wilcox's divisions from the left of the line and hustle them toward Cold Harbor. Heth was directed to remain on the left to support Early in an attack on Grant's right.[67] On reaching the vicinity of Cold Harbor Thursday afternoon, Wilcox dispatched Lane's and McGowan's brigades to join Breckinridge in dislodging the enemy from Turkey Hill, an eminence commanding the Confederate right.[68] This accomplished, Hill directed Wilcox to entrench almost to the Chickahominy while Mahone occupied a supporting line behind Breckinridge's troops to the left of Wilcox. During these operations Jim Lane was severely wounded by an enemy sharp-shooter,[69] and Colonel John Barry assumed command of the Fourth Brigade.[70]

While Hill anchored the Confederate right, Heth joined Early's two divisions in striking the Federal right flank and driving the bluecoats from their strong entrenchments to a strong second line at Bethesda Church. Here the parched and half-starved Confederates dug in as darkness halted hostilities.[71]

During the rainy night of Thursday, June 2,[72] the Army of Northern Virginia consolidated and strengthened its escalloped front which extended from Heth on the extreme left to Wilcox on the right. By dawn the six mile fortifications had been made virtually impregnable against any assault the nearby restless Federals might attempt. These preparations were well rewarded. Grant, repeatedly frustrated in his attempts to slip around Lee, now decided to hurl his 107,000 man Army of the Potomac

---

[66] *Ibid.,* 536.

[67] By May 29 Ewell had become so incapacitated from an intestinal ailment that Lee granted him a leave of absence and placed Early in temporary command of the Second Corps. O.R., *36,* Part 1, 846; Early, 363.

[68] O.R., *36,* Part 1, 1032.

[69] *N. C. Regts., II,* 574.

[70] S.H.S.P., *9,* 244; Wilcox MS, Report, 48.

[71] According to one participant, some units of the army had received only two rations since breaking camp on the North Anna. One issue consisted of three crackers and a small slice of pork. Two days later a single cracker was issued to each soldier. C.M.H., *III,* 464-65, 467; Early, 363; Alexander, 539.

[72] Welch, 99.

against the Army of Northern Virginia in a desperate headlong attempt to batter his way into Richmond.[73]

Through Friday's pre-sunrise mist[74] came the scattered fire of retiring pickets followed shortly by dense columns of charging bluecoats shouting "Huzzah! Huzzah!"[75] But the frenzied yells were quickly muted as line after line fell under short range cross-fire from Confederate batteries and a shower of musketry delivered by infantrymen who cheerfully bantered among themselves as they took deliberate aim through crevices in the breastworks.[76] Most of the assaults were checked fifty yards from the lines,[77] but one pierced a salient on Breckinridge's front whereupon Hill threw in Finegan's brigade of Mahone's division and a Maryland battalion to restore the break.[78]

Within ten minutes the main Federal threat had been repulsed. Hill, who had witnessed the enemy's attack on the right, showed one of Lee's couriers a portion of Hancock's 3,000 dead and wounded which lay heaped in front of the lines.[79] "Tell General Lee," he said excitedly, "it is the same all along my front."[80] In his ardor Hill mistakenly extrapolated the situation under his immediate surveillance to Wilcox's front where there had been no fighting because of a dense swamp which the enemy had made no attempt to penetrate.[81]

Later in the day Grant twice renewed his attack against Heth on Lee's left. Cooke's brigade bore the brunt of the heaviest fighting in this sector and successfully repelled the assaults. Still another attempt by enemy cavalry and infantry to turn Heth's left and threaten his rear was broken up by H. H. Walker's bri-

---

[73] O.R., *36*, Part 3, 426; B. and L., *IV*, 187. Exact figures of Lee's strength at this time are not available but it approximated 50,000. This figure is based upon Colonel Taylor's estimate of 78,400 as the aggregate of all troops engaged from the Wilderness to Cold Harbor. B. and L., *IV*, 187. Casualties for the corresponding period totalled 25,000. *R. E. Lee, III*, 397n, 446n.

[74] B. and L., *IV*, 139.

[75] W. C. Oates, *The War Between the Union and the Confederacy and Its Lost Opportunities*, 365.

[76] C.M.H., *III*, 468; B. and L., *IV*, 141.

[77] Alexander, 542.

[78] *Ibid.;* B. and L., *IV*, 142; S.H.S.P., *23*, 193.

[79] B. and L., *IV*, 187; C.M.H., *III*, 468.

[80] John. E. Cooke, *The Life of General Robert E. Lee*, 406.

[81] *N. C. Regts., IV*, 199; Wilcox MS. Report, 48.

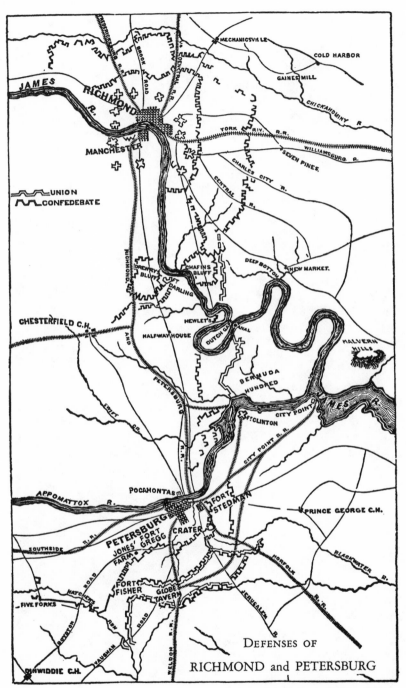

DEFENSES OF

RICHMOND and PETERSBURG

Adapted from *Confederate Military History.*

A. P. Hill's Troops Capture the Crater. From a painting by John A. Elder.

gade under Colonel Fry. Having thus acquitted itself, Heth's division rejoined the remainder of the Third Corps on the right.[82]

From Heth to Wilcox the Confederate line had held. Grant's blind frontal assaults netted him nothing but 7,000 casualties piled in front of Lee's lines where they lay exposed to the hot glare of a June sun. "It was not war; it was murder," wrote one Confederate officer.[83] Even among Grant's officers there was bitter agreement that "it was the dreary, dismal, bloody, ineffective close of the Lieutenant-General's first campaign with the Army of the Potomac, and corresponded in all its essential features with what had preceded it."[84] Grant himself subsequently reflected in his memoirs: "Cold Harbor is, I think, the only battle I ever fought that I would not fight over again under the same circumstances."[85]

---

[82] *Lee's Dispatches*, 213; Early, 363; O.R., *36*, Part 1, 1032.
[83] B. and L., *IV*, 141. Statement of Gen. E. M. Law.
[84] *Ibid.*, 212.
[85] U. S. Grant, *Personal Memoirs of U. S. Grant, II*, 276.

CHAPTER XIX

"What Is The Use Of Killing These Yankees?"

(Petersburg—Reams Station)

AFTER THE sickening slaugh-
ter of June 3 both sides confined hostilities to skirmishing,
sharpshooting, and artillery demonstrations which kept the troops
pinned down in the zig-zag trenches.[1] This respite afforded the
Confederates an opportunity to assess the new Federal commander
and his probable influence on the future course of the conflict.
Lee's officers concurred that Grant was "no strategist,"[2] but this
was scant comfort to the foot soldiers who, having fought almost
continuously since Grant assumed command, poignantly inquired:
"What is the use of killing these Yankees? It is like killing mos-
quitoes—two come for every one you kill."[3]

On June 6, Grant finally swallowed his pride and requested
a truce to permit withdrawal of the bloated Federal dead whose
nauseating odors blanketed the battlefield. While enemy litter-
bearers removed their fallen comrades, Breckinridge pulled his
troops out of the line and returned to the Valley which was being
overrun by a Federal force under General Hunter. Hill moved
Mahone's division into the vacated sector and placed Heth in
reserve.[4]

Slowly but steadily Grant's line drifted toward the Chickahominy. Then at daybreak on June 13 Lee learned that the enemy
trenches were empty. Confederate skirmishers advanced nearly
two miles without sighting any bluecoats whereupon Lee ordered
Anderson and Hill to hurry over the Chickahominy and pursue.[5]
Doggedly the Third Corps quick-stepped down the Charles City

[1] B. and L., *IV*, 219.
[2] *Ibid.*, 142.
[3] S.H.S.P., *14*, 531.
[4] *R. E. Lee, III*, 396.
[5] O.R., *36*, Part 1, 1035. Early left with the Second Corps before dawn on
June 13 to join Breckinridge in crushing Hunter, after which he proceeded on his
famous expedition to the outskirts of Washington. Early 371-72.

road toward Frayser's Farm where Hill and Longstreet had engaged McClellan on his retreat to the James during the Seven Days Battles.

Late in the afternoon Hill's vanguard made contact with enemy cavalry and infantry at Riddle's Shop, a smithy near Frayser's Farm.[6] When darkness ended the pursuit,[7] Lee disposed his attenuated army on a north-south line from White Oak Swamp to Malvern Hill thereby covering the eastern approaches to Richmond.[8] Lee ordered Hill to attack the next morning, but during the night the enemy vanished.[9] On the 15th Heth and Wilcox drove a screening force of enemy cavalry eastward four miles to Smith's Shop and took a number of prisoners. Late in the day Hill prepared to assail the rear of the retreating column with two of Heth's brigades and a detachment of cavalry, but when the cavalry failed to arrive in time he was forced to abandon this plan.[10]

During this period Lee was seriously handicapped in ascertaining Grant's positions and movements by the lack of cavalry, most of which was guarding the Virginia Central Railroad against an anticipated raid by Sheridan.[11] Although the commanding General suspected that the Army of the Potomac was heading for the James with the object of crossing and seizing Petersburg, he also had to guard against the possibility of an enemy march on Richmond. With the Army of Northern Virginia now reduced to less than 30,000,[12] Lee could neither assume the offensive nor afford to miscalculate his adversary's intentions.[13]

As indications mounted that Grant had moved his 110,000 man army across the James to demonstrate against Beauregard's small force at Petersburg, Lee cautiously began transferring his

---

[6] *Lee's Dispatches*, 228; *N. C. Regts., IV*, 200.
[7] *N. C. Regts., II*, 56.
[8] *Lee's Dispatches*, 239.
[9] *Ibid.*, 229.
[10] *Ibid.*, 240; O.R., *51*, Part 2, 1017.
[11] *Lee's Dispatches*, 222.
[12] *R. E. Lee, III*, 406; S.H.S.P., *14*, 538. Venable estimated the size of the army as 25,000 to 27,000 at this time.
[13] *Lee's Dispatches*, 231.

divisions to the south side of the James.[14] Hill's troops, bringing up the rear, crossed the pontoon bridge at Drewry's Bluff after midnight on June 18. As Powell Hill and his Chief-of-Staff rode southward along the dusty Petersburg Pike, the commander of the Third Corps voiced a pessimistic opinion that Lee would not be able to hold the line fronting Richmond and Petersburg with the small force at his disposal.[15]

Late Saturday afternoon the ragged, emaciated veterans of Hill's Corps reached Petersburg where they learned that Beauregard's vastly outnumbered defenders had skillfully and stubbornly frustrated the enemy's four-day campaign to capture the "back door" to Richmond.[16] That night Hill's men extended the Confederate right south of the town to the Weldon and Petersburg Railroad.[17] Perhaps because the army once again was safely and formidably reunited athwart Grant's path, weary Southerners remembered this night as "most brilliant and beautiful . . . with an exhilarating quality in it."[18]

With the arrival of Anderson's and Hill's Corps, "the spade took the place of the musket,"[19] and both sides spent Sunday and Monday strengthening and improving their lines. To protect themselves against mortar shells which the Federals now began lobbing into their lines, the Confederates constructed a labyrinth of deep, narrow trenches and mound-shaped "bomb-proofs" behind the front.[20] Although some of Hill's veterans predicted that they would have to swelter all summer in these lines, they were prepared "to endure anything rather than submit."[21]

Thus began the investment of Petersburg which Grant under-

---

[14] *R. E. Lee, III,* 439. At 4:30 on June 17, Lee sent the following message to Hill at Riddle's Shop: "General Beauregard reports large numbers of Grant's troops crossed the James River above Fort Powhatan yesterday. If you have nothing contradictory to this move, move to Chaffin's Bluff." B. and L., *IV,* 542. This was followed by another note at 10 P.M. from Lee's headquarters at Drewry's Bluff: "Move your command promptly at 3 A.M. to-morrow for Chaffin's Bluff. Cross the river and move to the Petersburg turnpike, there await further orders. Send to examine the bridges." S.H.S.P., *14,* 570.

[15] S.H.S.P., *20,* 202.

[16] D. Macrae, *The American At Home, I,* 170.

[17] C.M.H., *III,* 516.

[18] Alexander, 556.

[19] B. and L., *IV,* 544.

[20] Alexander, 560.

[21] Welch, 102.

took because, "Without a greater sacrifice of life than I was willing
to make, all could not be accomplished that I had designed north
of Richmond, I therefore determined . . . to move the army to
the south side of the James River, by the enemy's right flank, where
I felt I could cut off all his sources of supply except by the canal.[22]
The sources of supply to which Grant referred were the four
railroads radiating from Richmond and Petersburg. Most vulner-
able of these was the Weldon and Petersburg line which brought
troops and supplies from the seaboard states. Although Lee was
resigned to its ultimate loss, he hoped to keep the road open
until the summer crops could be harvested and shipped.[23]

Unobligingly, Grant immediately threatened this supply artery.
On Tuesday, June 21, he sent the II and VI Corps to extend the
Federal left toward· the railroad and also dispatched Wilson with
6,000 cavalry to destroy the line farther south and then sweep
northward.[24] Apprised of Grant's movements, Lee sent a mounted
force under his son Rooney to head off Wilson, while Hill started
Wilcox's and Mahone's divisions to the right to contest the advance of Federal infantry.[25]

Late Wednesday morning the enemy's front line comprising
three divisions of the II Corps pivoted on the right and swung
away from the supporting VI Corps in a maneuver designed to
envelop Hill. But as the two blue lines separated like the hands
of a clock, Mahone saw an opportunity to overwhelm the isolated
front line. As a civil engineer before the war he had surveyed this
region, and he now proposed to take three of his brigades together
with one of McIntosh's batteries by a concealed route and strike
the enemy's flank. Lee and Hill assented, whereupon the sallow
Virginian[26] rapidly led his men along a ravine to dense woods beyond the enemy's left division which was then moving into position.[27]

After forming in line of battle behind a strong skirmish line,[28]

---

[22] O.R., *36*, Part 1, 22.
[23] O.R., *42*, Part 2, 1194; S.H.S.P., *19*, 113.
[24] S.H.S.P., *2*, 272-73; C.M.H., *III*, 518; O.R., *40*, Part 1, 620-21.
[25] Alexander, 561.
[26] Sorrel, 276.
[27] S.H.S.P., *2*, 273.
[28] O.R., *40*, Part 1, 329, 366.

Mahone's yelling troops burst through the pines and fired a "pealing volley"[29] on the enemy's flank and rear. Completely surprised, the bluecoats fired a few shots and fled toward the line they had left that morning.[30] Several regiments surrendered in a body as panic spread along the disorganized front. Sensing a rout, Mahone's brigades under Sanders, Weisiger, and Wright pressed forward to curl up two divisions and overrun part of a third—capturing its battery which they turned on the defenders.[31]

Within an hour Mahone's whirlwind assault had swept the remainder of Hancock's II Corps more than a mile to a strong line of rifle pits and breastworks.[32] Here Mahone re-formed and deployed his brigades in sharp attacks at several points without success. Emboldened, the enemy rallied sufficiently to deliver a feeble counter-assault which was easily repulsed.[33] Meanwhile, Hill had ordered Wilcox's troops to support Mahone, but they arrived too late to renew the attack.[34] Mahone discerned the vulnerability of his advanced position in the abandoned enemy trenches, and he ordered his men to collect the wounded and retire to their original line.[35] The June 22 entry in the diary of the First Corps referred to Mahone's victory as "a handsome affair."[36] Certainly, the day's harvest of 1,742 prisoners, four light guns, eight standards, and a vast quantity of small arms[37] had a leavening effect on the morale of an army hungry for offensive exploits.

Grant, however, was undeterred by this costly repulse. On Thursday Hancock's II Corps reoccupied the lines from which it had been driven so ignominiously the previous day. Only this time Wright's VI Corps formed obliquely to the left of the II Corps to guard against another flank attack.[38] Later on this scorching June day, Wright advanced to the railroad, but before his wrecking force had done much damage Mahone arrived and drove

---

[29] S.H.S.P., *2*, 274.
[30] O.R., *40*, Part 1, 326-27.
[31] *Ibid.*, 326, 367.
[32] *Ibid.*, 326; O.R., *51*, Part 2, 1026.
[33] O.R., *51*, Part 2, 1026.
[34] *Ibid.*
[35] *Ibid.*, 1025.
[36] O.R., *40*, Part 1, 761.
[37] *Ibid.*, 750; S.H.S.P. *2*, 274.
[38] Alexander, 562.

the marauders back through the dense undergrowth.[39] During the night Perry's diminutive Florida brigade took a circuitous route and fell upon the enemy capturing 600 prisoners.[40] On Friday Hill finally halted Mahone's men who had gone without sleep for two nights.[41] Mahone's sudden display of zeal and skill impressed and reassured his corps commander who was entrusted with custody of the army's constantly threatened right.

While the Third Corps beat off infantry thrusts toward the Weldon and Petersburg Railroad, Wilson's bedizened cavalry squadrons struck the line at Reams Station about eight miles south of Petersburg. After tearing up several miles of track the Federal cavalry ranged westward to damage the Southside and the Richmond and Danville railroads. On his return Wilson was attacked during the afternoon of June 28 by Wade Hampton who had just joined forces with Rooney Lee. The running fight continued throughout the night as Wilson retreated toward Reams Station which he believed would now be in possession of the II and VI Corps.[42]

When Lee learned of Wilson's plight he sent Mahone with two brigades, two of Pegram's light batteries, and Fitz Lee's cavalry to intercept Wilson at Reams Station. While Hampton drove the harried raiders toward this depot at daybreak on the 29th, Fitz Lee assailed the Federal flank, and Mahone and Pegram closed the trap in front. After a brief, confused fight Wilson fled with those who could fight their way through the gray cordon of infantry and horse. Pressing forward through the heat and smoke, the Confederates took a thousand prisoners, all 12 of the enemy's guns, a thousand cringing fugitive negroes, plus stolen vehicles of all description crammed with plunder.[43]

*   *   *

Discouraged by the failure of conventional tactics to breach the Petersburg front, a regiment of Pennsylvania coal miners in Burnside's IX Corps conceived the novel stratagem of opening

[39] O.R., *40*, Part 1, 750; O.R., *51*, Part 2, 1027; C.M.H., *III*, 518.
[40] O.R., *40*, Part 1, 750; O.R., *51*, Part 2, 1028.
[41] O.R., *51*, Part 2, 1028.
[42] O.R., *40*, Part 1, 752; S.H.S.P., *2*, 274-75.
[43] Alexander, *562*; C.M.H., *III*, 518-19; S.H.S.P., *2*, 275-76.

a gap in the Confederate line by exploding a tremendous mine The Federal high command at first doubted the practicability of this project but finally approved it chiefly as a measure to occupy the men.[44]

Late in June, Colonel Henry Pleasants' 48th Pennsylvania Volunteers, 400 strong, began tunneling toward Elliott's Salient, a weak position just to the left of Hill's front, where the opposing lines narrowed to within two hundred yards of each other. Incessant enemy sharpshooting opposite this sector aroused Confederate suspicions, and Lee ordered his engineers to dig countermines. Four such shafts were sunk, but none intercepted or detected the 511-foot Federal gallery which passed twenty feet directly under the apex of the salient where it forked laterally to form a T.[45]

By July 23 the underground vault was ready for the placement of 320 powder kegs containing an 8,000 pound charge in which was concentrated the Federal hopes for a quick breakthrough.[46] But before giving the order to light the fuse, Grant sent Hancock's II Corps plus two divisions of Sheridan's cavalry to threaten Richmond in the hope that Lee would weaken the Petersburg defenses. Lee conformed by sending Anderson, Heth, and Rooney Lee's cavalry to head off Grant's diversionary movement. This left Hill with only Mahone's division and three of Wilcox's brigades which together with Johnson's and Hoke's divisions of Beauregard's command comprised a force of about 18,000 men to defend the ten mile Petersburg front.[47]

When Lee discerned that Grant's main assault would fall on Petersburg he issued orders on Friday night, July 29, for the city's defenders to be "ready to move at a moment's warning."[48] Despite this forewarning the men in the trenches were psychologically unprepared for the shock which shattered Elliott's Salient at 4:44 Saturday morning. With a burst resembling the simultaneous discharge of artillery, the eruption spewed skyward a

---

[44] B. and L., *IV*, 545 ff.
[45] Alexander, 563-65; B. and L., *IV*, 546, 548; S.H.S.P., *2*, 279.
[46] B. and L., *IV*, 548.
[47] Alexander, 566-68.
[48] S.H.S.P., *18*, 4.

mammoth column of flashing earth, splintered timbers, and mangled limbs.[49] As the dense cloud of white smoke billowed heavenward it uncovered a yawning crater 170 feet long, 60 feet wide and 30 feet deep.[50] Survivors recovering from the initial shock scampered to the rear, pursued by a deafening roar and fusilade from 150 enemy guns.[51]

Ten minutes after the explosion the dust had settled and a rising sun illuminated to 65,000 waiting bluecoats an undefended path to Petersburg which lay invitingly less than a mile away.[52] However, this day the fortunes of war did not wear blue. The commander of Burnside's leading division preferred to sit in a bomb-proof shelter behind the Union lines rather than direct the Federal advance into the "back door of Richmond."[53] Consequently, three Federal divisions swarmed into the crater and adjoining trenches where they foundered for four hours.[54]

At the sound of the explosion Powell Hill had leaped from his cot at Third Corps Headquarters to glimpse the rising column of smoke at Elliott's Salient. Then dressing quickly, he mounted Champ, his iron gray, and told Colonel Palmer: "I am going to Mahone's division, I will take his troops—all that can be spared—to the point of the explosion."[55] Then seeing that his Chief-of-Staff intended to accompany him, he instructed Palmer to remain at headquarters for any reports. With that he galloped furiously to Mahone's division which lay sprawled out four miles to the right of the salient.[56]

When Hill reached Mahone, the doughty little Virginian was inconspicuously withdrawing troops from their breastworks in compliance with orders he had just received from Lee to take two brigades to the salient.[57] Although Hill had bitterly resented and heatedly disputed Jackson's direct transmission of orders to subor-

---

[49] *Ibid.;* S.H.S.P., 2, 283; R. de Trobriand, *Four Years With the Army of the Potomac,* 608 ff.
[50] B. and L., *IV,* 551.
[51] *Ibid.;* Alexander, 569; S.H.S.P., *10,* 20.
[52] B. and L., *IV,* 545 ff.; Alexander, 568; S.H.S.P., 2, 293.
[53] B. and L., *IV,* 556.
[54] *Ibid.,* 551-56; C.M.H., *III,* 521.
[55] S.H.S.P., *20,* 203-04.
[56] Alexander, 568.
[57] S.H.S.P., 2, 289.

dinates in the Light Division, he did not question Lee's propriety in this emergency to send orders directly to Mahone. Instead, he simply ordered Pegram to accompany Mahone with two light batteries,[58] and then joined Lee near the salient to discuss the mounting crisis.[59]

The outlook was far from reassuring. Enemy flags studded the rim of the crater inside which a "forrest of glittering bayonets" was crammed.[60] Federal troops also occupied both flanks of the crater from which they had already launched several abortive assaults.[61] Only the accurate converging fire of Lee's sparse batteries coupled with musketry fire from surviving defenders on this sector barred the advance of Burnside's restive troops.[62]

After sizing up the situation the two commanders parted, and Hill rode back to hasten the Virginia and Georgia brigades which Mahone was hustling along a hidden ravine to a point opposite the crater.[63] Here Mahone formed his old brigade, now commanded by Colonel D. A. Weisiger, in line of battle in a hollow parallel to the enemy. It was now about 8:30,[64] and as the 800 grim veterans filed into position Mahone patted them affectionately on the shoulders and said, "Give 'em hell boys."[65]

The Virginia brigade had just formed and lay flat upon the ground in front of the hollow when an impatient Federal officer seized a stand of colors, vaulted the Federal breastworks to the left of the crater, and called on his men to charge. Mahone, realizing that it was imperative to stem this assault before it gained momentum, ordered the Virginians to charge.[66] The cheering regiments in perfect alignment double-quicked up the hill behind their tattered battle-flags which gleamed in the bright sunlight.[67] Supported by batteries, mortars, and sharpshooters, the gray line

---

[58] *Ibid.*

[59] S.H.S.P., *18*, 5.

[60] S.H.S.P., *2*, 290; S.H.S.P., *28*, 218.

[61] B. and L., *IV*, 554-57.

[62] Alexander, 569-71; C.M.H., *III*, 521; O.R., *40*, Part 1, 759.

[63] S.H.S.P., *2*, 289; J. S. Wise, *The End of an Era* (cited hereafter as *The End of an Era*), 357 ff.

[64] S.H.S.P., *18*, 6.

[65] N. M. Blake, *William Mahone of Virginia*, 56; S.H.S.P., *28*, 218.

[66] S.H.S.P., *2*, 291; *The End of an Era*, 357 ff.

[67] S.H.S.P., *18*, 10.

obediently reserved its fire until within ten paces of the enemy who at close range was found to include negroes as well as whites.[68] Infuriated at the idea of fighting negroes,[69] Weisiger's men delivered a deadly fire and rushed the foe with bayonets and clubbed muskets.[70] Within ten minutes the Federals had fled to their trenches and into the crater, whereupon the Virginians planted their own flags along parapets north of the immense pit.[71]

An hour after Weisiger's charge, Mahone ordered Wright's Georgia brigade to clear the enemy from a fifty yard spoke radiating south of the crater. The Virginia brigade cooperated in this maneuver by turning their freshly captured muskets on any bluecoats who ventured above the rim of the crater. However, Federal artillery raked the advancing Georgians so severely that the line deflected to the left where the men took shelter behind Weisiger.[72] Later, a second attempt to carry the enemy segment to the right also failed.[73]

It was now 11 o'clock.[74] The noonday sun was fearfully hot; wounded were crying for water which empty canteens could not relieve; and Mahone's cartridges were running low. The enemy essayed a spirited attack which was repulsed, but unless Hill's troops soon seized the crater and its adjoining works it would be only a matter of time before the Federals pushed their numerically superior forces through the thin defenders and took Petersburg.[75] Fortunately, Brigadier General Sanders' Alabama brigade, which Mahone had ordered up, arrived shortly and formed into line in the ravine from which the Virginians had charged earlier. The Alabamians were then instructed to head straight for the crater while the Sixty-First North Carolina regiment on the left and Colquitt's brigade to the right covered their flanks.[76]

---

[68] *Ibid.;* S.H.S.P., *20,* 219.
[69] S.H.S.P., *18,* 15.
[70] *The End of an Era,* 357 ff.
[71] B. and L., *IV,* 558; C.M.H., *III,* 521; S.H.S.P., *2,* 291-92; S.H.S.P., *18,* 15. An excellent eye-witness account of Weisiger's charge is recorded in S.H.S.P., *18,* 3 ff.
[72] S.H.S.P., *18.* 15; S.H.S.P., *28,* 219.
[73] S.H.S.P., *18,* 16.
[74] *Ibid.,* 17; S.H.S.P., *2,* 293.
[75] S.H.S.P., *18,* 17.
[76] *Ibid.,* 18; Alexander, 572.

Sharply at 1 o'clock the crouching line dashed forward in the face of surprisingly scattered opposition, and Sanders' troops quickly reached the crater. Thereupon, Confederate batteries ceased firing while forty volunteers from the Alabama brigade prepared to assault the disorganized mob of bluecoats inside the man-made volcano. But before this little band had completed its dispositions, a white handkerchief attached to a ramrod was hoisted above the edge of the crater and 1,101 despondent Federals (including a general whose cork leg had been shattered) crawled out of the pit to surrender and file to the rear.[77]

At 3:25 Lee reported to the War Department: "We have retaken the salient and driven the enemy back to his lines with loss."[78] Hill's men had mended the breach and narrowly averted a breakthrough to Petersburg. Although Powell Hill himself had responded promptly and surely to the crisis at the crater, he neither claimed nor received the major credit which deservedly went to Mahone who had personally directed this brilliant counter-offensive. Hill, who constantly strove to weld a strong esprit de corps within his command, was delighted at the complete metamorphosis that had transformed the lethargic Mahone of Gettysburg into the dynamic Mahone of the Crater. And when Mahone spoke of refusing his long overdue promotion to permanent rank of Major General in command of R. H. Anderson's former division, Hill enjoined: "You cannot think of declining."[79]

*   *   *

Following the battle of the Crater, Hill's troops enjoyed three weeks of comparative quiet punctuated by picket fire during the day and fiery trails of mortar shells at night.[80] As soon as the mortar shells or "lamp-pots" exploded, Hill's men dashed out to gather the fragments which they sold to Ordnance for a few cents with which to supplement their scant rations.[81] Despite the oppressive heat Hill ordered that all men be given some sort of

---

[77] B. and L., *IV*, 558n; S.H.S.P., *2*, 293.
[78] O.R., *40*, Part 1, 752.
[79] President Davis approved Mahone's promotion to Major General on August 3, to date from July 30. O.R., *42*, Part 2, 1156-57. *Lee's Lieutenants, III*, 553n.
[80] S.H.S.P., *2*, 294.
[81] S.H.S.P., *14*, 374.

constant duty to divert their attention from the wormy peas, shredded "uniforms," and general ennui.[82]

On Wednesday morning, August 18, mounted pickets reported the movement of Federal infantry toward the Petersburg and Weldon Railroad.[83] Beauregard, who was now in temporary command of the Petersburg defenses, ordered Hill to ascertain the enemy's dispositions while he sent to Lee for reinforcements from the Richmond front. Hill promptly dispatched Heth with two brigades and one of Pegram's batteries[84] which soon struck the enemy's exposed left flank near Globe Tavern and captured nearly a thousand prisoners.[85] Despite this momentary setback, the enemy, which proved to be Warren's V Corps supported by cavalry, rallied and retained their hold on more than a mile of the partially destroyed tracks.[86]

When Beauregard learned that at least three Federal divisions had effected a lodgement on the railroad, he ordered Hill to reinforce Heth with three of Mahone's brigades, three of Pegram's batteries, and Rooney Lee's cavalry which was just arriving from Richmond. The combined force was to assail Warren and dislodge him from the railroad.[87]

Hill quickly concentrated these units at the Davis House near Globe Tavern where he hurled Heth's men against Warren's left while Mahone slipped through the woods to assail the right flank.[88] Heth drove over 1,500 bluecoats from their breastworks into the muzzles of Mahone's advancing troops which had quietly collared the enemy's skirmishers and seized the front line in that sector.[89] Hill then withdrew and re-formed two of Mahone's brigades which had become disorganized in the thick undergrowth.[90] Again he ordered them forward, but reinforcements from Burnside's IX Corps were now at hand to support Warren in a counterattack

[82] Caldwell, 168.
[83] B. and L., *IV*, 568.
[84] O.R., *42*, Part 1, 858.
[85] C.M.H., *III*, 523.
[86] B. and L., *IV*, 568.
[87] O.R., *42*, Part 1, 858.
[88] C.M.H., *III*, 523.
[89] B. and L., *IV*, 569; Heth MS, 162.
[90] O.R., *42*, Part 1, 940.

which reeled back Hill's men.[91] Just before dark Hill instructed Heth to launch still a third attack which Warren also repelled.[92]

While Hill's foot soldiers butted the enemy's lines, Rooney Lee's cavalry strove to turn the Federal left but Federal horse drove them toward Reams Station.[93] Hence, although Hill had captured 2,700 prisoners and mauled Warren's corps he wrote regretfully that night to Beauregard: "My weakness prevented me from following it up as I would like to have done."[94]

The next day Warren withdrew and entrenched his troops on more open ground from which his artillery could sweep Hill's front.[95] Undaunted, Hill advanced Mahone under cover of Pegram's twelve guns against these bristling lines. But in the face of thirty cannonading guns the serried line recoiled. Mahone then quickly rallied his survivors and sent them against a narrow segment on the enemy's right. One brigade breasted the works only to be captured in a body, while the other units retired.[96] Mahone then carefully reconnoitered the front and reported to Hill that with two more brigades he could dislodge Warren before nightfall. Hill gave orders for the requisite troops to support Mahone, but the brigades arrived too late to make the projected attack advisable.[97] Consequently, Warren was able to maintain his tourniquet on the Petersburg and Weldon Railroad. Henceforth Lee's incoming supplies on this line had to be unloaded twenty miles south of Petersburg and transferred to wagons for transport to the city.[98]

Warren's success at Globe Tavern emboldened Grant to apply another clamp further down the railroad at Reams Station. He ordered two divisions of Hancock's II Corps augmented by Gregg's cavalry division to leapfrog over Warren's V Corps and destroy the tracks several miles south of the burned station house at Reams.[99] Hancock's men had begun tearing up the rails when they

---

[91] B. and L., *IV*, 569-70.
[92] *Ibid.*, 570.
[93] *Ibid.*
[94] O.R., *42*, Part 1, 940.
[95] B. and L., *IV*, 571.
[96] *Ibid.*; S.H.S.P., *2*, 296.
[97] S.H.S.P., *2*, 296n.
[98] *R. E. Lee*, *III*, 487.
[99] B. and L., *IV*, 571.

were abruptly interrupted on Sunday, August 22 by Hampton's cavalry which had been reconnoitering in the vicinity. After a sharp contest[100] Hampton notified Lee of Hancock's operations and urged that the commanding General dispatch infantry to cooperate in an assault on the exposed and isolated II Corps.[101]

Lee concurred with Hampton's recommendation, and on Tuesday, August 24, Hill withdrew 1,750 men[102] from their trenches around Petersburg and led them south along country roads to Armstrong's Mill,[103] about two miles west of Reams Station. Here the troops bivouacked for the night.[104] As Lee agreed with Hill that the failure to evict Warren from Globe Tavern was due to "the smallness of the attacking force",[105] he enjoined Hill to employ adequate troops to insure the success of the Reams expedition. Accordingly, Hill had taken Hampton's two cavalry divisions, eight infantry brigades, and a portion of Pegram's artillery battalion.[106]

Early Wednesday morning Hill directed Hampton to take the main body of cavalry around the enemy's left and lure Hancock southward along the railroad. Meanwhile the infantry, screened by the remaining cavalry, would approach the station across flat, wooded country and assail the opposite flank.[107] Hill's reconnaissance showed that the II Corps was disposed along a U which was intersected on each flank by the railroad. As Hill's troops approached the enemy's lines they discerned formidable breastworks consisting of an abatis of felled trees interlaced with wire.[108]

Hill posted Pegram's 8 guns in a position where they could enfilade and take in reverse the Federal lines at close range.[109] At 2 o'clock Hill ordered Wilcox to take two of his brigades which were up and attack Hancock's right flank. The assaulting column

---

[100] S.H.S.P., *19*, 114.
[101] *N. C. Regts., V*, 207.
[102] *N. C. Regts., II*, 448.
[103] Caldwell, 180.
[104] S.H.S.P., *19*, 114.
[105] O.R., *42*, Part 2, 1194.
[106] *N. C. Regts., V*, 208.
[107] B. and L., *IV*, 571; O.R., *42*, Part 1, 942-43.
[108] *N. C. Regts., II*, 258, 389.
[109] C.M.H., *III*, 523.

charged vigorously but unsuccessfully, and a number of killed and wounded were left within a few yards of the enemy lines.[110]

As the North Carolina brigades of Lane, Cooke, and MacRae arrived Hill ordered them to form behind sharpshooting skirmishers for another attack on Hancock's right.[111] At 5 o'clock Pegram shook the enemy breastworks and demoralized the raw defenders with a barrage of shot and shell at musketry range.[112] Meanwhile Hill's sharpshooters endeavored to silence the enemy's guns by picking off their tireless artillerists.[113] In the wake of Pegram's cannonade the yelling Tar Heel brigades moved forward over sharpened tree limbs and brushwood in what one participant labelled "the most brilliant *dash*—for indeed it was a dash—of the war."[114] On striking the enemy's breastworks, desperate hand-to-hand fighting ensued during which an aging veteran in Lane's brigade admonished: "Yankees, if you know what is best for you, you had better make a blue streak towards sunset."[115] As the blue-coats broke, General Heth, who had insisted on acting as a co-color-bearer, planted the flag of the Twenty-Sixth North Carolina regiment on the breastworks.[116]

Hancock personally attempted to stem the tide by drawing reinforcements from his left flank only to have that sector overrun by Hampton's alert dismounted cavalry.[117] Assailed on all sides Hancock abandoned his works leaving 2,150 prisoners, 12 stand of colors, 9 pieces of artillery, 3,100 stand of small-arms, and 32 horses in Confederate hands. Hill's loss totalled only 720 most of whom were in Lane's brigade.[118]

That night Hill's men proudly forwarded the captured guns to corps headquarters,[119] and jested that Grant would have to send

---

110 B. and L., *IV*, 572; *N. C. Regts.*, *V*, 208.
111 Caldwell, 180. Brigadier General William MacRae had been assigned command of Kirkland's brigade on January 27. *N. C. Regts.*, *II*, 385. This brigade was transferred from Heth to Mahone for awhile during the summer of 1864. *N. C. Regts.*, *IV*, 564.
112 B. and L., *IV*, 573; S.H.S.P., *19*, 117.
113 Caldwell, 180.
114 *N. C. Regts.*, *II*, 448, 575.
115 S.H.S.P., *9*, 354.
116 *N. C. Regts.*, *II*, 388-89.
117 *N. C. Regts.*, *V*, 210; B. and L., *IV*, 573.
118 *N. C. Regts.*, *V*, 211; O.R., *42*, Part 2, 940.
119 *N. C. Regts.*, *II*, 448.

Hancock back North to recruit his command.[120] Next morning Hill ordered Hampton's men to occupy the trenches while the infantry returned triumphantly to Petersburg.[121]

The engagement at Reams Station marked Powell Hill's outstanding tactical achievement as commander of the Third Corps. With an offensive dash reminiscent of the Light Division's hey-day, Hill had marched his men with customary promptness and fallen upon Hancock's isolated corps before it could effect a junction with Warren or Burnside.[122] Hill's plan of attack was well-conceived and brilliantly executed save for the use of inadequate troops in the initial assault. Although this success only temporarily discouraged further attacks on the railroad, Hill's harvest, which included a crop of prisoners exceeding his entire force, did much to boost sagging morale in the South at the same time it raised Democratic hopes in the North for a victory against Lincoln in the fall elections.

---

[120] *Ibid.*, 480.

[121] O.R., *42*, Part 1, 944; Caldwell, 181.

[122] General Orlando Wilcox's division of Burnside's IX Corps arrived shortly before dark, "but considering the utter demoralization of one of his (Hancock's) divisions, and the fatigue of all the brave men that had stood, Hancock did not think it wise to renew the fight that evening." Gen'l. Wilcox, B. and L., *IV,* 573.

CHAPTER XX

"He Is At Rest Now"

DURING THE MONTHS following his victory at Reams Station, Powell Hill watched with growing apprehension the inexorable approach of the eventuality he had forecast to Colonel Palmer as the two rode toward Petersburg in June. Then, Hill had confided to his Chief-of-Staff that he did not see how Lee could hold the extended Richmond-Petersburg front with the disparate force at his disposal.

As the summer campaign drew to a close, Grant abandoned further costly assaults on Lee's lines and concentrated on siege tactics. The besieger of Vicksburg now forged an impregnable cordon of forts connected by infantry parapets formidably aproned with ditches and abatis.[1] He then planned a series of coordinated feints against Richmond and Petersburg designed to pin down the attenuated defenders all along the front while the Federal left inched westward around Hill's line toward the Appomattox River. With Petersburg thus encircled Grant could deprive Lee's hungry army of supplies arriving from western Virginia via the Southside Railroad and at the same time stretch the Confederate line to the breaking point.[2] Lee fully recognized this calamitous threat and warned the Government: "If the enemy cannot be prevented from extending his left, he will eventually reach the Appomattox and cut us off from the south side altogether."[3]

Along the Third Corps' front which ran southwest of Petersburg, Hill had approximately 13,000 men[4] with which to bar Grant's envelopment. Heth held the right, Wilcox the left, and Mahone held his division in readiness as a mobile reserve.[5] Although Hill's ranks had been severely depleted by recent

---

[1] Alexander, 560-61.
[2] O.R., *42*, Part 2, 1213.
[3] O.R., *43*, Part 3, 1133.
[4] Monthly returns for the Army of Northern Virginia, August 31, 1864, listed 12,374 effectives and 1,071 officers in the Third Corps. O.R., *42*, Part 2, 1214.
[5] Caldwell, 194.

campaigns, their loss was partially compensated by the return of experienced commanders to their brigades. Kirkland, Lane, and McGowan had recovered sufficiently from their wounds to rejoin their commands in August.[6] Archer, Hill's gallant charter-brigadier in the original Light Division, reported for duty with the others, but his imprisonment following Gettysburg had so enfeebled him that he was able to serve only two months before succumbing to a fatal illness.[7]

Parallel to the Federal arc south of Petersburg, Hill set his men to work digging trenches and fashioning a bearded screen of chevaux-de-frise.[8] The bronzed troops labored daily from 8 to 4[9] railing all the while against the "able-bodied exempts" and the scant, undelectable ration of bread and meat.[10] Otherwise the men in the ranks appeared "as happy and lively as could be."[11] Many expected that Grant would soon launch another offensive in order to bolster "Old Abe's" candidacy. And although the Confederates unalterably opposed the Emancipator's military objectives, there was sentiment in favor of his re-election, because as one analyst in the Third Corps put it: "McClellan might have the Union restored, if elected. I should prefer to remain at war for the rest of my life rather than to have any connection with the Yankees."[12]

On Thursday, September 29, Grant undertook the extension of his left flank toward the Southside Railroad—prefacing this movement with a diversionary attack against Fort Harrison on the outer defenses of Richmond. On Hill's front Hampton's cavalry cushioned the initial impact of four Federal divisions thrusting westward.[13] The next day Hill sent Heth's and Wilcox's divisions to support Hampton. The opposing infantry collided at Jones Farm where after a short but stubborn fight the bluecoats retired in confusion, leaving the field littered with such welcome items as oil

---

[6] O.R., *42*, Part 2, 1185, 1189, 1190.
[7] *Ibid.*, 1207.
[8] S.H.S.P., *27*, 28.
[9] *N. C. Regts., II*, 390; Caldwell, 196.
[10] Welch, 107.
[11] *Ibid.*, 110.
[12] *Ibid.*, 114.
[13] C.M.H., *III*, 525.

cloths, blankets, and knapsacks.[14] As darkness fell the enemy rallied behind hastily improvised breastworks at the Pegram House almost two miles south of Jones Farm.[15]

After sleeping on their arms Hill's men advanced the following morning and drove the enemy from the Pegram House.[16] As the Yankees retreated in disorder, Major Wooten's sharpshooters of Lane's brigade dashed among the defenders and captured about 300—a larger number than he had in his whole command.[17] Lane's men then held the breastworks throughout the rainy day, returning again that evening to their lines at Jones Farm.[18] The enemy attacked Heth the next day and were repulsed.[19]

In this engagement known as the Battle of Jones' Farm and also as the Battle of Peebles' Farm, Hill checked Grant's thrust to the Southside Railroad, captured about 2,000 prisoners, and inflicted over 1,000 casualties with but slight loss.[20] Nevertheless, Grant had succeeded in extending his flanks three miles to ground on which his engineers soon began constructing Fort Fisher, an enormous earthen fort which securely anchored the Federal left.

Confronted with the constant threat of further enemy elongations opposite his front, Hill relied increasingly upon the services of Major Thomas J. Wooten of the Eighteenth North Carolina to obtain information about the enemy's movements and intentions. This North Carolinian, "young, cool and brave, but modest as a girl,"[21] specialized in "seine haulings" which netted prisoners for questioning at headquarters. Wooten's technique consisted in reconnoitering an appointed sector during the daytime. Then at a propitious hour—usually shortly before dawn—his selected trainees crawled in pairs through enemy picket lines and approached the rifle pits. At a predetermined signal, the sharpshooters rushed forward between the pits, fanned out on both sides and swept

---

[14] *N. C. Regts.*, *II*, 355, 481; S.H.S.P., *9*, 355.
[15] *N. C. Regts.*, *II*, 575, 669; Welch, 106.
[16] S.H.S.P., *9*, 356; O.R., *42*, Part 1, 859.
[17] *N. C. Regts.*, *II*, 669; *N. C. Regts.*, *IV*, 478; S.H.S.P., *9*, 356.
[18] *N. C. Regts.*, *II*, 481; S.H.S.P., *9*, 356.
[19] O.R., *42*, Part 1, 859.
[20] S.H.S.P., *2*, 297n.
[21] *N. C. Regts.*, *IV*, 476.

in defenders and plunder.[22] Wooten led his men on these dashing forays repeatedly without losing a single man,[23] although on one expedition his "catch" subsequently turned out to consist of seven Dutchmen whose "foreign gibberish" was incomprehensible at headquarters.[24]

During the latter part of October the Federals showed signs of renewing activity. North of the James, Grant again feinted toward Richmond where he was easily repulsed by Longstreet, who had recently resumed command of the First Corps. Simultaneously, the Federal commander dispatched three army corps together with cavalry, over 17,000 strong, westward across the Boydton Plank Road where they were to turn north and seize the Southside Railroad.[25]

On the morning of October 27, Burnside's IX Corps demonstrated against Hill's front while Hancock pushed two long flanking columns of his II Corps past Hampton's cavalry to the Boydton Plank Road. Hill, too ill to command in the field,[26] ordered Heth and Mahone to rush their divisions to the right and interpose them between the enemy and the Southside Railroad. Heth took charge of these operations, and by rapid marches arrived in time to confront Hancock as the bluecoats turned northward toward the railroad. Hancock, surprised at finding Hill's men across his path, halted and threw up breastworks.[27]

When Hancock ventured forth again later in the day, Heth organized a counterattack. Shortly after dark Mahone's troops sliced into a gap between the II Corps and one of Warren's divisions that was hurrying to Hancock's assistance. Then while Mahone assailed Hancock's right, Hampton's cavalrymen fell on the opposite flank which broke and retreated in confusion through the dense forest. However, Hancock managed to stay the rout with his superior numbers, and under cover of darkness withdrew to his fortified position on the Boydton Plank Road. Morning found

---

[22] Caldwell, 195-96; *N. C. Regts., II,* 59, 175.
[23] *N. C. Regts., IV,* 476; S.H.S.P., *9,* 354.
[24] *N. C. Regts., IV,* 479; S.H.S.P., *9,* 494.
[25] C.M.H., *III,* 525.
[26] S.H.S.P., *2,* 297n; "Sketches of Southern Generals," Part V.
[27] C.M.H., *III,* 525-26.

the Third Corps holding the approaches to the Southside Railroad and 700 prisoners.[28] Several days after this engagement Lee wrote Hill: ". . . I am much gratified at the results obtained, and pleased with the good conduct displayed by the officers and men. You have rendered a valuable service, and I desire to tender to you, and to the officers and men engaged, my thanks for what they have accomplished. . ."[29]

Early in November a cold spell ushered in another severe winter.[30] Hill's veterans who had endured privations in winter camps at Fredericksburg and Orange Court House now faced the bleakest winter of the war. At times Hill was unable to procure for his troops more than a sixth of a ration of corn meal and a quarter to a third of a pound of rancid Nassau bacon per day, and during one week the men went without meat of any kind.[31] When wheat flour was available, Mahone ordered his commissaries to bake it into light wholesome bread, but his men would have none of it. Instead, they preferred the hard chunks concocted by heating a mixture of flour and grease which they claimed stayed in a soldier's stomach and quenched his appetite.[32]

Several weeks before Christmas the Northern press whetted Confederate appetites by publishing descriptions of bountiful yuletide dinners which the people of the United States planned for their fighting men. Southerners proudly tried to follow suit but their efforts netted a pathetic fare exemplified in one of Hill's companies which received for the entire unit: 1 turkey drumstick, 1 rib of mutton, 1 slice of roast beef, 2 biscuits, and 1 slice of lightbread![33]

During this bleak period Hill's threadbare and cadaverous troops busied themselves with picket duty and the construction of additional breastworks which stretched ever farther to the right where Grant was uncoiling his blue line. In rifle pits, spaced ten yards apart, fully accoutered squads remained on duty all day.

[28] *Ibid.,* 526; S.H.S.P., *2,* 297-98.
[29] Letter from R. E. Lee to A. P. Hill, Oct. 31, 1864. Copy furnished to the author through the courtesy of The Virginia Historical Society.
[30] Alexander, 585; Welch, 114, 123.
[31] S.H.S.P., *2,* 299; Sorrel, 281; Caldwell, 197.
[32] Sorrel, 281.
[33] *N. C. Regts., IV,* 204.

After dark at least one soldier was required to remain awake with a rifle in his hand while the rest slept. On raw, blustery days the men huddled around blazing pines surreptitiously gathered from the 500 yard wooded strip between the picket line and breastworks.[34]

Grant further discomforted the Third Corps early in December by sending Warren's infantry and Gregg's cavalry to raid the Weldon and Petersburg Railroad near the North Carolina border. Hill promptly pulled his men out of the lines and marched them southward through blinding snow and chafing winds in pursuit of the marauding bluecoats. Hill's barefoot troops suffered intensely as they slid along slick sleety roads to within a few miles of Belfield. On learning that Warren had turned back, Hill about-faced his men who hurried to intercept their familiar adversary. Pegram and Cooke jostled Gregg's cavalry at Reams Station but were unable to overtake Warren's foot-soldiers.[35] As Hill's disconsolate veterans plodded the remaining distance toward Petersburg, one disgruntled soldier from Florida mused: "Ain't Florida a great place? There the trees stay green all the time, and we have oranges and lemons, and figs and bananas, and it is the greatest country for taters you ever did see."[36]

*   *   *

Heretofore the Army of Northern Virginia had endured severe privations and reverses with the reassuring hope that ample resources and superb leadership would bring ultimate victory. However, during the winter of 1864-65 Lee's despondent army was sustained only by its faith in the Confederate high command. Even this spark of optimism dimmed with the rapid encroachment of blue tides on other fronts. At the turn of the year Georgia and the Gulf states were in Federal hands; Sherman's victorious army was poised for its northward march to join Grant; and in the Shenandoah Valley, Sheridan had crushed Early. Cognizant of their country's desperate plight, Hill's veterans resignedly concluded

---

[34] *Ibid.*, 203; Caldwell, 194-95; Welch, 123.
[35] *N. C. Regts., II*, 450, 481, 576, 669-70; *N. C. Regts., IV*, 43, 205.
[36] S.H.S.P., *9*, 489.

that the Army of Northern Virginia, thinly spread along a 35 mile front, could sustain only one more campaign.[37]

Added to this grim outlook was the demoralizing influence of widespread desertion. Every day about a hundred men responded to pathetic appeals to return home and care for starving children or sick relatives. These importunities were coupled with assurances that deserters no longer were branded as dishonorable.[38] In a single fortnight 500 deserted from Heth's and Wilcox's divisions alone.[39] Alarmed lest the corps evaporate, a number of Hill's officers and men drafted and adopted resolutions reaffirming their faith in the cause, re-enlisting "for the war unconditionally and without reserve,"[40] and calling upon "all good people at home to give us their sympathy and support, to send us food to sustain life, and recruits to fill our wasted ranks."[41]

Despite failing health Powell Hill endeavored to maintain the tone of his command. The following contemporary account describes him during this period:

> Through the last winter Hill's face and form became familiar sights to the troops. He was constantly on the lines, riding with firm graceful seat, looking every inch a soldier. Like General Lee, he was rarely much attended. One staff officer and a single courier formed his usual escort, and often he made the rounds alone. Of ordinary height, his figure was slight but athletic, his carriage erect, and his dress plainly neat. His expression was grave but gentle, his manner so courteous as almost to lack decision, but was contradicted by rigidity about the mouth and chin, and bright flashing eyes that even in repose told another tale. In moments of excitement he never lost self-control nor composure of demeanor, but his glance was as sharp as an eagle's and his voice could take a metallic ring. Of all the Confederate leaders he was the most genial and lovable in disposition.[42]

Throughout the winter Hill enjoyed the company of his wife and two baby girls who stayed at J. M. Venable's cottage on the

---

[37] Caldwell, 198.

[38] Alexander, 585-86; Caldwell, 192; "Letters of Luther R. Mills," *N. C. Historical Review, IV,* 308, 1927.

[39] O.R., *46,* Part 2, 1254.

[40] S.H.S.P., *9,* 357-61.

[41] *Ibid.,* 493.

[42] *Annals of the War,* 703.

western fringe of Petersburg.[43] Here in the companionship of his family and friends he occasionally found time to shed the burdens of command and divert his thoughts from the approaching crisis which loomed so ominously.[44]

Early in February Grant took advantage of the coldest spell of the winter to extend and fortify his left flank still further to a point on Hatcher's Run three miles below Burgess' Mill.[45] The following month he established headquarters opposite the Third Corps to direct the final act of the Petersburg drama.[46]

Meanwhile, Powell Hill's health progressively deteriorated to such an alarming state that about March 20 Lee insisted he take a sick furlough to recuperate. Reluctantly, Hill left the front and journeyed with his wife and children to the refugee house of his cousin, Thomas Hill, Jr. on the James River just below the Bellona Arsenal.[47] During this respite Hill accompanied Colonel Hill, the Paymaster-General, to the latter's office in Richmond. As word of the General's presence in the capital spread, a number of prominent citizens called to pay their respects. When their conversation turned to the possible evacuation of Richmond, Hill became visibly annoyed and vehemently asserted that he did not wish to survive the fall of the capital.[48]

The nature of the malady which plagued Hill during the latter years of the war is nowhere disclosed in contemporary accounts, although there are numerous allusions to his ill health. Thus, G. W. Tucker, his chief courier, wrote: "During the entire winter of 1864-65 General Hill was an invalid. . ."[49] G. M. Sorrel, who assumed command of Wright's Georgia brigade in November, 1864, wrote: "His (Hill's) health was impaired toward the close

---

[43] This cottage was located north of an extension of Washington Street and across the road from corps headquarters at "Indiana." S.H.S.P., *11*, 565; communication from Floyd B. Taylor, Superintendent of Petersburg National Military Park.
[44] Chamberlayne, 291-92, 299; "Sketches of Southern Generals," V.
[45] B. and L., *IV*, 578; *N. C. Regts., II*, 390.
[46] B. and L., *IV*, 708.
[47] S.H.S.P., *11*, 565; S.H.S.P., *19*, 184-85; Pollard, 447; "Sketches of Southern Generals," Part V.
[48] S.H.S.P., *19*, 185.
[49] S.H.S.P., *11*, 565.

of the war."[50] Captain W. G. McCabe, Adjutant of Pegram's Battalion, stated: "Much he suffered during this campaign from a grievous malady. . ."[51] Pollard referred to Hill's health simply as "delicate and feeble."[52] Nor is there any account of his ailment in *The Medical and Surgical War of the Rebellion (1861-65)*.

In the absence of specific medical information, Dr. Douglas Southall Freeman has suggested that Hill's malady may have been psycho-somatic.[53] He bases this hypothesis on the premise that Hill's elevation to corps command imposed vast responsibilities which proved overburdening to the proud, conscientious Virginian. On the eve of battle, viz, Gettysburg, the Wilderness, and reportedly at Reams Station, this anxiety presumably induced an indisposition which markedly impaired his capacity as a field commander. However, it must be remembered that throughout his career Hill had been in delicate health. At West Point he repeated his third year because of illness; in the far South he contracted a severe case of yellow fever; and while courting Nelly Marcy his prospective mother-in-law objected to his suit on the basis that his "health and constitution had become so impaired, so weakened, that no mother could yield her daughter. . . unless to certain unhappiness."[54]

Moreover, Hill thrived on increased responsibilities during the first two years as he catapulted from Colonel of the Thirteenth Virginia Regiment to Major General in command of the Light Division. In the latter capacity his burdens during the Seven Days campaign approximated those of corps command. Therefore the record would seem to indicate that psycho-neurosis alone was not the cause of Hill's physical decline.

In an attempt to diagnose the nature of Hill's affliction in the light of current medical knowledge the author has consulted several medical authorities. The possibility that he may have suffered after-effects from his pre-war bout with yellow fever is unlikely in view of the fact that this disease normally produces

---

[50] Sorrel, 89.
[51] S.H.S.P., *2*, 302.
[52] Pollard, 446-47.
[53] *Lee's Lieutenants, III*, 442, 667.
[54] See supra, p. 20.

no mental or physical impairment following convalescence, and true relapses probably do not occur.[55] Contrariwise, extant evidence strongly suggests that Hill suffered from chronic malaria. Bouts of this disease in an individual chronically infected with the parasite are induced by undue fatigue, exposure, climatic changes, dampness, and lowered body resistance—all factors that were present in Hill's case. Interestingly, the pattern of his illness which shows evidence of symptoms that might border on psycho-neurosis or psycho-somatic disease is also rather true with chronic clinical malaria. In fact, the added responsibilities of corps command conceivably could stimulate the trigger mechanism for these malarial attacks.[56]

*   *   *

During Hill's absence General John B. Gordon, now commanding the remnants of Early's II Corps, undertook to shrink Grant's left by an attack on Fort Stedman opposite the eastern sector of Petersburg. If this maneuver proved successful Lee planned to detach reinforcements to General Johnston for an assault on Sherman, following which the Confederate forces would unite against Grant.

However, this ambitious strategy soon became a forlorn hope. Before dawn on March 25, Gordon's assault force succeeded in breaching the Federal front only to be thrown into confusion when the guides got lost.[57] Soon the bluecoats rallied and staged a vigorous counterattack which forced Gordon to retire with heavy loss.[58] The next day Lee notified Davis that the Richmond-Petersburg defenses would have to be abandoned and the entire Army of Northern Virginia consolidated with Johnston's army in North Carolina.[59]

While the defenders made preparations to evacuate these lines by April 10,[60] Grant massed Sheridan's cavalry and Warren's V

---

[55] R. C. Cecil, Ed., *Textbook of Medicine* (Seventh Edition), 20.
[56] *Ibid.*, 439; Communication from Dr. Robert Nye, Assistant Dean, Jefferson Medical College of Philadelphia.
[57] Gordon, 411; S.H.S.P., *2*, 300.
[58] C.M.H., *III*, 529; S.H.S.P., *2*, 300.
[59] *Lee's Dispatches*, 341 ff.
[60] O.R., *46*, Part 2, 1265.

Corps near Five Forks west of Hill's line. With this overwhelming force the Federal commander intended to seize the Southside Railroad and cut off Lee's line of retreat along the Appomattox River. When Lee discerned Grant's intention he dispatched Pickett's division and Fitz Lee's cavalry to counter this latest threat.[61]

When Hill learned of the enemy's operations beyond the right of the Third Corps, he cut short his furlough to resume command of his troops.[62] Arriving at Petersburg, he mounted Champ early on Saturday morning, April 1, and accompanied by his staff and couriers spent the clear, pleasant day inspecting his lines.[63] Wilcox still manned the left and Heth the right of Hill's six mile front extending from Fort Gregg to Burgess' Mill. Beyond Burgess' Mill 400 men of the Third Corps boldly stretched the line three miles further.[64] As Mahone's division had been withdrawn to defend the five mile Howlett Line north of the Appomattox River, Hill could oppose Grant with what in actuality was little more than a skirmish line on which the men were spaced 10-20 feet apart.[65]

While examining the defenses on the right late in the afternoon, Hill received foreboding news of Pickett's reverse at Five Forks. Slowly and deliberately he retraced his way along the breastworks, exchanging but few words with his party and the men in the trenches. About 9 o'clock in the evening he reached Fort Gregg where he paused some time, apparently lost in contemplation as he surveyed the closed palisade manned by a score of artillerists and 200 of Lane's infantrymen.[66] He noted with concern the unfinished line of rifle pits running to Fort Whitworth, an adjoining earthwork to the north. These partially constructed trenches provided a convenient foothold from which an enemy force could assail the parapet. Pensively he then led his party to corps headquarters where he checked the day's reports before joining his family at Venable's across the road.[67]

---

[61] C.M.H., *III*, 531.
[62] S.H.S.P., *11*, 565.
[63] *Ibid.*; S.H.S.P., *19*, 185; J. B. Jones, *A Rebel War Clerk's Diary*, *II*, 464; *Appleton's Cyclopaedia of American Biography*, III, 202.
[64] *R. E. Lee*, *IV*, 33, 43; S.H.S.P., *11*, 566.
[65] *R. E. Lee*, *IV*, 26, 41.
[66] S.H.S.P., *2*, 301.
[67] S.H.S.P., *19*, 67, 70. S.H.S.P., *11*, 565.

As Hill retired to snatch a few winks before the impending crisis, cannonading broke out on Wilcox's lines, and before long Federal artillery raked the entire front. About midnight the bombardment swelled so ominously that Major Norborne Starke, Hill's Acting Adjutant General, investigated the action and reported to Hill that matters looked very critical in front of the city.[68] Hill quickly threw on his gray surcoat and rushed to corps headquarters for any reports from Heth and Wilcox. When Colonel Palmer informed him that there was no news from either divisional commander, Hill rode through the fog to confer with Lee at the Turnbull House nearly a mile and a half west of Third Corps Headquarters.[69] With little formality Hill entered and sat down to discuss the disturbing situation with the commanding General who was resting on his bed.[70] They had not deliberated long when Colonel C. S. Venable of Lee's staff unceremoniously broke into the room and excitedly reported that teamsters and wagons were dashing madly down the road towards Petersburg, and that enemy skirmishers were in the rear of Hill's right.[71]

Powell Hill instantly bolted out of the house and mounted his dapple-gray steed with an air so "utterly reckless"[72] that Lee entreated Venable to caution the impetuous commander not to expose himself. When Venable caught up with Hill and relayed General Lee's concern, Hill expressed appreciation but insisted that he must join his men on the right.[73]

Southward galloped Hill and Venable, followed by two of Hill's couriers, Tucker and Jenkins. The party had proceeded but a short distance when it encountered two enemy infantrymen. The couriers immediately demanded and received their surrender, whereupon Hill said: "Jenkins, take them to General Lee."[74] Farther on the threesome watered their horses in a run as Hill peered ahead through the gray dawn with his field-glasses.[75]

While thus engaged the little group drew a straggling fire from

---

[68] *Ibid.*, 566.
[69] *Ibid.*
[70] S.H.S.P., *12*, 185-86.
[71] *Ibid.*, 186.
[72] *Ibid.*, 185.
[73] *Ibid.*, 184, 186.
[74] S.H.S.P., *11*, 567.
[75] *Ibid.; S.H.S.P., 12*, 186.

the direction of the Boydton Plank Road. Turning his gaze Hill espied about half a dozen friendly skirmishers retiring before the enemy's advance. Without delay he dispatched Venable to rally and deploy these men, but growing impatient at the slow progress of this operation he recalled Venable and the three pressed on until they spotted Poague's artillery battalion on a hill to the right. Hill then ordered Venable to deploy these guns against the enemy.[76]

Accompanied only by his chief courier, Hill now proceeded rapidly over the pine-studded terrain.[77] Alarmed at the risk his chief was taking, Tucker inquired: "Please excuse me General, but where are you going?" Hill replied: "Sergeant, I must go to the right as quickly as possible," and pointing toward the southwest, added "we will go up this side of the woods which will cover us until reaching the field in the rear of General Heth's quarters, I hope to find the road clear at General Heth's."[78]

Protectively, George Tucker drew his pistol and rode slightly ahead of Hill as they crossed the Boydton Plank Road and threaded their way through the sheltering woods. In the midst of his contemplation Hill suddenly realized his precarious situation, and, pulling astride of Tucker, he said: "Sergeant, should anything happen to me you must go back to General Lee and report it."[79]

As the two horsemen emerged from the woods into a field opposite Heth's headquarters, they discerned a sizable force on the Boydton Plank Road. Pausing only long enough to identify it through his glasses as an enemy unit, Hill pointed to the side of woods parallel to the road, and said: "We must keep on to the right."[80] Spurring forward, the twosome soon reached the edge of the woods. Slowing their mounts to a walk they noticed two bluecoats ahead of the main Federal body run behind a large oak tree and level their guns one above the other.[81]

Tucker glanced inquiringly to Hill on his right who drew his

[76] *S.H.S.P.*, *12*, 186.
[77] *Ibid.*
[78] *S.H.S.P.*, *11*, 567.
[79] *Ibid.*, 568.
[80] *Ibid.*
[81] *Ibid.*; *S.H.S.P.*, *20*, 350; *S.H.S.P.*, *27*, 36.

colt and declared: "We must take them." Tucker replied: "Stay there, I'll take them." But Hill advanced side by side with his handsome courier to within twenty yards of the tree when Tucker shouted: "If you fire, you'll be swept to Hell! Our men are here— surrender!" When the mounted pair had advanced to within ten yards and the two muskets remained horizonal, Hill peremptorily demanded: "Surrender your arms!" The crouching Federal covering Tucker lowered the stock of his gun but instantly raised it when his companion who was covering Hill cried: "Let us shoot them."[82] Both guns barked simultaneously—the bullet from the upper one snipping Hill's left thumb and passing directly through his heart.[83]

The bullet aimed at Tucker missed its mark, and as the faithful courier carried news of his chief's death to Lee he encountered Longstreet, Hill's mellowed antagonist, who grieved, "the Southern service has lost a sword made bright by brave work upon many heavy fields."[84] General Lee, upon learning of Hill's fate, shed tears and remarked heavily, "He is at rest now, and we who are left are the ones to suffer."[85]

TELL A. P. HILL

No Epitaph more noble or sublime
Hath e'er been writ in all the tide of time;
Nor yet can be. It doth all fullness fill
These—Death's undying words—"Tell A. P. Hill!"

Hill was already Fame's, and Jackson's death
Confirmed her verdict with his latest breath.
So LEE's last words, as his great heart grew still,
were Fame's and Jackson's own—"Tell A. P. Hill!"

"Prepare for action!" Ah, the action's done!
These three have met on fields beyond the sun.
But Fame endures, and shall endure until
Her trumpets cease to sound—"Tell A. P. Hill!"

W. W. SCOT

---

[82] S.H.S.P., *11*, 568; S.H.S.P., *20*, 351.
[83] S.H.S.P., *11*, 569; S.H.S.P., *19*, 185.
[84] D. B. Sanger and T. R. Hay, *James Longstreet*, 295.
[85] S.H.S.P., *11*, 184, 187.

Monument to A. P. Hill, Richmond, Va.

APPENDIX

Charge and Specifications preferred by Maj. Gen'l T. J. Jackson against Maj. Gen'l A. P. Hill.*

Charge—Neglect of Duty

Specification 1. In this that Maj. Gen'l A. P. Hill when he was directed by Maj. Gen'l T. J. Jackson to move early in the morning of August 8th, 1862, from Orange C. H. towards Culpeper C. H., by way of Barnetts ford, did fail to move in obedience to said order, but did continue in the vicinity of Orange C. H. until night, thus remaining a days march in rear of the position which he should have occupied. All this near Orange C. H., Va., on or about the 8th of August, 1862.

Specification 2. In this that Maj. Gen'l A. P. Hill, on the night of the 19th of August 1862, when he had been specially directed by Maj. Gen'l T. J. Jackson, to move his troops so soon as the moon should rise, via Somerville ford, did fail to obey said order, and thus rendered it necessary for Maj. Gen'l T. J. Jackson, about two hours after the designated time, to put the said troops in motion as they had not, up to that time, left camp. All this near Somerville ford, Va., on or about the time specified.

Specification 3. In this that Maj. Gen'l A. P. Hill did neglect to give all his brigade commanders the requisite orders for enabling him to move his division so soon as the moon should rise during the night of the 19th of Aug., 1862, as he had been directed by Maj. Gen'l T. J. Jackson. All this near Somerville ford, Va., on or about the time specified.

Specification 4. In this that Maj. Gen'l A. P. Hill in moving around Centreville on August 31st, 1862, did permit the head of his command to move too rapidly and notwithstanding his attention was called to it by Maj. Gen'l T. J. Jackson who required him to move more slowly. He subsequently during the same evening permitted the head of his column again to march too rapidly and allowed a large number of his men to straggle from ranks. All this on the march around Centreville, Va., on or about the time specified.

Specification 5. In this that notwithstanding Maj. Gen'l A. P. Hill was directed by Maj. Gen'l T. J. Jackson on the evening previous to leaving the vicinity of Drainesville to march at a fixed hour next morning Sept. 4th, 1862 and had about an hour for putting his division in motion he did not only fail to put them all in motion within the time prescribed but even to have his whole command ready to move within that time, though the road admitted of more troops being put in motion. All this near Drainesville, Va. on or about the time specified.

Specification 6. In this that Maj. Gen'l A. P. Hill having neglected to put his command in motion, on the morning of the 4th of Sept., 1862, as he had been directed by Maj. Gen'l T. J. Jackson, but apparently leaving the moving of part of his troops to their respective commanders, and the troops

---

* Reproduced from copy in the Virginia Historical Society.

not moving when they should it became necessary for Maj. Gen'l T. J. Jackson to put part of the troops in motion, in consequence of Maj. Gen'l A. P. Hill's neglect of duty. All this near Drainesville, Va., on or about the time specified.

Specification 7. In this that Maj. Gen'l A. P. Hill on Sept. 4th, 1862 did neglect to halt his leadingg brigade and rest it at the proper time as he had been directed by Maj. Gen'l T. J. Jackson and thus rendered it necessary for Maj. Gen'l T. J. Jackson to give the order directly to the brigade commander. All this on the march from Drainesville to Leesburg, Va., on or about the time specified.

Specification 8. In this that Maj. Gen'l A. P. Hill did on the 4th of Sept. 1862 ride in advance of the head of his column and permit men to straggle from his command without attemping to prevent it, instead of moving along his column and superintending its march, and requiring his staff officers to do the same. All this on the march from Drainesville to Leesburg, Va., on or about the time specified.

INDEX